Chemistry: A Novel (Textbook)

Chemistry:
A Novel (Textbook) – Vol. 1

R. Mark Matthews

RMARKMATTHEWS.COM

A person is fortunate to have one mentor
at the start of their career.
I had two, which I suppose puts me in the category of blessed.
The fact that they're also named Mark…
Well, that's just plain weird.

Dr. Mark Noble (U. of Louisville), who taught me how to teach,
& Dr. Mark Mason (U. of Toledo), who taught me how to think.

Whether or not they succeeded is probably up for debate.
I guess you're about to become the judge of that…

Volume 2

Chapter 13 Liquids & Solids
Chapter 14 Solutions
Chapter 15 Chemical Kinetics
Chapter 16 Chemical Equilibrium
Chapter 17 Acids & Bases (Part I)
Chapter 18 Acids & Bases (Part II)
Chapter 19 Thermochemistry (Part II)
Chapter 20 Electrochemistry
Chapter 21 Nuclear Chemistry

Prologue

I suppose I should start by explaining the title, because I'll be the first to admit that it's a pretty silly one.

It was always my intention to write a nontraditional textbook (at least by current standards), and when I decided to use a trade paperback format I jokingly considered calling it *Chemistry: A Novel*. I'm of the opinion that adding "A Novel" to the end of a title isn't really necessary these days, and might just border more on pretentiousness. I mean, besides the fact that bookstores—both physical and online—usually have a section that's clearly labeled "Fiction," when I see a thousand-plus page book by Stephen King called *Under the Dome*, my initial assumption isn't that it's a history of indoor sports arenas. I also liked the idea of someone accidentally picking this book up thinking that it was a romance novel or Chuck Palahniuk knock-off, only to learn some basic chemistry before they realized what they were actually reading. Hey, in a time where companies try to pass products off as "chemical-free," sometimes us chemistry teachers have to go to extreme lengths to educate.

What changed it from a joke to a legitimate title was the idea to parenthetically add the word "Textbook" at the end. I thought it worked on several levels. It conveyed my desire to put the focus more on reading instead of simply looking at graphs, pictures, or sample problems (more on that in a second), along with the idea that this was a "novel" approach to writing a general chemistry textbook (again, by current standards; those written seventy to eighty years ago didn't look much different from any other book). Plus, to steal a phrase from Trent Reznor, the title passed the "two week test," and over time the name just stuck.

As for why I'd even attempt to write a "novel" textbook in the first place, a while back I began to wonder how many students actually read the textbooks being used in their classes. I mean *really* read it. Not just a blurb or two, here and there. Not just the sample problems or figure captions. How many people actually sit down and read a textbook, even a single chapter, like they would any other book? I don't think any number would be low enough to surprise me, and I can't really blame anyone that doesn't. To be honest, I'm not sure that today's textbooks are actually designed to be read like a "regular" book. You're constantly being asked to divert your attention to a figure or a table that's somewhere else on the page, or the next page, along with various multicolored side-boxes with more sample problems or miscellaneous facts or vignettes. There just seems to be too many distractions, and too little "real estate" on an average textbook page actually devoted to *text* for someone to just sit back and *read* the darn thing.

Then there's the 800-pound gorilla riding the elephant in the room: college textbooks cost *a lot*. Antiques and collectibles aside, no book is worth $250. Period. I can buy the entire *Beatles* catalog for less than half that price. And I realize a general chemistry textbook normally covers two semesters. That's still $125 per course, more than four times the price of *Under the Dome* when it first came out in hardcover. I'm also aware of the argument that the used book market is a major reason for such prices, which is also the reason we have the cycle of putting out a new edition every three years (regardless of whether or not any significant changes have been made). Of course, that argument lost face with me when I learned that the Kindle version of my previous textbook was available for $150, about the same price as the device you'd be reading it on.

I'm not saying this book, or the ideas behind it, is better than the textbooks put out by the major publishers (though I certainly don't think that it's worse; I wouldn't have wasted many years of my free time writing it had I did). I'm mainly curious as to whether or not books like this can work anymore. Basically, this book—and the volume that follows—is a little experiment of mine. Needless to say, I hope it works, and whether you're a student taking general chemistry or someone who's just now realized that this isn't a going to be a romance novel, I hope it helps you have a better understanding of the world you live in, if only a little. If it's a failure, please accept my humble apologies. But look on the bright side: at least it didn't cost you the equivalent of two copies of the entire *Beatles* catalog. At worst, it probably only ran you a single copy of *The White Album*.

How to use this book

It feels a bit weird starting a book by telling you that the best way to use it is to actually *read* it. Then again, we live in a world where fast food restaurants and gas stations feel obliged to remind you that their coffee is hot, so I suppose it's not that unusual.

This book was written to be read just like any other book. That's the main reason I'm using the trade paperback format (though it did force me to split it into two volumes; Stephen King can get away with thousand page tomes, but I didn't think I could). It's also written in a way that—I hope—assists with its readability. I've split the material into "bite-sized" parts that are only a few pages long. Things like figures, graphs, or examples are embedded within the text itself, usually without labels or captions, in an attempt to keep the "narrative flow" going. The same is true for sample calculations, which are presented in a step-by-step fashion to mimic how I'd walk you through a problem if I were doing it in person.

Don't get me wrong. I love technology. I teach this class online (lecture and lab) and I, like scores of others—have done a few tutorial videos that are currently housed at YouTube (and might one day be incorporated into some electronic version of this book). And I enjoy trying to figure out new ways that technology can be used to help students "get" the concepts taught in a general chemistry course (trust me, us teachers really, really like it when that happens). Still, in my opinion, when it's all said and done nothing beats reading as a means of learning, at least until technology reaches the point where we can stick plugs into the back of our necks like they did in *The Matrix*. When you're watching a video, or listening to an instructor in class, it's pretty easy to tune out for minutes at a time or longer (especially when you have a phone in your hand; yes, teachers notice when you do that, even when we don't call you out on it). And you have more control over the pace at which you're learning when you read. With print, you can read or reread things as quickly or slowly as you need to, without having to rewind a video or ask a teacher to repeat what he or she just said (because you were messing with your phone. Did I mention how obvious that is?).

Of course, not everyone learns things in the same way, and there's no single right way (and to be honest, this book shouldn't be your only way to learn this stuff). But if you prefer other methods of learning, go for it. As long as it works, that is. If it doesn't, maybe you should reevaluate how you're trying to learn and how you can improve. And maybe, just maybe, that'll include picking up a book.

How to use the practice problems

I've taught many, many general chemistry courses during my career as a teacher, and one of the more common things I hear from students who are struggling is, "I've tried *all* the practice problems you've assigned, and I still did poorly on the last test."

My initial response is usually, "*How* are you doing them?" Because simply going through problems in the hope that it eventually clicks doesn't usually work, and in many cases what you end up doing—without even realizing it—is blindly copying problems from a solutions manual to your notebook. At that point, you've veered from practicing concepts to rote memorization, and if you don't believe anything I've said up to this point, believe this: you cannot memorize your way to a passing grade in a college-level chemistry course.

There are two types of problem sets in this book: Try It Yourself and Test Your Skills. Try It Yourself problems are placed within the chapters and—as the name implies—are there to give you a chance to practice the concepts you've just read about. It's important for you to try these problems before moving on to the next section. Most of the concepts covered in this book are usually progressive, with each one building or leading up to the next. Don't worry if you need to flip back and reread sections or look at my examples to assist you. That's expected (you only just read about the concepts, after all). Just make sure that when you don't get the right answer, you understand *why* you got it wrong. And if you feel like you "lucked" into the right answer or want to make sure you actually know what you just did, go through the problem again, only now pretend that you're trying to teach someone else how to work through the problem (or, if you have a study buddy, take turns playing tutor to the other). Aloud, if possible, so you can hear how well you're explaining the solution.

Once you've finished a chapter, and feel like you have a pretty firm understanding of the material, then it's time to try the Test Your Skills problems. The problems are divided into three starred sections. The one-star problems are meant to be fairly straight forward, oftentimes identical (or at least very similar) to the Try It Yourself questions. The two-star problems will usually require you to think a little more, as opposed to simply following the examples found within the chapter beat for beat, while the three-star problems are meant to not only test your understanding of what was covered in that specific chapter, but everything discussed in the book thus far. In an attempt to make it feel less like a "real" test, I've used goofy names for each starred section (though I'll admit it was mostly for my own amusement), and instead of simply assigning points to each question, I decided to use experience points (XP) and equally goofy "achievements," which fans of video games will be quite familiar with.

Unlike the Try It Yourself questions, try to solve the Test Your Skills problems without flipping back to the chapter or any notes you may have. You don't have to get every question correct to move to the next section, but if you don't meet the minimum amount of XP you should go back and reread the parts of the chapter that gave you the most trouble (maybe give the Try It Yourself problems another try, as well). Later, when you think you've gotten a better grip on the material, give the Test Your Skills problems another go. Just remember that you haven't really answered a question successfully until you *understand* how you got the correct answer. Again, general chemistry is a very progressive course, and it's important to not move on to the next topic until you have a firm understanding of the ones at hand. You'll get lost very quickly if you don't.

Chapter 1
Matter and Measurements

Part 1: Studying Chemistry

What is Chemistry?

Basically, chemistry is the study of matter. **Matter** can be defined as anything that has mass and takes up space. If that's the case, what *isn't* made of matter? Energy, perhaps, though many physicists—and, ironically, people who use certain recreational drugs—would tell you that matter and energy are two different versions of the same thing. Either way, chemistry really is an extremely broad field. It's no exaggeration to say that chemists study *everything*, be it living or inanimate, natural or synthetic, on this planet or beyond.

Classifying Matter

Matter is generally split into two categories: substances and mixtures. A **substance** has its own distinct properties that never change from one sample to another. **Elements** are the simplest types of substances (though not the simplest forms of matter; more on that in the next chapter), while **compounds** are substances made up of two or more elements. Water, as you probably already know, is a compound composed of the elements hydrogen and oxygen. It's often possible to separate a compound into its elements, but it has to be done chemically (i.e., some type of reaction). We'll discuss elements and compounds more in Chapter 3.

A **mixture** is a combination of two or more substances. The substances that make up a mixture can usually be separated by physical means, such as filtration (separating by size) or distillation (separating by boiling point). A **homogeneous mixture** is one that has a constant composition throughout (*homo-* = same). In other words, if you took a homogeneous mixture and split it into three samples, the percent breakdown of each substance would be the same for all three mixtures. Conversely, a **heterogeneous mixture** doesn't have a constant composition (*hetero-* = different), even if it looks that way to the naked eye. A general trend that helps us distinguish between the two types of mixtures is known as "clear/cloudy rule." Homogeneous mixtures tend to be clear while heterogeneous mixtures are cloudy. Freshly brewed tea and most hard liquors would be examples of homogeneous mixtures (don't confuse *clear* and *colorless*; something can be clear and still have a color), while orange juice and milk are heterogeneous mixtures ("homogenized" milk is still technically heterogeneous). This rule doesn't work as well for mixtures of solids, such as alloys (a mixture of two or more metals), which could be one type or the other depending on how it's prepared.

Studying Matter

When chemists—and scientists in general—study the world or attempt to solve a problem, they use an approach commonly referred to as the **scientific method**. The first step is to simply make an observation and question it (which is why it's often said that we're all born scientists, as anyone who's ever been around a child five or younger can attest to). If enough people make the same type of observation, it can lead to the formation of a **scientific law**. In many cases, these laws are mathematical in nature, but can often be expressed in general terms. Newton's law of gravity is a good example of this. An important thing to remember about scientific laws is that they only state that certain things seem to always happen, but they don't explain *why or how* they're happening. That's where the rest of the scientific method comes in.

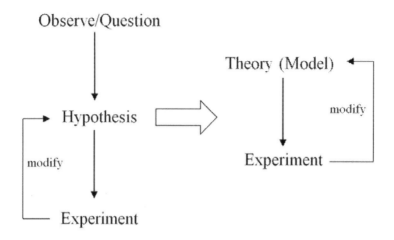

In order to answer (or attempt to answer) the questions that come from your observations, you begin by forming an educated guess, or **hypothesis**. You would then try to devise a series of experiments to test your hypothesis, after which you'd probably discover that you were right about some things and wrong about others. So you'd go back and tweak your hypothesis a bit, retest it, tweak it some more, and so on.

Once enough experimentation has been done, and you feel that you've developed a good understanding of what you're studying, the next step would be to develop a **theory** (or *model*). Theories are scientists' attempts to explain the laws of the natural world (the *why* and *how* parts, in other words). People will often confuse the terms *theory* and *hypothesis.* In general, a hypothesis is formed before you do any experimentation and the theories come afterwards.

But it doesn't end there. After the theory is developed (and probably published in a scientific journal), more experimentation can be done to further test and modify it. This cycle can continue for a few years, an entire career, or several lifetimes. Einstein, for example, developed a theory over a hundred years ago that said space curves and the speed of light is constant. Today, many of the scientists he inspired continue to test and examine his ideas.

Part 2: Properties of Matter

Mass & Density

Mass is a measure of how much matter is in a given object. It's often confused with a similar term, **weight**, which is a measure of the force of gravity between two objects (you and this planet, for instance). You're probably already familiar with the "Earth vs. Moon" example of the difference between mass and weight: even though you'd weigh less on the Moon than you would on Earth, your mass would remain the same. That said, unless you're doing experiments on more than one planet, the two are pretty interchangeable. There's nothing wrong, for example, with saying something weighs ten grams instead of saying that it has a mass of ten grams.

A related term is **density**, which describes the amount of mass per volume (e.g., grams/milliliter). When a petroleum company has an oil spill in the ocean, you'll notice that the oil floats on the water. That's because most oils have a lower density than water. Ice floats because when water freezes, the water molecules expand, lowering the amount of mass per volume, which in turn lowers its density. By the way, water is one of the few substances whose solid floats on its liquid. In most other cases, the molecules are more tightly packed as a solid, increasing its density.

Extensive & Intensive Properties

An **extensive property** is one that varies with amount. Mass and volume are examples of extensive properties. The more of a substance you have, the more it will weigh and the more space it will occupy. Conversely, an **intensive property** is independent of amount (remember: *in*tensive = *in*dependent). Common examples include density, melting points, and freezing points. For example, no matter how much water you have, its density will be 1.00 g/mL. Notice that the ratio of two extensive properties (such as mass and volume) is often an intensive property (density).

Physical & Chemical Properties/Changes

A **physical property** can be measured without having to change the identity of what you're examining. Take mass, for instance. When you step on a scale to weigh yourself, you're still the same person you were before (though your mood might be different, depending on what the scale says). Volume's another example. When you measure a cup of sugar, it's *still* sugar.

On the other hand, there are some properties that actually require an identity change in order to measure it, which we call **chemical properties**. Flammability is a good example. Let's say you want to see if gasoline is flammable, so you light a match and attempt to burn it (hopefully, you already know that it is; if not, I'm probably legally obligated to ask you not to find out on your own). As you'll learn in Chapter 4, when something burns it undergoes a combustion reaction, converting the gasoline into mostly carbon dioxide and water vapor. The identity of the matter you studied has changed (and possibly part of the matter that makes up your skin; I told you not to try it). One hint that you're measuring a chemical property is that it will probably involve some sort of chemical reaction.

Now, let's say you wanted to test the flammability of water (again, I hope you know already, but in this case feel free to try all you want). You light a match, set it in the water...and the match fizzles out. It's still water, but a negative test result doesn't mean we weren't measuring a chemical property, since a positive test would have resulted in a change in identity.

Another related set of terms is physical and chemical changes. A **physical change** is one that doesn't result in an identity change, such as boiling and freezing. When water melts or freezes or boils, it's still water. It's just undergoing a phase change. A **chemical change**, however, *will* result in a change in identity. For example, when iron rusts, it's no longer iron, but has reacted with oxygen and water to form an iron-oxygen compound. As it was with chemical properties, notice that chemical changes also involve a *chemical* reaction of some sort.

Try It Yourself

Read the Prologue for tips on using these problems effectively.

P1. The following list are things many people encounter during a typical day. Identify each as an element, compound, homogeneous mixture or heterogeneous mixture. Some of these may require a quick internet search to have a better understanding of its composition.

a) "Black" coffee, b) Coffee with cream, c) Vitamin C, d) Blood, e) Water, f) Gasoline, g) Helium, h) Table sugar (sucrose), i) Aluminum foil, j) Polyvinylchloride (PVC), k) Air, l) Fog

(See Appendix for answers)

Part 3: Measurements

Accuracy & Precision

Whether you're in a lab or at home, the measurements you make are only as good as the instrument you're making them with. A properly working instrument is dependent on two factors: its accuracy and its precision. **Accuracy** is a term that describes how close a measurement is to a known or accepted value. Notice I didn't say that it was close to the "actual" value because—technically speaking—every measurement that's made with an instrument has *some* degree of error. Electronic balances, for example, have to be calibrated periodically (using a set of standard weights) to ensure proper accuracy. **Precision**, on the other hand, describes how close repeated measurements are to one another. For example, let's say you use a balance to measure the mass of a solid. If the balance has good precision, reweighing the solid a second time (or third, fourth, etc) should give the same mass.

A dartboard analogy is often used to illustrate the difference between these two terms:

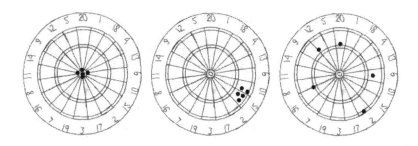

We're assuming the player is intending to hit the bullseye each time, making it our "known or accepted value" (I'm aware of things like triple 20's; let's not get carried away here). On the first board all five darts hit the bullseye, showing good accuracy as well as good precision. On the second board, the accuracy is poor, but the precision is high, while the third lacks both precision and accuracy.

Significant Figures

When making a measurement with an instrument, it's usually not possible to obtain an exact value. Sure, it may look like you have "exactly" 10.0-mL in that graduated cylinder. As mentioned in the previous section, every instrument will have some degree of error, even when it's used properly. **Significant Figures** are the digits in a measurement or calculation that have the highest degree of certainty.

When making a measurement yourself, the number of significant figures will depend on the instrument you're using. Weighing a sample on a balance that goes out to the second decimal place will have fewer significant figures than one that goes out to the fourth. When you're looking at measurements made by others—a table of data, for instance—you'll have to decide how many significant figures are being presented. In either case, the following rules are used for determining significant figures:

1. Numbers that are known to be **exact** have zero uncertainty, which means they are "infinitely significant." For example, if you count 30 people in a room, then your measured value is *exactly* 30, which means you could technically write an infinite number of zeros after the decimal point (30.0000000000...). Counting aside, if you didn't make a measurement yourself, you should assume a given number has been rounded unless you're specifically told it's an exact value.

2. Nonzero numbers are always significant. Simply put, if it's not a zero, it's assumed to be significant. The number 236, for example, has three significant figures.

3. Leading zeros (those left of the first nonzero number) are *never* significant. The reason is fairly simple: if you show a number such as 0.005213 in scientific notation, the leading zeros aren't written (5.213×10^{-3}). They're essentially placeholders, making them insignificant. As such, this number has a total of four significant digits (the other four nonzero numbers)

4. Zeros between two nonzero numbers are *always* significant. In the number 0.0309, the two leading zeros are not significant (see rule 3), but not the one between the 3 and the 9. That zero isn't just a placeholder since it doesn't disappear when you switch to scientific notation (3.09×10^{-2}). Therefore, this number has three significant figures.

5. Trailing zeros (zeros after the last nonzero number) are *only* significant if there's a decimal point present. Take the number 23,000 as an example. Unless you're specifically told that this number is exact, with no decimal point you should assume that it was rounded to the thousands place and those three zeros are just placeholders, giving the number two significant figures. If you or whoever made the measurement wanted to make it clear that it was actually rounded to the ones place, and those zeros are in fact significant, you should write it as 23,000.0, for a total of six significant figures. This rule also applies to numbers that are less than one. For example, 0.030290 has a total of five significant figures: the three nonzero numbers, the middle zero, and the zero at the end. Significant zeros should also be included in numbers written in scientific notation. In fact, scientific notation can help emphasize when trailing zeroes are (2.30000×10^{4}) or aren't (2.3×10^{4}) significant.

Significant Figures and Calculations

Even with simple calculations, usually not all of the digits in your raw answer have the same degree of certainty. It's therefore necessary to round your answer to the appropriate number of significant figures. How you do that depends on the type of operation being performed.

Addition and Subtraction

For addition or subtraction, find the number with the fewest decimal places and round your answer to that decimal point. For example, in the following calculation

$$\begin{array}{r} 12.5 \\ + \ 0.384 \\ \hline 12.884 \end{array}$$

Both numbers have the first decimal place in common, so we'd round the number to 12.9. We do this because we simply don't know what follows the 5 in that first number, so our certainty is lower for the last two digits of our answer.

$$\begin{array}{r} 12.5?? \\ + \ 0.384 \\ \hline 12.8?? \end{array}$$

When you're adding or subtracting numbers that are written in scientific notation, it's usually helpful to convert them to either standard notation or a common power of ten. Otherwise, you might have trouble finding the common decimal point. In the following calculation, for example,

$$\begin{array}{r} 1.45 \times 10^4 \\ + \ 3.015 \times 10^6 \end{array}$$

we can convert the two numbers so they're both on the order of, say, 10^5.

$$0.145 \times 10^5$$
$$\underline{+ \; 30.15 \times 10^5}$$
$$30.2\underline{9}5 \times 10^5 \quad = 30.30 \times 10^5$$
$$= 3.030 \times 10^6$$

If you're not comfortable enough with scientific notation to do that, you can just use standard notation, though it might help to highlight the placeholder zeros somehow.

$$14,\mathbf{500}$$
$$\underline{+ \; 3,015,\mathbf{000}}$$
$$3,02\underline{9},500 \quad = 3,030,000$$
$$\text{or } 3.030 \times 10^6$$

Multiplication and Division

With multiplication and division, you find the number with the fewest significant figures and round your answer to that many digits. The reasons are similar to those discussed for addition/subtraction. In the following calculation, for instance,

$$18.44 \times 0.0021 = 0.038724$$

the second number only has two significant figures, so our final answer will be rounded to 0.039.

When performing a long string of operations where only one rounding rule applies (addition/subtraction *or* multiplication/division), don't round after each operation. Instead, punch everything into your calculator at once and then round off your final answer at the end.

$$541 \times 20.10 \div 15 = 720$$

If you have a problem that includes mixed operations, round after each applicable rule. For example, let's say we have to calculate

$$(3.00 \times 0.3044) - (0.0744 \times 2.3)$$

Before we can subtract, we have to multiply each set of numbers, so we'll do that first, rounding off according to the rule for multiplication/division.

$$(0.913) - (0.17)$$

Now we subtract, using its rule for rounding.

$$0.913 - 0.17 = 0.7\underline{4}3 = 0.74$$

Try It Yourself

P2. How many significant figures are in each of the following numbers? Explain.
a) 20.1, b) 0.049, c) 1,800, d) 3.301×10^6, e) 89.07010

P3. Perform the following calculations, rounding your answer to the appropriate number of significant figures.
a) $45.1 + 77.18$
b) $1,190 + 452$
c) $5,722 \times 0.04$
d) $542 \div 6.1$
e) $(13.5 + 0.88 - 7.20) \div (0.903 - 0.10)$

Part 4: Units of Measurement

SI Units

Scientists have globally adopted a set of standard units known as **SI units** (SI stands for *Système International*). SI units that we'll often use in this book include…

Measurement	SI Unit	Symbol
energy	Joule	J
mass	kilogram	kg
length	meter	m
time	second	s
temperature	Kelvin	K
amount	mole	mol
volume	liter	L

Technically, liter isn't the SI unit of volume (officially, it's cubic meters, m^3), but it is the most commonly used unit of volume in a laboratory, so it's what we'll use in this book. Casing is important with unit symbols. For example, the symbol of meter is a lowercase *m*. An uppercase *M* is used for a different unit—molarity—that we'll introduce in Chapter 5.

You're probably already familiar enough with the metric system to know that it's a base-ten (decimal) system, with each power of ten having its own prefix. Commonly used prefixes in chemistry include the following:

Prefix	Symbol	Power of 10
tera-	T	10^{12}
giga-	G	10^9
mega-	M	10^6
kilo-	k	10^3
centi-	c	10^{-2}
milli-	m	10^{-3}
micro-	μ	10^{-6}
nano-	n	10^{-9}
pico-	p	10^{-12}

Notice that the power of 10 goes with the base unit (1 nm = 10^{-9} m, 1 kg = 10^3 g, etc.). Also notice that, like unit symbols, casing is also important with metric prefixes (mega- is a capital *M* while milli- is a lowercase *m*). Finally, going back to our previous discussion on significant figures, it should be noted that metric conversions are exact relationships. A kilogram, for instance, is exactly 1000 grams.

Absolute vs. Relative Scales

Units can be created in one of two ways. Some are **absolute scales** with an "absolute zero," but most units we work with are **relative scales** that are measured against some agreed-upon point of reference. The Celsius scale, for instance, is based on the freezing and boiling points of water. Why? Because 18th century astronomer Anders Celsius thought it was a good idea, though he originally gave the *boiling point* a value of 0 and the freezing point 100. It wasn't until after his death that the scale was flipped. Water is used as the reference in several other common units of measurement. A gram was originally defined as the mass of one milliliter of water, which is why its density is usually given as 1 g/mL.

Heat vs. Temperature

Heat is a quantitative measure of energy. In other words, you can measure how much heat something possesses (we'll discuss the role energy plays in chemical reactions in Chapter 7). The SI unit for measuring energy is the Joule (J), though another commonly used unit is the calorie (cal). Technically, though, this isn't the calorie you're familiar with. That would be the "food calorie" (Cal), which is actually a kilocalorie. 1 kcal = 1 Cal. Confusing, right? But since neither is the SI unit we won't be working with either of them much in this book.

Temperature, on the other hand, is a relative measure of how hot and cold something is. Sure, you can measure it, but it's not a quantitative value. Look at it this way: say you have a cup of freshly brewed coffee and a carton of ice cream. Which one is hotter? The coffee, of course. But which has more heat? Remember, a unit for heat is the calorie, and if you're drinking a cup of coffee with more calories than an entire carton of ice cream, you're putting *way* too much sugar and cream in your mocha latte. Again, heat is a quantitative measurement, while temperature is relative. Just because something is hotter doesn't necessarily mean that it has more heat.

Units of Temperature

In the U.S., temperatures are commonly measured in Fahrenheit (°F), but the majority of the world—including the scientific community—uses the Celsius scale (°C). As such, the Fahrenheit unit will be essentially ignored in this book. While we usually measure in Celsius, most temperature-based calculations are done using the SI unit, Kelvin (K). You can easily convert between the two using the following equation

$$K = °C + 273.15$$

Unlike the other two temperature scales, Kelvin is an absolute scale with an *absolute zero*, the lowest possible value for that measurement. At 0 K there is zero heat, making it the lowest temperature possible. This means that there are no negative temperatures in the Kelvin scale, which is why we tend to use it in calculations (as we'll see in Chapter 6). Also, being an absolute scale means it relates heat and temperature better than the other two. For example, doubling your temperature from 50-100°C isn't necessarily doubling the amount of heat, but on the Kelvin scale (50-100 K) it is.

Part 5: Converting Between Units

Dimensional Analysis

For the first seven chapters of this book, the majority of calculations we'll be discussing will be nothing more than converting one type of unit to another. A common method for performing conversions is **dimensional analysis**. The idea behind dimensional analysis isn't that different from a shortcut you were probably taught for multiplying fractions: if a number appears in the denominator of one fraction and the numerator in another, the number effectively cancels outs.

$$\frac{1}{\cancel{2}} \times \frac{\cancel{2}}{3} = \frac{1}{3}$$

This trick also works with whole numbers, since they can be written in fraction form as that number over 1.

$$3 \times \frac{2}{3} = \frac{\cancel{3}}{1} \times \frac{2}{\cancel{3}} = 2$$

Conversion factors can also be shown as fractions. For example, 1 kg = 1000 g can be written as

$$\frac{1 \text{ kg}}{1000 \text{g}} \text{ or } \frac{1000 \text{ g}}{1 \text{ kg}}$$

With dimensional analysis, we convert between units by taking one or more conversion factors, written as fractions, and multiplying them in a way that cancels out any unwanted units.

For example, let's say you're driving down the interstate doing a comfortable 75 miles per hour (mi/hr). How far will you have driven after 2 hours? Odds are you can do this one in your head—150 miles—because you're familiar enough with these types of units that you knew to multiply. Using dimensional analysis, we see that the reason you multiply is because this removes the unwanted *hours* unit

$$\frac{75 \text{ mi}}{1 \text{ hr}} \times 2 \text{ hr} = 150 \text{ mi}$$

Here's another one you've probably done on a long car ride: suppose you've traveled 150 miles at an average speed of 50 mi/hr, how many hours have you been driving? Again, you're probably familiar enough with these units to know that you divide 150 by 50, for a time of 3 hours. Setting this up as a dimensional analysis calculation, we see that dividing allows the unwanted unit of length to cancel out, leaving only the desired unit of time.

$$150 \text{ mi} \times \frac{1 \text{ hr}}{50 \text{ mi}} = 3 \text{ hr}$$

As we progress through this course, we'll be doing similar calculations, but they'll involve conversions that are less familiar to you than miles and hours. Instead of trying to learn when you multiply and when you divide for each type of calculation (which involves memorization, something you should try to avoid in a general chemistry class), use dimensional analysis to first get rid of the unwanted units. Once you do, the multiplication and division takes care of itself.

Common Conversion Factors
(Imperial units are U.S. values)

1 in = 2.54 cm (exactly)
1 yard (yd) = 0.9144 m
1 mi = 1.609 km
1 Angstrom (Å) = 10^{-10} m
1 ounce (oz) = 28.35 g
1 pound (lb) = 453.6 g

1 pint (pt) = 473.2 mL
1 gallon (gal) = 3.785 L
1 mL = 1 cm^3
1 cal = 4.184 J (exactly)

More Conversion Examples

Example: What is 25.0 pounds in units of grams?

From the above table, we see that 1 lb = 453.6 grams. In fraction form, this would be written as

$$\frac{1\text{ lb}}{453.6\text{g}} \quad \text{or} \quad \frac{453.6\text{ g}}{1\text{ lb}}$$

For pounds to cancel, we need it in the bottom part of our conversion factor, so we'd use the one on the right.

$$25.0\text{ \cancel{lb}} \times \frac{453.6\text{ g}}{1\text{ \cancel{lb}}} = 11{,}300\text{ g}$$

Example: Convert 385 mm to μm

From our table of metric prefixes in Part 4, we see that 1 mm = 10^{-3} m and that 1 μm = 10^{-6} m. Instead of doing any extra work to try and fudge two conversion factors into one, it's usually easier to simply do a two-step conversion. First we'll get rid of the mm unit

$$385\text{ \cancel{mm}} \times \frac{10^{-3}\text{ m}}{1\text{ \cancel{mm}}}$$

and then use the other conversion factor to get rid of the meter unit.

$$385\text{ \cancel{mm}} \times \frac{10^{-3}\text{ \cancel{m}}}{1\text{ \cancel{mm}}} \times \frac{1\text{ μm}}{10^{-6}\text{ \cancel{m}}}$$

Once you have the desired unit, you can whip out your calculator, multiplying and dividing as needed.

$$385 \text{ mm} \times \frac{10^{-3} \text{ m}}{1 \text{ mm}} \times \frac{1 \text{ μm}}{10^{-6} \text{ m}} = 3.85 \times 10^5 \text{ μm}$$

Example: Convert 18.50 lb/in² to g/cm².

We have two units to convert: pounds to grams, and square inches to square centimeters. We'll take each one at a time. First we'll convert pounds to grams like we did earlier.

$$\frac{18.50 \text{ lb}}{1 \text{ in}^2} \times \frac{453.6 \text{ g}}{1 \text{ lb}}$$

Now we'll convert square inches to square centimeters. From our table of conversion factors, we know that 1 in = 2.54 cm,

$$\frac{18.50 \text{ lb}}{1 \text{ in}^2} \times \frac{453.6 \text{ g}}{1 \text{ lb}} \times \frac{1 \text{ in}}{2.54 \text{ cm}}$$

but inches and square inches are two different units. The easiest way to fix this is to square everything in the conversion factor.

$$\frac{18.50 \text{ lb}}{1 \text{ in}^2} \times \frac{453.6 \text{ g}}{1 \text{ lb}} \times \frac{1^2 \text{ in}^2}{2.54^2 \text{ cm}^2}$$

Now that we have a gram unit on the top half and square centimeters at the bottom, we're ready to calculate the answer.

$$\frac{18.50 \text{ lb}}{1 \text{ in}^2} \times \frac{453.6 \text{ g}}{1 \text{ lb}} \times \frac{1^2 \text{ in}^2}{2.54^2 \text{ cm}^2} = 1,301 \text{ g/cm}^2$$

Try It Yourself

P4. Show the two ways that each of the following conversion factors can be written as fractions: a) 1 pt = 473.2 mL, b) 1 gal = 3.785 L, c) 1 ng = 10^{-9} g, d) 1 cal = 4.184 J

P5. Complete the following conversion strings and solve.
a) 48.5 in × ———— = _____ cm
b) 83.4 J × ———— = _____ cal
c) 105 nL × $\dfrac{L}{}$ × $\dfrac{}{L}$ = _____ mL
d) 80.30 m × ———— × ———— = _____ mi

P6. Perform the following conversions.
a) 40.02 gal to L, b) 93.0 kg to pounds, c) 603 in to μm, d) 1.5 x 10^6 m to mi

P7. Want more practice? Pick a number between 1 and 100 (or any maximum number you like), then a letter between A to Z. Using dimensional analysis, convert that number between one of the units from the following table, based on the letter you chose. If you really want to mix things up, go online and find a website with a random number and letter generator (there's a nice one at random.org).

A. pounds to grams
B. pounds to kilograms
C. kilograms to milligrams
D. ounces to grams
E. ounces to milligrams
F. nanograms to milligrams
G. stone to pounds
 (1 stone = 6.35 kg)
H. stone to kilograms
I. feet to meters
J. miles to kilometers
K. inches to centimeters
L. millimeters to picometers
M. nanometers to micrometers

N. centimeters to Angstroms
O. square feet to square meters
P. teaspoon to milliliters
Q. gallons to liters
R. pints to liters
S. cups to milliliters
T. nautical leagues to meters
 (1 n.l. = 5.56 km)
U. cubic feet to liters
V. cubic inches to milliliters
W. microliters to nanoliters
X. picoliters to centiliters
Y. Celsius to Kelvin
Z. Kelvin to Celsius

There are numerous websites that have conversion calculators you can use to check your answers (onlineconversion.com, for example).

Learning Beyond

A few things to explore the next time you're bored and online:

- **Luis & Walter Alvarez**: The father-son team that gave us the theory that dinosaurs were wiped out by an asteroid, which is often cited as a great example of the scientific method in action.
- **Mars Climate Orbiter**: Often cited as an example of why the U.S. should finally adopt the metric system.
- **Imperial to Metric Approximations**: If the U.S. joined the rest of the world and switched to the metric system, it wouldn't be as difficult as some might think. See for yourself.

Test Your Skills

See the Prologue for an overview of this section. Answers can be found in the Appendix

★ Crawling

1. Fill in the blanks:
a) _____ mixtures are usually clear in appearance, while _____ mixtures are usually cloudy.
b) In the scientific method a _____ is formed before doing any experimentation, while a _____ is formed after.
c) A student measures the mass and volume of an object three times in order to determine its density. All three trials were close to one another, showing good _____, but he forgot to calibrate his balance, which affected the _____ of his mass measurements.

XP: +3 each

2. Identify the following as chemical or physical changes.
a) Water boiling, b) Grating cheese, c) Paper burning, d) The digestion of food, e) Gelatin congealing in the refrigerator, f) Beer fermenting, g) Silver tarnishing

XP: +3 each

3. Determine the number of significant figures in each of the following numbers.
a) 206, b) 3,000, c) 2.0030, d) 9.04×10^5, e) 0.007008, f) 89,040, g) 0.0000021,

XP: +3 each

4. Perform each of the following calculations, rounding your answer to the appropriate number of significant figures.

a) 2.0 + 7.14

b) 405 + 820

c) 25 + 1.55

d) 0.025 − 0.0111

e) 1,339,930 − 6,300

f) 1.9 × 3.14

g) 2.01 × 19.001

h) 5.020 × 4

i) 2,321 ÷ 6.3

j) 6,300,000 ÷ 142

k) 5.03 ÷ 0.00030

XP: +4 each

5. Perform each of the following calculations, rounding your answer to the appropriate number of significant figures.

a) 10.2 + 3.002 + 0.44

b) 338.0 + 19.0 + 3.10

c) 71.08 + 30.0 − 14.20

d) 1,770 − 133 + 900

e) 90.10 × 7.0 ÷ 0.044

f) 6.00 ÷ 0.110 × 8.2

XP: +4 each

6. Rewrite the following conversion factors as fractions.

a) 1 yd = 0.9144 m

b) 1 mg = 0.001 g

c) 1 mi = 1.609 km

d) 1 μL = 10^{-6} L

XP: +3 each

7. Complete the following dimensional analysis strings by canceling out the appropriate units.

a) Feet (ft) to cm: $\text{ft} \times \dfrac{\text{in}}{} \times \dfrac{}{\text{in}} = \text{cm}$

b) pL to μL: $\text{pL} \times \dfrac{\text{L}}{\text{pL}} \times \dfrac{}{} = \text{μL}$

c) mg to kg: $\text{mg} \times \dfrac{}{\text{mg}} \times \dfrac{\text{kg}}{} = \text{kg}$

XP: +4 each

8. What unit(s) remains in each of the following dimensional analysis strings?

a) $\text{nm} \times \dfrac{\text{m}}{\text{nm}} \times \dfrac{\text{pm}}{\text{m}} = $ ___

b) $\text{lb} \times \dfrac{\text{kg}}{\text{lb}} \times \dfrac{\text{g}}{\text{kg}} \times \dfrac{\text{mg}}{\text{g}} = $ ___

c) $\dfrac{\text{mi}}{\text{hr}} \times \dfrac{\text{km}}{\text{mi}} \times \dfrac{\text{m}}{\text{km}} \times \dfrac{\text{hr}}{\text{min}} \times \dfrac{\text{min}}{\text{s}} = $ ___

XP: +4 each

9. Perform the following conversions:
a) 49 miles to km
b) 18 ft to cm
c) 190.0 gal to liters
d) 9,003 lb to kg
e) 2.01 mg to μg
f) 4.066×10^5 oz to kg
g) 19 stone to lb (1 stone = 6.35 kg)
h) 75.0 pints to liters
i) 8.093×10^{-12} cm to Angstroms
j) 58.3 °C to K
k) 455.0 K to °C

XP: +4 each

★ XP: ___

If it's 147 or greater you're ready to start...

★★Walking

10. For each of the following, determine which has the lower density.
a) Air or helium
b) Air or carbon dioxide
c) Crude oil (say, from a spilled tanker) or sea water
d) A ship's anchor or sea water

XP: +3 each

11. Read the following and identify the properties being described as extensive, intensive, chemical or physical. Some properties can fall under more than one category.

A 250 mL sample of a reddish-brown liquid was analyzed. It had a mass of 775 g, giving it a density of 3.1 g/mL. The liquid solidified at -7.2 °C and boiled at 59 °C. It was highly corrosive to most plastics, and was air-sensitive, so it had to be stored in a closed glass bottle. It didn't react with water, however, but its solubility is very low (less than 1 mg per mL water).

XP: +5 for each property

12. Which of the following are extensive properties and which are intensive properties?
a) Tire pressure is often measured in **pounds per square inch**.
b) The **Scoville scale** is used to measure the amount of capsaicin in peppers (the chemical responsible for their "hot" taste).
c) The purity of gold jewelry is measured in **carats**
d) A bottle of juice has 100 **calories per serving**
e) Jack Daniel's whisky is commonly sold as 80 **proof**, or 40 % alcohol **by volume**.

XP: +3 each

13. Perform each of the following calculations, rounding your answer to the appropriate significant figures.
a) $(109 + 20.08) \times (4.0 + 0.59)$
b) $(3.020 + 18.3) \times (4.10 - 1.003)$
c) $(802 - 41.0) \times (0.083 - 0.0271)$
d) $(661 + 80) \div (10.0 - 6.3)$
e) $(1{,}350 + 500) \div (182 - 16.3)$
f) $(283 \times 1.2) + (50.04 \times 0.29)$
g) $(19.10 \div 4.01) + (310 \times 0.409)$
h) $(331 \times 10) - (1{,}504 \div 70.3)$
i) $(42{,}300 \div 108.6) - (11{,}984 \div 221.40)$
j) $(18.308 + 5.04) \times (31.9 - 9.008) \div (58.03 - 42.1)$
k) $(1900 \div 33) - (2201 \div 88) + (103 \times 91)$

XP: +4 each

14. Perform the following conversions using dimensional analysis.

a) The phrase "40 acres and a mule" refers to General William Sherman's attempt to provide land to freed slaves who had joined him during his famed March to the Sea. An acre is equal to 43,560 square feet. Using this conversion factor, convert 40.0 acres to units of square meters.

b) Rocky IV nemesis Ivan Drago threw punches that clocked in at 2,150 lbs/in^2 (which is why whatever he hits, he destroys). Convert this value to kg/m^2.

c) According to Amazon.com, the hardcover edition of *Harry Potter and the Deathly Hallows* is 9.1 × 6.0 × 2.4 inches and weighs about 2.5 pounds. Use these measurements to approximate the book's density in g/mL

XP: +5 each

★★ XP: _____   Total XP: _____

If your Total XP is 220 or greater, take a shot at…

★★★Sprinting

15. Perform each of the following calculations, rounding your answer to the appropriate significant figures.

a) $4.0 \times 10^4 + 3.20 \times 10^5$

b) $6.10 \times 10^7 + 8.990 \times 10^6 - 1.88 \times 10^5$

c) $(4.7 \times 10^4)(2.1 \times 10^3)$

d) $(6.060 \times 10^{-6}) \div (8.00 \times 10^{-8})$

e) $(7.90 \times 10^8)(6.8 \times 10^5) + (3.00 \times 10^4)(5.017 \times 10^6)$

XP: +10 each

16. Perform the following conversions, which come from an alternate dimension that I just made up. Assume they use the same metric system we do.

a) 1,309 jordans (j) to jabbars (jb); 1 jb = 0.23 j

b) 187 shazbots (sz) to kilofraks (kf); 1 sz = 3.85 f

c) 9.010 lucies (l) to centiethels (ce); 1 e = 83.12 l
d) 8.66×10^7 millichiefs (mc) to kratos (k); 1 k = 120.8 c
e) 5.0 gagas (⚷) to germanottas (g); 1 ⚷ = 11.5 kg (exactly)
f) 18.2 j/f^2 to jb/sz^2
g) 10.50 k/g^3 to c/⚷ ^{3}

XP: +10 each

★ ★ ★ XP: _____   Total XP: _____
If your total XP is 307 or greater: Level up!

Achievement Unlocked: Mind over Matter
Completed Chapter 1

You're now ready to learn about elements.

Chapter 2
Atoms & Elements

Part 1: The Origins of Chemistry

Instead of jumping straight into atoms and elements, we'll begin with a brief history of how chemistry—as it's known today—came to be. Like most fundamental ideas of science, the story of the atom, from its earliest known origins to its universal acceptance, is a long one (it's customary to start with the ancient Greeks, but the idea is even older than that). Understanding this journey and others like it is important because you'll not only have a better appreciation of the world we live in, but it might also help you put some perspective on some of today's more hotly debated scientific issues.

What follows is really just scratching the surface of chemistry's history. For a more detailed account (yet still accessible to nonscientists), I would highly recommend *The Chemical Tree* by William H. Brock or *Creations of Fire* by Cathy Cobb & Harold Goldwhite.

The Ancient Greeks

One of the many things the ancient Greeks (5th – 3rd century BC) are famous for is their interest in philosophy. **Natural philosophers**, as the name implies, focused on understanding nature and the world they lived in. Two such philosophers were Leucippus and Democritus, two of the earliest known believers of **atomism**, the idea that the world is composed of small indestructible building blocks we now call atoms. In fact the word atom comes from the Greek word *atomos*, which means "uncuttable."

While the idea of the atom is at least 2500 years old, it's only been widely accepted for less than two hundred. Why so long? Simply put, it took the human race a couple of thousand years just to get a firm understanding of what matter actually *was*. Until that was accomplished, dealing with the issue of what matter was made of would be putting the proverbial cart in front of the horse. During this two millennia time span, there were several other theories that dominated. Some believed that matter wasn't composed of building blocks, but was "infinitely divisible." There were also several theories centered on the idea that matter was composed of just a handful of basic elements, such as the well-known "Earth, Air, Water, and Fire" theory.

The Alchemists

Alchemy was an early form of chemistry, dating back as early as 300 B.C. in China (Chinese alchemists are credited for inventing gunpowder and fireworks) to the European alchemists of the late 17th century. The primary trait that distinguishes alchemists from chemists is basically one of principle. While chemists, like most scientists, are generally interested in serving mankind and sharing what they learn with others, alchemists were more secretive and self-serving (it was common practice for alchemists to write their notes in codes only they could decipher), and would often include as much mysticism in their work as science.

In general, alchemists were interested in two mythical substances: the **philosopher's stone**, which could turn cheap metals into gold, and the **elixir of life**, which granted long-life or perhaps even immortality. Those who consider themselves to be "Potterphiles" might recognize these terms, as the true title of the first Harry Potter book/movie is *Harry Potter and the Philosopher's Stone* (in the book, J.K. Rowling actually lumps the two together, with the philosopher stone being required to produce the elixir of life). When the book finally came to the U.S., the American publishers thought it best to change its name to *Harry Potter and the Sorcerer's Stone*, out of concerns that the original title would be too confusing to children. Of course, fast forward a few years and billions of dollars later, any other concerns they may have had about the series magically disappeared (pun intended), as there seemed to be no problems selling books to kids that were as thick as a Stephen King novel (and nearly as horrific). But I digress…

Notice that both goals of alchemy involve *transmutation*, the conversion of one type of matter to another (turning one metal into another metal and turning diseased flesh into healthy flesh). Needless to say, no known alchemist actually discovered either of these, but some would occasionally stumble upon a way to make a metal *look* like gold, on the surface at least, or might *claim* to have developed some colored liquid that would grant long-life. This didn't do much for the general reputation of alchemy and by the start of the eighteenth century most alchemists were generally looked at as "pseudo-scientists" and held in fairly low regard by the scientific community.

That being said, alchemists did make some positive contributions to science. For example, they developed or perfected many common laboratory techniques that are still used today, such as the 8th century alchemist Abu Musa Jābir ibn Hayyān, who Westerners traditionally refer to as Geber (a variation of his middle name, Jābir). He is widely regarded as one of the earliest known adopters of the scientific method and is credited for discovering several of today's most common acids, such as nitric and sulfuric acid, as well as distillation and crystallization techniques that are still used by modern chemists.

Alchemists were also one of the first to endorse the use of mineral-based, non-herbal chemicals to treat disease (as opposed to a good bleeding from the local barber). One of western Europe's most famous alchemists, Paracelsus (1493-1541, born Philippus Theophrastus Aureolus Bombastus von Hohenheim) was a strong proponent of combining chemistry with medicine. Two of his more notable discoveries include the analgesic properties of ether and the use of mercury to treat syphilis. Of course, we now know that mercury's toxic, but hey, during the remainder of his patients' short lives they were syphilis-free (or so they thought).

Finally, if you think alchemy is a dead practice, consider the following. In the last hundred years, not only have we learned that atoms naturally change from one element type to another, but it's now possible to convert known elements to brand new ones. The difference between then and now is that alchemists were trying to perform such transmutations *chemically* whereas modern chemists use *nuclear* reactions (more on this in Chapter 21). And in case you're wondering, it is possible to change other elements into gold, but the fraction of a penny's worth of gold you're able to collect won't quite cover the costs required to run the cyclotron you'll need to do it. As for the elixir of life ... well, most of us may not be looking to live *forever*, but have you checked your grandparents' medicine cabinet lately? Don't laugh. Yours will undoubtedly look worse when you're their age.

Part 2: Modern Chemistry

Chemistry, as we know it today, didn't really begin to come into its own until the early 18th century, making it the youngest of the "big three" of science (chemistry, biology and physics). This was probably due in some small part to the less-than-respectable reputations of alchemists, but as we mentioned in Part 1, it wasn't until the 1700's that scientists had a firm enough understanding of how matter behaved to actually tackle the issue of what it was made of. Plus, from a technological standpoint, it wasn't until this period that people could make measurements on an accurate enough scale to properly observe changes of a chemical nature. As chemists began to have a better understanding of matter, several scientific laws began to emerge, such as...

The Law of Conservation of Mass

Antoine Lavoisier (1743-1794) is widely considered to be the "father of modern chemistry." Among his many early contributions to the field is his development of the **law of conservation of mass**, which states that matter is neither created nor destroyed during a chemical reaction. Matter cannot disappear or appear from nowhere. When a chemical reaction occurs, all the matter that was present at the beginning has to be accounted for in the end.

One of the earliest observations that led to this law came from a substance known in Lavoisier's time as "red calx." When this solid is heated, it transforms to the familiar silver liquid we call mercury. However, the mass of mercury formed is always smaller than the initial mass of red calx. Fifty grams of red calx, for instance, will only produce forty-six grams of mercury.

$$\text{Red calx} \quad \rightarrow \quad \text{Mercury}$$
$$50g \qquad\qquad\qquad 46g$$

This loss of mass puzzled Lavoisier and his fellow scientists at the time, but eventually he realized that a second element was also forming, which Lavoisier called oxygen. This and experiments like it soon led to the discovery of the gas phase of matter. Today, red calx is more commonly known as mercury (II) oxide (our modern naming system will be discussed in Chapter 3). A modern way to represent the heating of mercury (II) oxide is shown below, which we'll formally introduce in Chapter 4.

$$2HgO(s) \rightarrow 2Hg(l) + O_2(g)$$
$$50.0g \qquad 46.3g \qquad 3.7g$$

Lavoisier also exemplifies the typical chemist of the 18th century. During this time chemistry was more of a hobby than a job (it would be some time before universities made chemistry part of the standard curriculum). What's more, one had to be wealthy enough to afford the necessary lab space and equipment. Unfortunately for Lavoisier, whom you may have correctly guessed to be French, his main occupation was tax collector. If you happen to be a history buff, you may have also noticed the year of his death. He, like Louis XVI and Marie Antoinette, was arrested and publically executed by guillotine during the French Revolution's "Reign of Terror."

To end this section on a slightly less morbid note, one popular myth about Lavoisier was that he remained a scientist to his literal end. As the story goes, Lavoisier's last contribution to science was to test how long the brain could function after being separated from the body. Before his execution, he asked an assistant to find a spot near the front. When he was laid in the guillotine, Lavoisier began to blink his eyes repeatedly and his assistant's job was to count the number of times they blinked after the guillotine's blade fell. Needless to say, the story's probably not true. The logistics of the whole thing aside (the severed head usually fell into a basket, which prevented any prolonged counting to be done), there are no known records of such an experiment being requested or performed.

The Law of Definite Proportions

The law of definite proportions (also known as the law of constant composition) states that a compound will always contain the same elements in the same, fixed proportions. Take the reaction between lead and sulfur, for instance, which combine to form lead sulfide. Because the three substances have significantly different colors (lead is grey, sulfur yellow, and lead sulfide black), one could easily react the two elements and separate the resulting compound from any unreacted starting material. For this reaction, the two elements will completely react with one another when the lead/sulfur ratio is about 6.5:1. In other words, it takes 6.5 grams of lead to completely react with 1 gram of sulfur, which according to the law of conservation of mass should form 7.5 grams of lead sulfide.

6.5 g lead + 1 g sulfur = 7.5 g lead sulfide

This ratio remains constant, even if you repeat this reaction with a larger amount of lead; it will simply remain unreacted afterwards.

10.0 g lead + 1 g sulfur = 7.5 g lead sulfide + 3.5 g lead

The same is true if you increase the initial amount of sulfur

6.5 g lead + 3 g sulfur = 7.5 g lead sulfide + 2 g sulfur

Lead sulfide seems to only form in this constant, fixed mass ratio.

This is how an 18th century chemist would prove the law of definite proportions. A more modern explanation would be that lead sulfide forms in a fixed *numeric* ratio of one lead atom per sulfur atom (PbS). Another example is the well-known formula of water: H_2O. All water is composed of a fixed ratio of two hydrogen atoms per oxygen atom.

This law is often credited to another French chemist, Joseph Proust (1754-1826), but Proust apparently led a less interesting life (and died a less interesting death) than Lavoisier. Compare their Wikipedia entries and see for yourself. So we'll just move on to...

The Law of Multiple Proportions

As Proust's law of definite proportions became more widely accepted, many scientists, most notably English chemist John Dalton (1766-1844), expanded the idea further into **the law of multiple proportions**, which says two elements can combine in *different* fixed proportions to form *different* compounds. For example, carbon and oxygen combines in a 3:4 mass ratio to form carbon monoxide.

3 g carbon + 4 g oxygen = 7 g carbon monoxide

Varying the amounts of carbon and oxygen can lead to results that are similar to the lead/sulfur example in the previous section. However, if you double the amount of oxygen, you form a different compound: carbon *dioxide*.

3 g carbon + 8 g oxygen = 11 g carbon dioxide.

The law of definite proportions is still obeyed: carbon monoxide only forms in a 3:4 ratio while carbon dioxide's is 3:8. A modernized version of this example would be that carbon monoxide forms in a 1:1 ratio of atoms (CO) while carbon dioxide is 1:2 (CO_2).

Dalton's Atomic Theory

In the late 18th century, chemists were finally at the point where they could investigate the big question about matter: what was it made of? Finally, after at least two and a half millennia, many scientists were beginning to accept the idea of the atom. One of the atom's largest proponents was Dalton, who in 1801 published what we know today as **Dalton's atomic theory.** The theory can be summarized as follows:

1. Matter is made up of indivisible and indestructible particles called atoms.
2. All atoms of a given element are identical and have the same mass. Different elements have different atoms with different properties.
3. Compounds are formed from atoms and form in fixed proportions.
4. During a reaction, atoms aren't created or destroyed, but rearranged.

The first part of the theory essentially restates the Greek idea that matter is made of atoms, while the second part tries to explain why different elements have different properties. The last two parts attempt to explain the three laws I mentioned earlier using the idea of the atom.

At this point, let's look back at our earlier discussion on the scientific method from Chapter 1. Notice how it's being followed by scientists of the 18th century. Observations led to scientific laws. Chemists questioned these observations, formed hypotheses, and these ideas were tested experimentally. Finally, at the turn of the century, Dalton proposed a theory on why these observations were occurring, which scientists continue to test and modify to this day.

However, don't assume that everyone immediately jumped on board Dalton's "atomic bandwagon." Even after Dalton published his theory, there were still those who were skeptical of the atomic theory of matter and the debate continued for much of the century to follow. For the most part, however, Dalton's theory has stood the test of time, but as we said in Chapter 1, theories continue to be tested and modified over time, and Dalton's is no exception. As chemistry entered the 20th century, it was discovered that atoms were not only destructible, but most will decompose naturally (more on that when we get to nuclear chemistry in Chapter 21). It was also later discovered that atoms are actually divisible, as we'll see next.

Part 3: The Atom

At the turn of the 20th century there was a virtual explosion of scientific and technological breakthroughs: humans learned to fly, motion pictures were born, and Einstein's "miracle year" of 1905 sparked a new era of physics. This was also the dawn of a new era for chemistry with the discovery of the three "subatomic" particles that make up an atom: protons, neutrons and electrons. While it is true that smaller particles have been discovered (such as quarks), these "fundamental" particles are, for the most part, the sole fascination of modern physicists. Even today, most chemists have little or no need to concern themselves with quarks or bosons (not yet, anyway). In all fairness to physics, however, it was the physicists of the early 1900's who are responsible for the discovery of the three subatomic particles, some of whom will be mentioned in the pages to follow (and were awarded Nobel Prizes for their efforts).

Electrons and Protons

In 1897, J. J. Thomson (1856-1940) discovered the first subatomic particle, which we know today as the electron. **Electrons** are negatively charged particles, based on their attraction to the positive poles of a magnet. In the early 1910's, Robert Millikan (1868-1953) found that the charge of a single electron, in units of coulombs, was -1.602×10^{-22} C. Millikan also went on to calculate the mass of a single electron, which is an even smaller value: 9.1×10^{-28} grams.

Atoms are neutral particles, so if negatively charged electrons are present there must also be something in an atom that carries a positive charge. As Millikan was determining the charge and mass of an electron, Ernest Rutherford (1871-1937), with the help of Hans Geiger (1882-1945) and Ernest Marsden (1889-1970), performed a series of experiments that led to the discovery of a positively charged particle that Rutherford dubbed the

proton. Their work also revealed that these protons lie in an extremely dense area of the atom known as a **nucleus** that's surrounded by a "cloud" of electrons (we'll talk about this cloud in greater detail in Chapter 8).

A proton's charge is equal to an electron's, but with opposite sign: $+1.602 \times 10^{-22}$ C. Working with such small numbers can be rather tedious, so for convenience's sake the charge of a single proton or electron is assigned a relative value of 1. Protons are $+1$ and electrons are -1. For example, an atom with 11 protons and 11 electrons would have a total positive charge of $+11$ and a total negative charge of -11, which would make the atom neutral overall. As we'll see later, it's quite common for atoms to have an unequal number of protons and electrons, giving the atom an overall net charge. Such atoms are known as **ions**. Ions with a net positive charge are called **cations** while those with a negative charge are **anions**. In these cases, using relative charges of ± 1 becomes incredibly more convenient than values in coulombs. An ion with 11 protons and 10 electrons, for instance, would be a cation with an overall charge of $+1$.

Comparing masses, a proton is considerably heavier than an electron—by a factor of almost two thousand—with a mass of 1.67×10^{-24} grams. It's still a tediously small number to deal with when talking about atoms and elements in general, though. It would help to use a relative scale, similar to what we did with charges, but even though the electron's mass is smaller, it's more common to assign the relative value of 1 to a proton's mass, for reasons that should become clearer in a moment. Unlike our relative values of charge, this mass has a unit associated with it. The mass of a proton is normally given as 1 **atomic mass unit** (or amu, for short) or 1 dalton (Da), after the aforementioned chemist. Because an electron's mass (5.45×10^{-4} amu) is so much smaller than a proton's, it's essentially insignificant and usually ignored.

The main characteristic of a proton is that it gives an atom its identity. All atoms of a given element have the same number of protons. All hydrogen atoms, for example, have just one proton. If you're somehow able to put another proton into that atom's nucleus, it's no longer a hydrogen atom. It's an atom of helium. The term **atomic number** is used to describe the number of protons in a given element. It's simply a matter of convenience: Instead of saying "Hydrogen is the atom with one proton in its nucleus while helium is the atom with two protons in its nucleus," we can simply say "Hydrogen is atomic number 1 and helium's atomic number 2."

Neutrons

Rutherford's theory of an atomic nucleus was not widely accepted at first, for a very simple reason: like charges *repel*, so how could a proton-filled nucleus possibly stay intact? Another problem arose when scientists began comparing the masses of atoms with these newly discovered protons and electrons. For example, helium, on average, is four times heavier than hydrogen, but only has twice the number of protons (remember that an electron's mass is insignificant). If Thomson, Millikan, and Rutherford were correct, then how can one account for this discrepancy in mass?

Rutherford hypothesized that a neutral, third particle existed, which was eventually discovered in 1932 by James Chadwick (1891-1974). **Neutrons**, as the name implies, are neutral particles with no overall charge that are also found in the nucleus. Generally speaking, neutrons behave as "atomic glue" that keeps the positively charged nucleus stable. Nuclei without the proper number of neutrons will lead to an unstable atom that will undergo radioactive decay (again, more on that in Chapter 21). The mass of a neutron is equal to a proton, 1.67×10^{-24} g, so it's also said to have mass of 1 amu (their masses actually vary past the third significant figure, but since we're talking about the 26th decimal place, it's usually acceptable for us to think of them as being equal).

Because the mass of electrons are negligible, and since both protons and neutrons are given an arbitrary value of 1, one only needs to count the number of protons and neutrons to determine an atom's mass in amu, which is commonly known as the **mass number**. For example, the vast majority (over 99%) of hydrogen nuclei contain nothing but a single proton in its nucleus, giving them a mass number of 1 amu. A similar percentage of helium atoms have two protons and two neutrons, making their mass number 4 amu.

Unlike protons, atoms of the same element can have a different number of neutrons, which means that—contrary to Dalton's original theory—not all atoms of a given element will have the same mass. We call atoms that are of the same element, but have different masses, **isotopes**. For example, while most isotopes of helium have a mass of 4 amu, some only have one neutron in its nucleus, and therefore have a mass number of 3 amu.

	Electrons	**Protons**	**Neutrons**
Location:	Outside nucleus	Nucleus	Nucleus
Charge:	-1	+1	0
Mass:	Negligible	1 amu	1 amu
Affects:	Charge	Identity, mass and charge	Mass

Finally, while most of the atom's mass is in the nucleus, most of its space is actually occupied by electrons. A common example that's used to convey this point is to imagine going to any major football stadium (NFL, NCAA Division I, or—on the off chance that this book sells overseas—FIFA) and standing in the middle of the field. You would represent the nucleus while the rest of the field and the spectator seats represent the electron cloud.

Isotope Symbols

For most of the concepts discussed in the book, we deal with an element's atoms as a whole and aren't concerned about any isotope in particular, but not always. When it is necessary to refer to a specific isotope (as will be the case in Part 4, as well as most of Chapter 21), it's commonplace to use the following format

$$^A_Z X$$

where X is the element's symbol (which we'll discuss in Part 4), A is the mass number, and Z is a commonly used symbol for atomic number. For example, carbon (atomic number 6) has three main isotopes: one with six neutrons (for a total mass number of 12 amu), one with seven (13 amu), and one with eight (14 amu). To distinguish between these three isotopes, we'd write them respectively as

$$^{12}_6C \quad ^{13}_6C \quad ^{14}_6C$$

You'll sometimes see isotope symbols written without the atomic number (^{12}C, ^{13}C, ^{14}C), particularly in cases where the intended reader or audience is assumed to have an understanding of atoms and the periodic table.

When referring to isotopes by name, it's simply the element name followed by the mass number.

$$^{12}_6C \quad \text{carbon-12}$$
$$^{13}_6C \quad \text{carbon-13}$$
$$^{14}_6C \quad \text{carbon-14}$$

One notable exception is with the three isotopes of hydrogen: $^1_1$ H, $^2_1$H, and $^3_1$H. Because 99.99% of hydrogen is hydrogen-1, its usually referred to simply as "hydrogen." Hydrogen-2 and

56

hydrogen-3 are more commonly known by the names deuterium and tritium, respectively.

Finally, while thinking of atom masses in terms of the number of protons and neutrons works fine for practically everything we discuss in this book, keep in mind that masses in amu are not exact values (see Chapter 1). In other words, the mass of a helium-4 isotope isn't *exactly* four times greater than hydrogen-1. Mass numbers are a general way of expressing an atom's mass for the sake of convenience, but it is possible to determine atom masses with a greater degree of accuracy than simple whole numbers. To do this, carbon-12 was chosen as the standard reference. Only this isotope is said to have an exact mass (12.00000...) and all other isotope masses are measured relative to it.

Try It Yourself

P1. An atom has 48 electrons, 72 neutrons, and 50 protons.
    a. What is its atomic number?
    b. What is its mass number?
    c. What is the charge of this atom?
    d. What is the isotope symbol of this atom?
    e. What is the name of this isotope?

P2. Iodine-123 is an important isotope in the field of medical imaging.
    a. What is its mass number?
    b. What is its atomic number?
    c. How many neutrons are in the nucleus?
    d. If the atom is neutral, how many electrons are present?
    e. Write the isotope symbol of this atom?

P3. A common fuel source for nuclear power plants is the uranium isotope $^{238}_{92}U$.

a. What is the name of this isotope?
b. What is its atomic number?
c. What is its mass number?
d. How many neutrons are in the nucleus?
e. If the charge of the atom was +6, how many electrons are present?

Part 4: The Periodic Table

During the 19th century, as the field of chemistry continued to grow, there was an increasing need for a common, unified method of symbolizing and organizing the elements. Dalton came up with a way to represent the known elements using circular symbols,

but the idea didn't catch on with his fellow chemist, who saw all those little circular symbols to be as confusing as they probably are to you. Eventually, there was a general agreement to simply use letters (more on that later).

The person considered to be the "father" of the periodic table was 19th century Russian chemist Dmitri Mendeleev (1834 – 1907). Mendeleev, like other chemists at the time, knew there was a pattern, or periodicity, within the known elements. Sodium (Na), for example, had similar chemical properties to lithium (Li). The next heaviest element after sodium, magnesium (Mg), had similar properties to the next heaviest element after lithium, beryllium (Be). Inspired by the solitaire card games of his day, Mendeleev fashioned a set of cards using the different elements known at the time and attempted to organize them based on this known periodicity. He soon realized that this worked best when gaps were left in certain parts of his table. A copy of his table is given below (the numbers are the atomic weights of each element, which we'll introduce momentarily).

			Ti = 50	Zr = 90		? = 180
			V = 51	Nb = 94		Ta = 182
			Cr = 52	Mo = 96		W = 186
			Mn = 55	Rh = 104,4		Pt = 197,4
			Fe = 56	Ru = 104,4		Ir = 198
		Ni = Co = 59		Pd = 106,6		Os = 199
H = 1			Cu = 63,4	Ag = 108		Hg = 200
	Be = 9,4	Mg = 24	Zn = 65,2	Cd = 112		
	B = 11	Al = 27,4	? = 68	Ur = 116		Au = 197?
	C = 12	Si = 28	? = 70	Sn = 118		
	N = 14	P = 31	As = 75	Sb = 122		Bi = 210?
	O = 16	S = 32	Se = 79,4	Te = 128?		
	F = 19	Cl = 35,5	Br = 80	J = 127		
Li = 7 Na = 23		K = 39	Rb = 85,4	Cs = 133		Tl = 204
		Ca = 40	Sr = 87,6	Ba = 137		Pb = 207
		? = 45	Ce = 92			
		?Er = 56	La = 94			
		?Yt = 60	Di = 95			
		?In = 75,6	Th = 118?			

For example, Element Ur (today known as indium, In) didn't seem to fit immediately after aluminum (Al), but in the next column over. Mendeleev concluded, with remarkable foresight, that another element—one that had yet to be discovered—belonged in the space between aluminum and indium, so he left it and other spots like it blank (marked with a "?" in the above table). Furthermore, he went on to predict the properties of these undiscovered elements, most of which turned out to be spot on. For example, six years after Mendeleev unveiled his table in 1869, the element gallium (Ga) was discovered, fitting perfectly into the aforementioned gap between aluminum and indium.

	Mendeleev's prediction	Gallium's properties
Atomic weight	68	69.9
Density	5.9	5.9
Melting point	"low"	30°C
Formula of oxide	Ea_2O_3	Ga_2O_3

For those unfamiliar with the Celsius scale, 30°C is 86°F, a very low melting point for a metal. It will melt in the palm of your hand.

The Modern Periodic Table

Our current table is essentially the same as the one developed by Mendeleev with a few modifications. Rows and columns have been switched, plus we've discovered several elements since then, which have required us to expand it a bit.

1	2	3	4	5	6	7	8	9	10	11	12	13	14	15	16	17	18
1 H 1.008																	2 He 4.003
3 Li 6.941	4 Be 9.012											5 B 10.81	6 C 12.01	7 N 14.01	8 O 16.00	9 F 19.00	10 Ne 20.18
11 Na 22.99	12 Mg 24.31											13 Al 26.98	14 Si 28.09	15 P 30.97	16 S 32.07	17 Cl 35.45	18 Ar 39.95
19 K 39.10	20 Ca 40.08	21 Sc 44.96	22 Ti 47.87	23 V 50.94	24 Cr 52.00	25 Mn 54.94	26 Fe 55.85	27 Co 58.93	28 Ni 58.69	29 Cu 63.55	30 Zn 65.39	31 Ga 69.72	32 Ge 72.64	33 As 74.92	34 Se 78.96	35 Br 79.90	36 Kr 83.80
37 Rb 85.47	38 Sr 87.62	39 Y 88.91	40 Zr 91.22	41 Nb 92.91	42 Mo 95.94	43 Tc (98)	44 Ru 101.1	45 Rh 102.9	46 Pd 106.4	47 Ag 107.9	48 Cd 112.4	49 In 114.8	50 Sn 118.7	51 Sb 121.8	52 Te 127.6	53 I 126.9	54 Xe 131.3
55 Cs 132.9	56 Ba 137.3	57 La 138.9	72 Hf 178.5	73 Ta 180.9	74 W 183.8	75 Re 186.2	76 Os 190.2	77 Ir 192.2	78 Pt 195.1	79 Au 197.0	80 Hg 200.6	81 Tl 204.4	82 Pb 207.2	83 Bi 209.0	84 Po (209)	85 At (210)	86 Rn (222)
87 Fr (223)	88 Ra (226)	89 Ac (227)	90 Rf (261)	105 Db (262)	106 Sg (266)	107 Bh (264)	108 Hs (277)	109 Mt (268)	110 Ds (281)	111 Rg (272)	112 Cn (285)	113 Uut (286)	114 Uuq (289)	115 Uup (289)	116 Uuh (293)	117 Uus (294)	118 Uuo (294)

58 Ce 140.1	59 Pr 140.9	60 Nd 144.2	61 Pm (145)	62 Sm 150.4	63 Eu 152.0	64 Gd 157.3	65 Tb 158.9	66 Dy 162.5	67 Ho 154.9	68 Er 167.3	69 Tm 168.9	70 Yb 173.0	71 Lu 175.0
90 Th 232.0	91 Pa 231.0	92 U 238.0	93 Np (237)	94 Pu (244)	95 Am (243)	96 Cm (247)	97 Bk (247)	98 Cf (251)	99 Es (252)	100 Fm (257)	101 Md (258)	102 No (259)	103 Lr (262)

The rows of the periodic table are known as **periods,** while columns are referred to as **groups.** While the information on a periodic table can vary, most will at least have the following information:
1. The element's symbol
2. The atomic number (written above the element symbol)
3. The atomic mass (written below the element symbol)

Atomic Mass

The **atomic mass** of an element (also known as *atomic weight*) is the weighted average of the naturally occurring isotopes of an element. Unlike the type of averaging you're probably used to (the *mean* average), where you simply sum up and divide by the total number, in a weighted average some values are factored in or "weighted" more heavily than others. In the case of atomic mass, more abundant isotopes of an element are weighed more heavily.

Chlorine, for example, has two naturally occurring isotopes: chlorine-35, whose mass to four significant figures is 34.97 amu (remember, only carbon-12 has an exact mass) and chlorine-37, which has a mass of 36.97. Chlorine-35 makes up 75.77% of the chlorine found in nature while the other 24.23% is chlorine-37. The mean average would treat each mass equally ("fifty-fifty")

$$\frac{34.97 + 36.97}{2} = 35.97$$

or, shown another way,

$$(34.97)(0.50) + (36.97)(0.50) = 35.97$$

To find the weighted average, you multiply each mass by its percent abundance (as a fraction) and then add the two together.

$$(34.97)(0.7577) + (36.97)(0.2423) = 35.45 \text{ amu}$$

Looking at the periodic table, you'll see that 35.45 is given as the atomic mass of chlorine.

Why use a weighted average instead of the mean? For starters, the calculations that we'll be doing in the next chapter will be much more accurate. In more general terms, a weighted average is a better representation of how an element's isotopes

62

are distributed in nature. Look back at the atomic mass of chlorine. Of the two isotopes, the atomic mass lies closest to chlorine-35, the more abundant isotope.

As another example, let's look back at the three isotopes of hydrogen: ^1_1H, ^2_1H, and ^3_1H. Using the mass numbers for simplicity, the mean average of these three isotopes is 2

$$\frac{1 + 2 + 3}{3} = 2$$

However, as we mentioned in Part 3, 99.99% of hydrogen is hydrogen-1 ("hydrogen"). An extremely small percentage (less than 0.01%) of hydrogen isotopes are deuterium, and tritium only exists in trace amounts. An average value of 2 is a highly inaccurate representation of how hydrogen is found in nature. It's much better to factor in the percent abundances of these three isotopes, giving us an atomic mass of 1.008 amu.

Organizing the Groups

There have been three different ways to organize the groups of the modern periodic table and all three are still used to some degree. There are two competing "A/B" systems in use, where some of the groups are labeled with A's and some with B's. There is also a system where all of the columns are simply labeled 1-18, which is popular in most scientific journals. So aluminum (Al), for example, might be considered a group 3A, a group 3B or a group 13 element, depending on which table you use. Of these three we will work exclusively with the A/B system shown below, where the taller columns are labeled with A's and skinny part in the middle are labeled B's. There are several reasons we'll use this particular system, which you'll see as we progress through the book.

1 1A	2 2A											13 3A	14 4A	15 5A	16 6A	17 7A	18 8A
1 H 1.008		3B	4B	5B	6B	7B	8B	8B	8B	1B	2B						2 He 4.003
3 Li 6.941	4 Be 9.012	3	4	5	6	7	8	9	10	11	12	5 B 10.81	6 C 12.01	7 N 14.01	8 O 16.00	9 F 19.00	10 Ne 20.18
11 Na 22.99	12 Mg 24.31											13 Al 26.98	14 Si 28.09	15 P 30.97	16 S 32.07	17 Cl 35.45	18 Ar 39.95
19 K 39.10	20 Ca 40.08	21 Sc 44.96	22 Ti 47.87	23 V 50.94	24 Cr 52.00	25 Mn 54.94	26 Fe 55.85	27 Co 58.93	28 Ni 58.69	29 Cu 63.55	30 Zn 65.39	31 Ga 69.72	32 Ge 72.64	33 As 74.92	34 Se 78.96	35 Br 79.90	36 Kr 83.80
37 Rb 85.47	38 Sr 87.62	39 Y 88.91	40 Zr 91.22	41 Nb 92.91	42 Mo 95.94	43 Tc (98)	44 Ru 101.1	45 Rh 102.9	46 Pd 106.4	47 Ag 107.9	48 Cd 112.4	49 In 114.8	50 Sn 118.7	51 Sb 121.8	52 Te 127.6	53 I 126.9	54 Xe 131.3
55 Cs 132.9	56 Ba 137.3	57 La 138.9	72 Hf 178.5	73 Ta 180.9	74 W 183.8	75 Re 186.2	76 Os 190.2	77 Ir 192.2	78 Pt 195.1	79 Au 197.0	80 Hg 200.6	81 Tl 204.4	82 Pb 207.2	83 Bi 209.0	84 Po (209)	85 At (210)	86 Rn (222)
87 Fr (223)	88 Ra (226)	89 Ac (227)	104 Rf (261)	105 Db (262)	106 Sg (266)	107 Bh (264)	108 Hs (277)	109 Mt (268)	110 Ds (281)	111 Rg (272)	112 Cn (285)	113 Uut (286)	114 Fl (289)	115 Uup (289)	116 Lv (293)	117 Uus (294)	118 Uuo (294)

58 Ce 140.1	59 Pr 140.9	60 Nd 144.2	61 Pm (145)	62 Sm 150.4	63 Eu 152.0	64 Gd 157.3	65 Tb 158.9	66 Dy 162.5	67 Ho 154.9	68 Er 167.3	69 Tm 168.9	70 Yb 173.0	71 Lu 175.0
90 Th 232.0	91 Pa 231.0	92 U 238.0	93 Np (237)	94 Pu (244)	95 Am (243)	96 Cm (247)	97 Bk (247)	98 Cf (251)	99 Es (252)	100 Fm (257)	101 Md (258)	102 No (259)	103 Lr (262)

The A groups—using the A/B system above—are collectively referred to as the **main group elements**, while the B groups are called the **transition elements** (or transition *metals*, since we'll soon see that all of these elements are classified as metals). Technically, for reasons we're not quite ready to discuss, group 2B—Zn, Cd, Hg, and Cn—isn't "officially" a transition group, but in a general chemistry course it's often considered as such (to be honest, it's not the only little white lie you'll be told; it's just one of the few times I'm actually admitting it).

The bottom two rows, which you may already know as the "lanthanide and actinide series" are officially called the **inner transition elements**. An older term is *rare earth elements*, but these days many of these elements are fairly common. Uranium (U) and plutonium (Pu), for example, are used to fuel nuclear power plants while many household smoke alarms contain a small amount of americium (Am).

Most groups are referred to by the first element in its group (boron group, carbon group, etc), except the following four that still use traditional names:

Group 1A*   Alkali metals
Group 2A   Alkaline earth metals
Group 7A   Halogens
Group 8a   Noble gases,
            Rare gases,
            or Inert gases
*except hydrogen

Metals, nonmetals, metalloids

An element is classified as a **metal** if it has the following three characteristics:
1. It has a luster (or will if you polish or clean it)
2. It's bendable or malleable (flattens into sheets)
3. It's a good conductor of electricity.

As you can see in the figure below, the majority of elements are classified as metals.

3 Li 6.941	4 Be 9.012																
11 Na 22.99	12 Mg 24.31	3 3B	4 4B	5 5B	6 6B	7 7B	8 8B	9 8B	10 8B	11 1B	12 2B	13 Al 26.98					
19 K 39.10	20 Ca 40.08	21 Sc 44.96	22 Ti 47.87	23 V 50.94	24 Cr 52.00	25 Mn 54.94	26 Fe 55.85	27 Co 58.93	28 Ni 58.69	29 Cu 63.55	30 Zn 65.39	31 Ga 69.72					
37 Rb 85.47	38 Sr 87.62	39 Y 88.91	40 Zr 91.22	41 Nb 92.91	42 Mo 95.94	43 Tc (98)	44 Ru 101.1	45 Rh 102.9	46 Pd 106.4	47 Ag 107.9	48 Cd 112.4	49 In 118.7	50 Sn				
55 Cs 132.9	56 Ba 137.3	57 La 138.9	72 Hf 178.5	73 Ta 180.9	74 W 183.8	75 Re 186.2	76 Os 190.2	77 Ir 192.2	78 Pt 195.1	79 Au 197.0	80 Hg 200.6	81 Tl 204.4	82 Pb 207.2	83 Bi 209.0			
87 Fr (223)	88 Ra (226)	89 Ac (227)	104 Rf (261)	105 Db (262)	106 Sg (266)	107 Bh (264)	108 Hs (277)	109 Mt (268)	110 Ds (281)	111 Rg (272)	112 Cn (285)	113 Uut (286)	114 Fl (289)	115 Uup (289)			

58 Ce 140.1	59 Pr 140.9	60 Nd 144.2	61 Pm (145)	62 Sm 150.4	63 Eu 152.0	64 Gd 157.3	65 Tb 158.9	66 Dy 162.5	67 Ho 154.9	68 Er 167.3	69 Tm 168.9	70 Yb 173.0	71 Lu 175.0
90 Th 232.0	91 Pa 231.0	92 U 238.0	93 Np (237)	94 Pu (244)	95 Am (243)	96 Cm (247)	97 Bk (247)	98 Cf (251)	99 Es (252)	100 Fm (257)	101 Md (258)	102 No (259)	103 Lr (262)

A **nonmetal** can simply be defined as having none of the characteristics of a metal. You can't give it a luster, they can't be bent or flattened, and they're usually poor conductors of electricity. The nonmetals are highlighted in the following figure:

					2 He 4.003
	6 C 12.01	7 N 14.01	8 O 16.00	9 F 19.00	10 Ne 20.18
		15 P 30.97	16 S 32.07	17 Cl 35.45	18 Ar 39.95
			34 Se 78.96	35 Br 79.90	36 Kr 83.80
				53 I 126.9	54 Xe 131.3
					86 Rn (222)
					118 Uuo (294)

There's a third set of elements that exhibit some properties of a metal and some of a nonmetal (which properties will vary for each element). These are known as **metalloids**. Silicon is a good example of a metalloid. It does have a luster, but it's not malleable, and is a *semi*conductor of electricity. Metalloids can be thought of as an "overlap region" of the metals and nonmetals. The following elements are generally regarded as metalloids, though some consider polonium to be a metal while the properties of elements 116 and 117 are still being investigated.

5 B 10.81					
	14 Si 28.09				
	32 Ge 72.64	33 As 74.92			
		51 Sb 121.8	52 Te 127.6		
			84 Po (209)	85 At (210)	
			116 Uuh (293)	117 Uus (294)	

The Elements

There are currently 118 known elements. The first 94 on the periodic table (hydrogen through plutonium) can be found naturally, though some, such as technetium and plutonium are extremely rare and only exist in trace amounts. Elements of atomic number 95 and up are synthetic ("man-made").

Each element is represented by a one or two-letter symbol. Several common elements, like the following, simply use the first letter of their name.

Hydrogen	H
Carbon	C
Nitrogen	N

Several elements take the first letter, plus either the second...

Helium	He
Cobalt	Co
Nickel	Ni

or another letter in its name.

Magnesium	Mg
Chlorine	Cl
Platinum	Pt

If an element's symbol seems odd (to English speakers, anyway), it's usually because the symbol is based on the name in another language. Examples include...

Copper	Cu	Latin, *Cuprum*
Tin	Sn	Latin, *Stannum*
Lead	Pb	Latin, *Plumbum*
Mercury	Hg	Greek, *Hydragyrum*
Tungsten	W	Swedish, *Wolfram*

Notice that the first letter of the symbol is always capitalized and the second letter—when present—is lowercase. This is to avoid any unnecessary confusion. For example, Cu is the symbol for copper. If you write "CU," you're actually writing the formula for a compound made of carbon and uranium. Likewise, silver is Ag, while "AG" is a compound made of two elements that don't actually exist.

Most elements are **monatomic**, meaning they exist as individual atoms. All metals are monatomic. A piece of metallic iron, for example, is made up of individual iron atoms. The elements of the noble gas group (8A) are also monatomic. There are, however, several important elements that are actually **diatomic**, meaning they exist as two-atom molecules.

Hydrogen	H_2
Nitrogen	N_2
Oxygen	O_2
Fluorine	F_2
Chlorine	Cl_2
Bromine	Br_2
Iodine	I_2

So while a helium balloon contains individual helium atoms, a balloon filled with hydrogen would consist of diatomic (two-atom) molecules of H_2. Likewise the oxygen and nitrogen in the air you're breathing is actually O_2 and N_2.

There are also a few elements that are **polyatomic**, existing as molecules of three or more atoms. Two common examples are phosphorus (P_4) and sulfur (S_8).

Try It Yourself

P4. Silicon has three naturally occurring isotopes:

isotope	mass (amu)	natural abundance (%)
silicon-28	27.98	92.23
silicon-29	28.98	4.683
silicon-30	29.97	3.087

Using this information, calculate the atomic mass of this element.

P5. Boron has two naturally occurring isotopes: boron-10 and boron-11. Given its atomic mass of 10.81, which isotope would you expect to be the more abundant?

P6. Identify each of the following:
a) The element in period 3, group 5A
b) The alkali metal of the second period
c) The halogen of the fourth period
d) The two nonmetals in the fifth period
e) The three main group metals of the third period
f) The nonmetal of group 4A

Learning Beyond

1) Not every scientific theory stands the test of time. Here's a few that you might be interested in:
- The phlogiston theory
- The "plum-pudding" model of the atom
- The caloric theory of heat
- The geocentric model of astronomy
- The theory of luminiferous ether (or aether)

2) If you'd like to know more about the work that led to our current model of the atom, check out the following:

- Thomson's cathode ray experiments
- Millikan's "oil drop" experiment
- Rutherford's "gold foil" experiment

3) There have been several attempts to "improve" the periodic table. Search the internet for "alternate periodic tables" to see what I mean.

Test Your Skills

★Padawan

1. A piece of iron is left outside and eventually begins to rust. The rusted iron weighs more than it did originally. Which law rules out the possibility that the rusted metal is still pure iron?

XP: +4

2. A 25 g sample of limestone (calcium carbonate) is heated, forming 14 g of quicklime (calcium oxide) and a gas. How many grams of gas should have formed? Which law is your answer based on?

XP: +4

3. If 50 g of sodium reacts with 77 g of chlorine to form table salt (sodium chloride)
a) how grams of table salt should form? Which law is your answer based on?
b) how many grams of chlorine would be required to react with 200 g of sodium? Which law is your answer based on?

XP: +4 each

4. Complete the following table

Atom	A	B	C	D
Protons	15	26	___	51
Neutrons	17	___	113	___
Electrons	16	23	___	___
Mass number	___	56	190	125
Charge	___	___	+4	-2

XP: +3 for each blank

5. What are the names and isotope symbols of the four isotopes in question 4.

XP: +3 each

6. How many protons and neutrons are in each of the following isotopes: a) $^{10}_{4}$Be, b) $^{40}_{18}$Ar, c) $^{62}_{28}$Ni, d) $^{109}_{47}$Ag, e) $^{199}_{80}$Hg

XP: +3 each

7. Magnesium has three naturally occurring isotopes.

Mass (amu)	Percent abundance (%)
23.99	78.99
24.99	10.00
25.98	11.01

Use this information to verify the element's atomic mass of 24.31 that's shown on the periodic table.

XP: +4

8. Match each element with its appropriate classifications.

a. Aluminum (Al) _____
b. Chlorine (Cl) _____
c. Iron (Fe) _____
d. Lead (Pb) _____
e. Magnesium (Mg) _____
f. Neon (Ne) _____
g. Oxygen (O) _____
h. Uranium (U) _____

A. Alkali metal
B. Alkaline earth metal
C. Halogen
D. Noble Gas
E. Main group element
F. Transition element
G. Inner transition element
H. Monatomic element
I. Diatomic element

XP: +3 each

★XP: _____

If your XP is 68 or greater, you're ready to become a...

★★Knight

9. Complete the following table:

Isotope Symbol	$^{32}_{16}S$	___	___	___
Isotope Name	___	iodine-123	___	___
Atomic number	___	___	92	19
Mass number	___	___	238	___
No. of neutrons	___	___	___	22

XP: +3 for each blank

10. Write isotope symbols for each of the following:
a) silicon-32, b) bromine-81, c) calcium-44, d) arsenic-75

XP: +4 each

11. Using our modern version of the periodic table, identify each of the following elements from Mendeleev's original version.
a) The unknown (?) element after zirconium (Zr) in the first row
b) The unknown (?) element between silicon (Si) and tin (Sn)
c) Element "J" in the next to last column, between tellurium (Te) and cesium (Cs)
d) The unknown (?) element below calcium (Ca)

XP: +4 each

12. Identify each of the following elements using the current periodic table: a) The alkali earth metal in period 4, b) The halogen in period 3, c) The inert gas in period 6, d) The third transition metal in period 5, e) The seventh inner transition metal in period 7

XP: +4 each

13. A student who likes leaving the CAPS LOCK button on (a favorite on internet message boards and emails from elderly relatives) wrote the following five elements. What element was he trying to show? What elements are actually being shown?
a) SI, b) HF, c) PB, d) CO, e) IN

XP: +4 each

14. Copper has two naturally occurring isotopes: copper-63 and copper-65. If copper-63 has a mass of 62.93 amu and a natural abundance of 69.17%, what is the mass (to four significant figures) and percent abundance of copper-65?

XP: +5

15. What's the difference between Cl_2 and $2Cl$?

XP: +4

★★ XP: _____   Total XP: _____

If your total XP is 161 or greater, then you just might have what it takes to become a...

★★★Master

16. Sulfur has been known since ancient times (originally known as "brimstone"). However, until Lavoisier showed otherwise, many thought that sulfur was a compound and not an element. Suggest a method that Lavoisier may have used to prove that it wasn't a compound.

XP: +10

17. Using its mass number, calculate the mass of a nitrogen-14 nucleus in units of a) grams, b) micrograms, c) picograms.

XP: +10 each

18. An isotope is found to be 4.6613 times heavier than that of carbon-12. a) Calculate the mass of this isotope. b) If it's percent abundance is high, what is a possible identity of this isotope?

XP: +10 each

19. When writing an isotope symbol, why is it acceptable to omit the atomic number (^{A}X), but not the mass number ($_{Z}X$)?

XP: +5

74

20. Boron has two naturally occurring isotopes: boron-10 and boron-11. Using only the periodic table, determine which isotope is the most stable. Explain your answer.

XP: +10

21. Gallium has two stable isotopes: gallium-69 and gallium 71. The masses of these two isotopes—to four significant figures—are 68.93 and 70.92 amu, respectively. Use these masses along with gallium's atomic weight (69.73 amu) to calculate the percent abundance of each isotope.

XP: +10

22. In the sentences below, which are referring to the elemental form of oxygen (O_2) and which are referring to oxygen atoms (O)?
a) Animals require oxygen to live.
b) Carbon dioxide is composed of two oxygens and one carbon.
c) Oxygen gas was a by-product of a reaction.

XP: +5 each

★ ★ ★ XP: _____   Total XP: _____

If your total XP is 228 or greater: Level up!

Achievement Unlocked: Elementary, Watson!
Completed Chapter 2

You're now ready to learn about compounds.

Chapter 3
Molecules & Compounds

Part 1: Introduction to Compounds

Chemical Formulas

The most common way to show a compound is as a **molecular formula**, which simply shows the type and number of each element in a given compound. You're probably familiar with these to some degree already, such as the formula for water: H_2O. Notice that the number of a given atom is shown as a subscript, written to the right of its symbol, though we don't bother with a subscript when there's only one.

Compounds can also be represented as **structural formulas,** which shows how the atoms are bonded together and, depending on how detailed you draw it, what the molecule looks like in 3D space. A common type of structural formula is a Lewis structure, which we'll discuss in Chapter 10.

These days, various types of computer-generated structures are also common, such as "ball-and-stick" and "space-filling" structures, as they're commonly called, as well as ribbon-like structures for larger biological compounds. In most cases, such structures are based on experimental data to accurately portray a molecule's shape, which we'll talk more about in Chapter 10.

Molecular Mass

Determining the mass of a compound isn't any different from adding up the change in your pocket (assuming you still carry cash, that is). Let's say you have two dimes and a nickel.

You know a dime is worth 10 cents and a nickel's worth 5 cents, giving you a total of 25 cents

$$2(\$0.10) + \$0.05 = \$0.25$$

In the case of a water molecule, a quick peek at the periodic table tells us that each hydrogen has a mass of 1.008 amu and oxygen is 16.00 amu. Following the significant figures rule for addition (since we're adding up our atomic masses), this gives us a total mass of 18.02 amu

$$2(1.008 \text{ amu}) + 16.00 \text{ amu} = 18.02 \text{ amu}$$

When calculating the molecular mass of a compound, you should use at least four significant figures for an element's atomic mass and round up using the rules for addition.

Organic vs. Inorganic Compounds

Organic compounds are those based on the element carbon. Originally, an organic compound was defined as compounds made from living things, but over time chemists reached a point where they could routinely make these types of compounds in a lab, so the definition had to be redefined.

Compounds based on the other elements are **inorganic compounds**. Now, with one class of compounds based on 117 elements and the others based on just one, it would be easy to assume that there are far more inorganic compounds than organic, but it's quite the opposite. There are roughly half a million known inorganic compounds and between 20 to 30 *million* organic compounds. How do you get that many compounds from one element? One reason is carbon has a unique ability to form long chains of itself (C-C-C-C-C-C-C...), an ability known as *catenation*. These chains can be hundreds of atoms long or more, something no other element can do. The next closest is silicon and it can only make chains of a little more than a dozen atoms.

Organic compounds, by their very nature, are inherently more complex compounds to deal with. As such, the vast majority of concepts covered in this book will be illustrated using inorganic compounds. If you're a college student (I'm assuming most of you reading this are), your major may require you to become more familiar with organic compounds later in your studies, most likely a year from now.

Part 2: Ionic Compounds

Ionic compounds, as the name implies, are compounds composed of ions. These ions can be **monatomic** (charged atoms) or **polyatomic** (charged molecules). Because ionic compounds are neutral overall, one ion will carry a positive charge (a cation) and the other will carry a negative charge (an anion). A few examples of ionic compounds that you might already be familiar with are given below.

Common name	Cation	Anion
Table salt	Na^+	Cl^-
Lye	Na^+	OH^-
Baking Soda	Na^+	HCO_3^-
Quicklime	Ca^{2+}	O^{2-}
Limestone	Ca^{2+}	CO_3^{2-}
Milk of magnesia	Mg^{2+}	OH^-

Notice that we show an ion's charge as a superscript in the upper right corner of its chemical symbol (if monatomic) or molecular formula (if polyatomic). Charges are usually written number first (2+, 2-, etc), except for charges of +1 or −1, where only the sign is written.

The distinguishing feature of ionic compounds is they don't actually exist as individual molecules. For example, there's technically no such thing as a "table salt molecule." Rather, these types of compounds exist as a three-dimensional network of ions (known as a **crystal lattice)** that extends throughout the entire compound. In table salt, for example, each sodium ion is actually interacting with six chlorine ions (and vice versa). The following figure shows a section of table salt's crystal lattice (sodium is in grey, chloride in white).

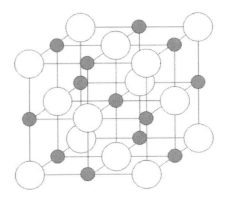

This "wall of ions" would actually extend further in all three dimensions, making up the entire crystal. Not every ionic compound has a crystal lattice with one ion interacting with six of the other, though. That will vary, depending on the relative charges and sizes of the two ions.

Monatomic Ions

For the most part, metals tend to form cations while nonmetals tend to form anions. Most of the main group elements (the *A* groups) are **constant charge elements**, meaning they typically form just one type of ion in nature. Using the A/B grouping system discussed in Chapter 2 (Part 4), we see a relationship between the common charge of several elements and the group that it's in.

- Metals of groups 1A-3A usually form cations with a charge equal to its group number. Examples: Na^+, Mg^{2+} and Al^{3+}.
- Nonmetals of groups 5A-7A usually form anions with a charge equal to its group number minus 8. Examples: F^-, O^{2-}, and N^{3-}
- Group 4A elements are a mixture of the above trends. Carbon and silicon commonly form −4 ions. Germanium, tin, and lead commonly form +4 ions (though other ions are known).

- Group 8A elements don't usually form ions (or compounds, in general).

Variable charge elements have more than one common charge. Iron ions, for example, have two common charges, Fe^{2+} and Fe^{3+}. Most of the transition metals are variable charge elements, having two or more common charges. There are only two transition metals that are usually considered to be constant charge elements: silver is usually a +1 cation while zinc ions are usually +2. Otherwise, you may assume that all other transition metals are variable charge elements

Finally, while hydrogen usually forms ions with a +1 charge (one of the reasons it's placed above the alkali metals), it can also have a -1 charge, depending on what the other ion in the compound is. For example, when dissolved in water, HCl forms H^+ and Cl^- (sort of; more on than in Chapter 5), but the compound LiH is composed of Li^+ and H^- ions.

Polyatomic ions

Like atoms, molecules can also have an unequal number of protons and electrons. A molecule with an overall charge (positive or negative) is called a **polyatomic ion**. A few common polyatomic ions are shown in the following table:

Cations:

Ammonium	NH_4^+	Mercury (I)	Hg_2^{2+}

Anions:

Carbonate	CO_3^{2-}	Nitrate	NO_3^-
Bicarbonate	HCO_3^-	Nitrite	NO_2^-
(hydrogen carbonate)			
Phosphate	PO_4^{3-}	Cromate	CrO_4^{2-}
Hydrogen phosphate	HPO_4^{2-}	Dichromate	$Cr_2O_7^{2-}$
Dihydrogen phosphate	$H_2PO_4^-$	Permanganate	MnO_4^-
Perchlorate	ClO_4^-	Cyanide	CN^-
Chlorate	ClO_3^-	Hydroxide	OH^-
Chlorite	ClO_2^-	Peroxide	O_2^{2-}
Hypochlorite	ClO^-	Acetate	$C_2H_3O_2^-$ or $CH_3CO_2^-$
Sulfite	SO_3^{2-}		
Sulfate	SO_4^{2-}		
Bisulfate	HSO_4^-		
(hydrogen sulfate)			

You might have noticed that most of the anions on this list are a combination of oxygen and some other nonmetal, which are often referred to as *oxyanions*. Examining these oxyanions a little further, we can see a couple of trends. First, oxyanions based on the same element have the same charge, such as nitrate (NO_3^-) and nitrite (NO_2^-). With the four chlorine-based oxyanions, the middle two are chlorate (ClO_3^-) and chlorite (ClO_2^-). Also, adding a hydrogen to an anion lowers the overall charge by 1, as it is with CO_3^{2-} and HCO_3^-. However, this doesn't mean that compound is composed of H^+ and CO_3^{2-} ions (more on that a little later in the chapter).

Formulas of Ionic Compounds

Since ionic compounds aren't individual molecules, you can't really show it as a molecular formula since the number of ions in the crystal lattice depends on the size of the crystal. Instead, we use a variation of the molecular formula known as an **empirical formula**, where we only show the simplest ratio of each element in the compound. For example, with table salt, no matter how big the crystal lattice ends up being, you're always going to have one Na^+ ion for every Cl^-. Because ionic compounds are neutral overall, the ions must have a net charge of zero. For this to happen with table salt, the sodium/chlorine ratio must be 1:1, giving an empirical formula of NaCl.

$$Na^+ + Cl^- \rightarrow NaCl$$
$$+1 + (-1) = 0$$

Ionic formulas are always written cation first, anion second. Also, since it's technically incorrect to say you have a "molecule" of NaCl, it's better to use the term *formula unit*.

Example: What is the empirical formula of a compound made from aluminum and fluorine ions?

Aluminum, being a group 3A element, should form an Al^{3+} ion. Since fluorine is in group 7A, it will form a F^- ion. For every one aluminum ion, it looks like you'll need three fluorine ions.

$$Al^{3+} + 3\ F^- \rightarrow AlF_3$$
$$+3 + 3(-1) = 0$$

The Crossover Method

A quick way to come up with an ionic formula is commonly called the **crossover method**, where the charge of cation becomes the subscript of the anion, and vice versa. Doing this with the previous example gives us

$$Al^{3+} \quad F^- \rightarrow AlF_3$$

Can you see why it's called the crossover method?

Example: What is the formula for a compound made of Ti^{4+} and oxygen ions?

First, notice you had to be told what the charge of titanium is, since it's a transition metal and predicted to be a variable charge element (which it is). Oxygen, on the other hand, only has one common charge, O^{2-}, since it's a member of group 6A. Doing the crossover method gives us

$$Ti^{4+} \quad O^{2-} \rightarrow Ti_2O_4$$

Remember, though, that an empirical formula is the *simplest* ratio. A 2:4 ratio can be simplified to 1:2.

$$Ti^{4+} \quad O^{2-} \rightarrow Ti_2O_4 \rightarrow TiO_2$$

Keep in mind that titanium is *still* +4 and oxygen is still -2; we're only simplifying the subscripts. And like our previous example, we can check our formula by making sure the charges add up to zero.

$$Ti^{4+} + 2\,O^{2-} \rightarrow TiO_2$$
$$+4 + 2(-2) = 0$$

Also remember that ionic compounds *aren't* individual molecules, so this compound isn't made of TiO_2 molecules *or* Ti_2O_4 molecules. It's a big crystal lattice that has one Ti ion for every two O ions.

Compounds with Polyatomic Ions

Let's say you have a compound made of Mg^{2+} and nitrate ion, NO_3^-. Using the crossover rule, magnesium will have a subscript of 1 and nitrate a subscript of 2. To clearly show that there are two nitrate ions for every magnesium ion, we put parentheses around the polyatomic ion and place the subscript on the outside.

$$Mg^{2+} \quad NO_3^- \rightarrow Mg(NO_3)_2$$

However, if the polyatomic ion only needs a subscript of 1, there's no need to write the parentheses.

$$Mg^{2+} + SO_4^{2-} \rightarrow MgSO_4 \; not \; Mg(SO_4)$$

Hydrated Compounds

Some solids, ionic compounds in particular, contain gaps in their crystal lattice that are large enough to trap water molecules. When that happens the compound is said to be **hydrated**. For example, the compound $NiCl_2$ will often contain six water molecules per formula unit. There are two ways to show a compound is hydrated. First, you can include the water as part of the compound's formula, like so:

$$NiCl_2 \cdot 6H_2O$$

Another way is to add this information to the compound's chemical name, which we'll discuss in Part 4.

Unless you're specifically given this information in the formula or name, it either means the compound is **anhydrous** ("without water") or it's simply not important for the topic at hand. Many hydrated compounds can be made anhydrous simply by heating the solid. The gaps in the crystal lattice remain, however, so many anhydrous compounds will rehydrate by absorbing moisture from the air. Such compounds have practical uses as *desiccants*, which trap moisture to prevent it from building up. This is why clothing and shoe manufacturers place those little packets of silica gel in their products, and why some restaurants mix rice into their salt shakers.

When determining the molecular mass of a compound, it's important to factor in the mass of water. Think about the last time you were out in the rain, or jumped into a pool fully clothed (or whatever you kids do for fun these days). Water makes your clothes heavier, right? The same thing happens when anhydrous compounds become hydrated. Anhydrous $NiCl_2$, for example, has a molecular mass of

$$58.69 + 2(35.45) = 129.59 \text{ amu}$$

but as $NiCl_2 \cdot 6H_2O$, you must also include mass from water.

$$58.69 + 2(35.45) + 6(18.02) = 237.71 \text{ amu}$$

Try It Yourself

P1. Determine the formulas for the six compounds given in the table at the start of this section (table salt, lye, etc.)

P2. Calculate the molecular mass of each of the following compounds:
a) CO, b) PF_3, c) Na_2SO_4, d) $Fe(NO_3)_2$, e) $ZnCl_2 \cdot 5H_2O$

P3. Determine the charge of the metal in each of the following compounds:
a) $CoCl_2$, b) NiN, c) Cu_2S, d) $Pt(SO_4)_2$, e) CrO_3

Part 3: Covalent Compounds

In an ionic compound, one element (or compound, in the case of polyatomic ions) gets rid of one or more electrons, forming a cation. These electrons are taken by another element (or compound) to become an anion. In table salt, for example, sodium atoms give up an electron to become Na^+ and each chlorine atom will take an electron to become Cl^-.

$$Na \quad Cl \rightarrow Na^+ \quad Cl^-$$

Electrostatic forces bring these oppositely charged ions together, forming a crystal lattice.

On the other hand, **covalent compounds** aren't formed from the complete taking or giving up of electrons. Instead they are *shared* between atoms, and these shared electrons are known as **covalent bonds**. Unlike ionic compounds, covalent compounds do exist as individual molecules, which is why they're also referred to as *molecular compounds*. Water is a covalent compound, composed of individual molecules of H_2O where oxygen is sharing electrons with two atoms of hydrogen (see the Lewis structure shown in Part 1). Another example you may be familiar with is "dry ice," the common name for solid carbon dioxide, CO_2. In this frozen version of CO_2, the crystal lattice is formed from billions of CO_2 molecules stacked together.

Polyatomic Ions Revisited

Not only are polyatomic ions charged molecules, they're charged *covalent* molecules. Sulfate (SO_4^{2-}), for example, isn't made up of sulfur and oxygen ions. Rather, it's a molecule where one sulfur atom is sharing electrons with four oxygen atoms. At some point during its formation it picked up two extra electrons, giving it a net charge of -2. Why it has two extra electrons is a discussion we'll save for later.

Ionic or Covalent?

If you need to predict whether a given compound is ionic or covalent, a general rule of thumb (one that works well enough for a general chemistry course, anyway) is that ionic compounds are usually identified by the presence of either a metal or ammonium ion, NH_4^+. In this text, and most general chemistry courses, ammonium is typically the only cation you encounter that isn't a metal, though you'll encounter many more if you have to take organic chemistry. Covalent compounds are usually composed of two or more nonmetals, though some may include metalloids. Keep in mind that there are exceptions to this, but overall we'll ignore those in this book for convenience's sake (actually, if you look closely, you'll actually see a couple of exceptions in that list of polyatomic ions I gave you a few pages back).

In Chapter 9, we'll discuss why certain compounds form as ionic while others are covalent, but we can get a general sense from what's been covered so far. At the start of Part 2, it was mentioned that metals usually form cations and nonmetals anions. If two nonmetals, like carbon and oxygen, try to come together to form a compound, they can't *both* be anions. Like charges repel! If neither atom is willing to give up electrons and form a cation, their only choice is to play nice and share.

Formulas of Covalent Compounds

Because covalent compounds aren't made of ions, it's not possible to predict the formula as easily as you can with ionic compounds. In fact, two nonmetals can usually combine in several different ways. Nitrogen and oxygen, for example, can combine to form, among others, the compounds: NO, NO_2 and N_2O.

Earlier, we saw that ionic compounds are always shown as empirical formulas, in the simplest cation/anion ratio, because such compounds don't actually exist as individual molecules. Covalent compounds, however, *do* exist as individual molecule, which means they're represented by their complete, *molecular* formula. For example, sulfur and fluorine can combine to form the compound S_2F_{10}. You wouldn't simplify the formula to SF_5. That compound doesn't normally exist. Here's an even better example: the sugar glucose has the molecular formula $C_6H_{12}O_6$. If you wrote it as CH_2O, you'd actually be writing the molecular formula of formaldehyde. One of these is used by the body to make energy, while the other is used by biology classes to preserve dead frogs and fetal pigs. Hopefully, you can see the importance of not getting these two mixed up.

Try It Yourself

P4. Predict whether each of the following compounds is ionic or covalent: a) LiCl, b) SO_2, c) Cu_3PO_4, d) NH_4Br, e) C_2H_6O

Part 4: Naming Compounds

As mentioned earlier, this book (and most general chemistry courses) will primarily focus on inorganic compounds. Overall, inorganic compounds are relatively simpler and therefore better suited for an introductory text such as this. Perhaps the best example of this is with naming. While the nomenclature (naming) of inorganic compounds can be reasonably covered in a few pages, as we'll do momentarily, trying to do the same with organic compounds would require an entire book (in a typical first-semester organic course, most will introduce naming a little bit at a time, chapter-by-chapter, and you still end up just scratching the surface by semester's end).

Naming Ionic Compounds

As we discussed in part 2, the cation is always written first, so it would make sense that the same would be true of its name. The name of the cation is simply the name of the element or polyatomic ion. If the anion is monatomic, we drop the last syllable (or two, depending on what will sound better) and add the suffix "–ide." The most commonly encountered monatomic anions are

N^{3-}	nitride	F^-	fluoride
P^{3-}	phosphide	Cl^-	chloride
O^{2-}	oxide	Br^-	bromide
S^{2-}	sulfide	I^-	iodide

Examples: KCl is potassium chloride, Li_2S is lithium sulfide

Polyatomic names aren't modified. You wouldn't, for instance, change phosphate's (PO_4^{3-}) name to phosphide because that's the name given to the monatomic ion, P^{3-}.

Examples: Li_2SO_4 is lithium sulfate, $Ca(OH)_2$ is calcium hydroxide

For the most part, the –ide suffix denotes a monatomic ion while polyatomic ions use an –ate or –ite suffix. There are exceptions (see our list in Part 2 of a few common ones), but most of those are older names that pre-date this system and changing their names just to fit the system probably wouldn't be worth the resulting confusion. After all, if most people—including nonscientists—know CN^- as cyanide, it might be a good idea to leave its name alone.

Notice that there's no need to identify the number of each ion present in the formula. Given what we talked about in Part 2, we don't have to. For example, to find the formula of magnesium nitride, we recall that magnesium and nitrogen are both constant charge ions (Mg^{2+} and N^{3-}). From there we can use the crossover method to determine its formula Mg_3N_2.

$$Mg^{2+} \diagdown \diagup N^{3-} \to Mg_3N_2.$$

A good naming system should be as simple as possible. With ionic compounds, including the number of each ion would just be superfluous information that cluttered up the name.

Variable Charge Metals

However, we do run into a problem when the metal is a variable charge element. For example, based on what we've discussed thus far, FeO would be called *iron oxide,* but there's another iron-oxygen compound that has the formula Fe_2O_3. We can't call both compounds iron oxide, as it would be much too confusing.

An older method for handling variable charge elements involves using the root of the element's Latin name and different suffixes for each charge. Typically, the higher charge gets the –ic suffix while lower one uses –ous. In the case iron, Fe^{3+} would be given the name *ferric* and Fe^{2+} would be *ferrous*. While you'll still see this naming convention occasionally used for some compounds, it's a fairly outdated system. Besides the fact that learning more than one name for an element seems—let's be honest—silly, we now know that several metals can easily form three, four, or *more* different ions. We only have two suffixes, and coming up with a new system based on Latin names and multiple suffixes may be more trouble than it's worth.

The modern way to differentiate between compounds with variable charge metals is to simply show the cation charge as a roman numeral after the element's name. This does require us to figure out the metal's charge, but since nonmetals are typically constant charge elements and the charges have to add up to zero, it's just a matter of figuring it out algebraically. For example, since oxygen is a group 6A element, its charge should be –2. This means the iron in FeO has to be +2.

$$Fe + O = 0$$
$$Fe + (-2) = 0$$
$$Fe = +2$$

Therefore, we'll name this compound iron (II) oxide (pronounced "iron two oxide"). In the case of Fe_2O_3, iron has to have a +3 charge for the compound to be neutral,

$$2Fe + 3O = 0$$
$$2Fe + 3(-2) = 0$$
$$2Fe = +6$$
$$Fe = +3$$

so we'll call it iron (III) oxide ("iron three oxide")

But remember, you *only* use roman numerals for variable charge elements. There's no need, for example, to call KCl "potassium (I) chloride" because in nature potassium ions are always K^+.

Naming Covalent Compounds

Most inorganic covalent compounds are *binary* compounds, composed of two types of atoms, so the naming convention is very similar to the one used for ionic compounds. As before, the name of the first element is just that element's name and the second element is renamed using the –ide suffix (in Chapter 10 you'll learn why the first atom is shown first).

Remember, though, that two nonmetals can usually combine in different ratios to form different compounds, similar to what we saw earlier with variable charge metals. For example, phosphorus and chlorine can form molecules of either PCl_3 or PCl_5. As it was with our two iron oxides, we can't call both of these compounds "phosphorus chloride," but this time there are no ion charges to help us tell the two apart. What we do instead is use prefixes to note the number of each element. The first ten prefixes are given below, many of which you're probably already familiar with.

Number	Prefix
1	mono-
2	di-
3	tri-
4	tetra-
5	penta-
6	hexa-
7	hepta-
8	octa-
9	nona-
10	deca-

We usually don't use the prefix "mono" for the first element shown. If there's no prefix, it's assumed that there's only one. This means PCl_3 is called phosphorus trichloride and PCl_5 is phosphorus pentachloride.

Examples: SF_4 is sulfur tetrafluoride, S_2F_{10} is disulfur decafluoride

If the prefix- ends with an *a* and the element begins with a vowel, the *a* of the prefix is sometimes dropped.

Examples: N_2O_4 is dinitrogen tetroxide, N_2O_5 is dinitrogen pentoxide

Finally, remember that prefixes are *only* used for covalent compounds. In our earlier example, there was no need to call Mg_3N_2 "trimagnesium dinitride." We don't use prefixes for ionic compounds because we can get that cation-anion ratio using the ion charges and the crossover method. That's the official rule, anyway. There are a few ionic compounds—especially those that have been used industrially for decades or longer—that still "unofficially" use prefixes in their name.

Naming Hydrated Compounds

If a compound is hydrated, you name the compound as you normally would, then add "[prefix]hydrate" at the end, using the above prefixes to note the number of waters per formula unit.

Examples: $LiCl \cdot H_2O$ is lithium chloride monohydrate, $BaCl_2 \cdot 2H_2O$ is barium chloride dihydrate.

Compounds with Common Names

There are several compounds that go by traditional, common names instead of the previously mentioned system, usually because that's what we've been calling them for centuries or longer. The two you'll encounter the most in a general chemistry course are ammonia (NH_3) and, of course, water (H_2O). A few others were mentioned in Part 2 of this chapter.

Try It Yourself

P5. Complete the following table

Formula	First name	Last Name
CaS	_____	sulfide
SO_2	sulfur	_____
Na_2O	_____	oxide
P_2O_5	diphosphorus	_____
$NiSO_4$	nickel (II)	_____
$NiCl_4$	_____	chloride
NCl_3	_____	trichloride
MgF_2	_____	_____
SF_6	_____	_____
Cu_3PO_4	_____	_____

P6. Look back at the table of common ionic compounds given in the beginning of Part 2 and determine their chemical names.

Test Your Skills

★ Button-masher

1. Write the molecular formulas for a molecule with…
a) one nitrogen and three oxygens
b) two sulfurs and ten fluorines
c) one bromine and five fluorines
d) five carbons and twelve hydrogens
e) six carbons, twelve hydrogens and two oxygens

XP: +4 each

2. Calculate the molecular mass of each of the following compounds:
a) NO, b) F_2, c) CS_2, d) $Cu(NO_3)_2$, e) NaH, f) $(NH_4)_2O$, g) Na_3PO_4

XP: +3 each

3. For each of the compounds in question 2, predict whether it will be ionic or covalent.

XP: +3 each

4. What are the common charges of each of the following elements?
a) Ca, b) S, c) K, d) P, e) Cl

XP: +3 each

5. Determine the charge of the metal in each of the following compounds.
a) $MnCl_2$, b) FeS, c) Ni_3P_2, d) $CuNO_3$, e) VO_2

XP: +4 each

6. Complete the following table

	I^-	O^{2-}	N^{3-}
Li^+	LiI	_____	_____
Fe^{2+}	_____	_____	_____
Al^{3+}	_____	_____	_____

XP: +4 each

7. Name each of the compounds from questions 6.

XP: +4 each

8. Name each of the following compounds.
a) CCl_4, b) S_2Br_{10}, c) NO_2, d) SeI_6, e) $BrCl_5$

XP: +4 each

9. Name each of the following compounds.
a) $NiCl_2·6H_2O$, b) $MgBr_2·4H_2O$, c) $CaSO_4·2H_2O$,
d) $Ba(OH)_2·8H_2O$

XP: +4 each

★XP: _____

If your XP is 151 or higher, it's time to switch to…

★★Combos

10. Write the molecular formula for each of the following:

a)

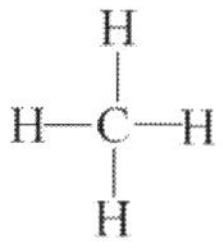

$$H-\overset{\displaystyle H}{\underset{\displaystyle H}{C}}-H$$

b)

$$Cl-\overset{\displaystyle Cl}{\underset{\displaystyle Cl}{P}}\overset{Cl}{\underset{Cl}{}}$$

98

c) 
$$\begin{array}{c} O \\ \| \\ H-C-H \end{array}$$

XP +4 each

11. Why is it technically wrong to say "a molecule of table salt?"

XP: +4

12. Complete the following table:

	NO_3^-	SO_4^{2-}	PO_4^{3-}
NH_4^+	_____	_____	_____
Cu^{2+}	_____	_____	_____
Ga^{3+}	_____	_____	_____
Mn^{4+}	_____	_____	_____

XP: +4

13. Name each of the compounds from question 12.

XP: +4

14. Write formulas for each of the following compounds:
a) disulfur decafluoride, b) ammonium permanganate, c) chromium (VI) perchlorate, d) sodium carbonate decahydrate, e) tetraselenium tetranitride, f) triphosphorus pentiodide, g) nickel (IV) cyanide, h) nitrogen trioxide

XP: +4 each

★★ XP: _____   Total XP: _____

If your total XP is 259 or greater, don't just stand there…

★★★Finish Him!

15. Why isn't it possible for a polyatomic ion, such as nitrate (NO_3^-), to be made up of monatomic ions?

XP: +5

16. Is it possible for a molecular formula to also be an empirical formula? If so, give an example. If not, explain why?

XP: +5

17. Write formulas for each of the following compounds
a) calcium dihydrogen phosphate. b) ammonium sulfite, c) mercury (I) chloride, d) potassium peroxide

XP: +5 each

18. Name the following compounds.
a) NH_4HCO_3, b) $Hg_2(NO_3)_2$, c) MgH_2, d) AgH_2PO_4, e) $TiCr_2O_7$

XP: +5 each

19. Once you understand how inorganic compounds are named, you'll find that your ability to read the ingredient list of commercial products has improved significantly (yet another example of why learning this stuff isn't just for passing exams). When you do, you may notice that some compounds tend to break the rules we've just discussed. Many times, it's because they're common names that predate our current system (much like the polyatomic ions that have the –ide suffix). A few examples are

a) Calcium dichloride, often used to deice roads in the winter.
b) Titanium dioxide, commonly used as a pigment in wide range of products, such as paints, foods, and sunscreens.
c) Nitrous oxide (N_2O), also known as "laughing gas," which is used both as an anesthesia and a racing fuel.
d) Chromium trioxide, which is used in chrome-plating.

How would we name these compounds using the rules discussed in this chapter?

XP: +5 each

20. When it comes to the toxicity of chemicals, one thing to remember is that it's not just the identity of the chemical that's

important, but the amount as well. For example, sodium fluoride, the active ingredient in many brands of toothpaste, was once the active ingredient in many rodenticides ("rat poisons") as well. For an average human, the lethal dosage of sodium fluoride is around 5.0 g. If a 130 g tube of toothpaste is 0.243 % sodium fluoride, how many tubes would you need to ingest at once to reach the lethal dosage?

XP: +10

21. An unknown compound was thought to be either calcium carbonate or barium carbonate (MCO_3, M = Ca^{2+} or Ba^{2+}). A 20.0 g sample of the compound was heated, where it decomposed into of the metal oxide (MO) and carbon dioxide gas. The mass of the metal oxide was 11.2 g. Identify the compound using concepts discussed in this and the previous chapter (but not Chapter 4, if you've already read ahead).

XP: +10

★★★XP: _____   Total XP: _____

If your total XP is 330 or greater: Level up!

Achievement Unlocked: It's So Formulaic
Completed Chapter 3

You're now ready to learn about chemical reactions.

Chapter 4
The Mole &
Chemical Equations

Part 1: The Mole

The mole unit (usually abbreviated as "mol") is a counting unit. Chances are you're already familiar with another type of counting unit: the dozen. If you have a dozen of anything (eggs, doughnuts, etc.), you have 12 of them, right? The mole is used in the same way, only this counting unit is much, *much* bigger: 6.022×10^{23} with four significant figures. Writing this number using standard notation would look like this:

$$602,200,000,000,000,000,000,000$$

So, if you have a dozen eggs, you have 12 eggs. If you have a mol of eggs, you have 6.022×10^{23} eggs, which would be enough to cover the entire planet, several miles deep. Obviously, the mole unit is not practical when dealing with "normal-sized" things, but when you're dealing with atoms that are around 10^{-28} grams, it's extremely useful. You probably drink at least a mol of water when you take a sip from a drinking fountain.

The number 6.022×10^{23} is often referred to as **Avogadro's number**, after chemist Amedeo Avogadro (1776 – 1856). He didn't come up with the number, but the work he did played a large part in its development, so it was named in his honor. Also, the number wasn't just made up because chemists needed a really big counting unit. It's currently based on the number of atoms in 12 grams of carbon-12, which we mentioned in Chapter 2 is our standard for determining atom mass.

Molar Mass

Molar mass is the mass (in grams) per mole of a substance, giving it units of grams per mol (*g/mol*). For example, one mole of carbon atoms has a mass of 12.01 grams, making its molar mass 12.01 g/mol. A mole of sulfur has a mass of 32.07 g, for a molar mass of 32.07 g/mol. If you take a quick peek at the periodic table, you'll notice that these are also the atomic masses of these two elements. This isn't a coincidence, mind you; it's just part of the mole's history that we're skipping over. What this means for us, though, is that molar mass and atomic mass are essentially the same thing, just expressed in different units.

$$1 \text{ g/mol} = 1 \text{ amu}$$

As you'll see once we get to chemical equations, it's much more beneficial to think of atomic weights on the "mol scale," in units of g/mol, instead of atomic mass units. After all, unlike eggs in a kitchen, you can't exactly count out how many atoms you'll need for a reaction, but you can weigh something on a balance. *Molar mass gives us the ability to easily convert between a unit of mass (grams) and a counting unit (moles).* For example, if a reaction requires 0.20 moles of sodium, you can use the element's molar mass (22.99 amu, or 22.99 g/mol) to convert this amount to a mass in grams, using dimensional analysis (Chapter 1).

$$0.20 \text{ mol Na} \times \frac{22.99 \text{ g Na}}{1 \text{ mol Na}} = 4.6 \text{ g Na}$$

Example: How many moles of sodium chloride are in a 7.00g sample?

In Chapter 3, we learned that finding a compound's molar mass is as easy as adding up the change in your pocket.

Na	22.99
Cl	35.45
NaCl	58.44

We can then convert "g NaCl" to "mol NaCl" using dimensional analysis

$$7.00 \; \cancel{\text{g NaCl}} \times \frac{1 \; \text{mol NaCl}}{58.44 \; \cancel{\text{g NaCl}}} = 0.120 \; \text{mol NaCl}$$

Notice that when I'm setting up these types of calculations, I include the identity of the element or compound along with the unit. That can be especially useful with conversions that involve several steps. For example...

Example: How many moles of oxygen are in 12.0 g of carbon dioxide?

First we can convert g CO_2 to mol CO_2 using its molar mass

$$12.0 \; \cancel{\text{g } CO_2} \times \frac{1 \; \text{mol } CO_2}{44.01 \; \cancel{\text{g } CO_2}}$$

Looking at the compound's formula, we see that there are two oxygen atoms per molecule. This 2:1 ratio is true regardless of whether we're talking about a single molecule, a dozen molecules or a mole of CO_2.

- 2 O atoms per 1 CO_2 molecule
- 24 O atoms (2 doz) per 12 CO_2 molecules (1 doz)
- 1.204×10^{24} O atoms (2 mol) per 6.022×10^{23} CO_2 molecules (1 mol)

⎤ 2:1 ratio

Therefore, we can use this ratio to convert mol CO_2 to mol O.

$$12.0 \; \cancel{\text{g } CO_2} \times \frac{1 \; \text{mol } CO_2}{44.01 \; \cancel{\text{g } CO_2}} \times \frac{2 \; \text{mol O}}{1 \; \cancel{\text{mol } CO_2}} = 0.545 \; \text{mol O}$$

Example: Calculate the number of helium atoms in a 9.50 g sample.

Like our previous example, we start by converting grams of the chemical given to moles

$$9.50 \; \cancel{\text{g He}} \; \times \frac{1 \; \text{mol He}}{4.003 \; \cancel{\text{g He}}}$$

and since 1 mol of anything equals Avogadro's number

$$9.50 \; \cancel{\text{g He}} \; \times \frac{1 \; \text{mol He}}{4.003 \; \cancel{\text{g He}}} \times \frac{6.022 \times 10^{23} \; \text{He atom}}{1 \; \cancel{\text{mol He}}}$$

$$= 1.43 \times 10^{24} \; \text{He atoms}$$

Summing Up

Looking back at the past few examples, notice that we're essentially doing the same types of conversions again and again.

To covert between...	use
moles and individual number	Avogadro's Number
grams and moles	molar mass
moles within a compound	the compound's formula

Over the next several chapters, we'll be performing similar calculations, adding a couple more conversion factors along the way, but ultimately they're all just variations of what we've been doing up to this point.

Try It Yourself

P1. How many dozens are in the number 1,188? How many moles?

P2. How many dozens are in the number 5.20×10^{24}? How many moles?

P3. A piece of copper has a mass of 5.00 g. How many moles of copper is this? How many atoms?

P4. Calculate the mass (in grams) of a) 5.81 mol K, b) 0.9920 mol SO_2

P5. Calculate the mass (in grams) of a) 8.22×10^{24} Al atoms, b) 3.44×10^{25} Br_2 molecules

P6. How many moles of chloride are in 7.3 g $CaCl_2$?

Part 2: Percent Composition & Elemental Analysis

Percent composition refers to the mass percentage of an element in a given compound. It's essentially the same percentage math you've undoubtedly done before. For example, glucose ($C_6H_{12}O_6$) has a total molar mass of 180.16 g/mol. It has 6 carbons in its formula, each with a mass of 12.01 g/mol. The percentage of this compound's mass that comes from carbon would be

$$\frac{6 \times 12.01 \text{ g/mol}}{180.16 \text{ g/mol}} \times 100 = 40.00\% \text{ C}$$

The same can be done with the other two elements.

$$\frac{12 \times 1.008 \text{ g/mol}}{180.16 \text{ g/mol}} \times 100 = 6.714\% \text{ H}$$

$$\frac{6 \times 16.00 \text{ g/mol}}{180.16 \text{ g/mol}} \times 100 = 53.29\% \text{ O}$$

Notice that the percentages add up to 100%, as you'd expect them to.

Since percent composition is expressed as a mass percentage, any amount of sugar you have will be 40.00% C, 6.714% H, and 53.29% O by mass. If, for instance, you had 38.0 g of sugar, the masses of each element in the sample would be

$$38.0 \times 0.4000 = 15.2 \text{ g C}$$
$$38.0 \times 0.06714 = 2.55 \text{ g H}$$
$$38.0 \times 0.5329 = 20.25 \text{ g O}$$

Again, this is the same percentage math you've undoubtedly done before, much in the same way those conversions in Part 1 were similar to the conversions discussed in Chapter 1. Don't let the fact that this is a chemistry book make you think any differently (that's true for a lot of what we do here, by the way).

Elemental Analysis

With many compounds, it's possible to experimentally determine the percent composition of a compound, a process commonly referred to as **elemental analysis**. It's one of the many methods used by chemists to verify the identity of a new or unknown compound. Here, the percent composition of a compound is used to determine or confirm its empirical formula, which is essentially the opposite of what we did earlier. Notice that I said *empirical formula*, not its molecular formula. That's because any compounds with the same atom ratio will have the same percent composition. Formaldehyde (CH_2O), for example, has the same ratio of atoms as sugar (1 C: 2 H: 1 O), so it also has the same percent composition.

$$\frac{12.01 \text{ g/mol}}{30.03 \text{ g/mol}} \times 100 = 40.00\% \text{ C}$$

$$\frac{2(1.008 \text{ g/mol})}{30.03 \text{ g/mol}} \times 100 = 6.714\% \text{ H}$$

$$\frac{16.00 \text{ g/mol}}{30.03 \text{ g/mol}} \times 100 = 53.29\% \text{ O}$$

Determining the molecular formula requires additional information, which we'll discuss a little later.

Example: Determine the empirical formula of a compound that's 62% C, 10.4% H and 27.5% O.

Step 1: Find the mass of each element in a 100.0 g sample.

You can actually pick *any* mass and end up with the same formula in the end, but using 100.0 g just makes things easier, since 62% of 100 is 62, and so on.

$$100.0 \text{ g} \times 0.62 = 62 \text{ g C}$$
$$100.0 \text{ g} \times 0.104 = 10.4 \text{ g H}$$
$$100.0 \text{ g} \times 0.275 = 27.5 \text{ g O}$$

As you can see, when we use 100 g, we're basically just replacing the "%" with a "g."

Step 2: Convert grams of each element to moles

Since a chemical formula is a *numeric* ratio, we need to convert our masses to a numeric (counting) unit, which can easily be done using molar mass.

$$62 \text{ g C} \times \frac{1 \text{ mol C}}{12.01 \text{ g C}} = 5.2 \text{ mol C}$$

$$10.4 \text{ g H} \times \frac{1 \text{ mol H}}{1.008 \text{ g H}} = 10.3 \text{ mol H}$$

$$27.5 \text{ g O} \times \frac{1 \text{ mol O}}{16.00 \text{ g O}} = 1.72 \text{ mol O}$$

Step 3: Determine the element ratio of the compound.

The easiest way to convert the amounts from step 2 into a ratio is to divide each number by the smallest—1.72 in this case.

$$\frac{5.2}{1.72} = 3.02 \approx 3 \text{ C}$$

$$\frac{10.4}{1.72} = 5.99 \approx 6 \text{ H}$$

$$\frac{1.72}{1.72} = 1 \text{ O}$$

Our C:H:O ratio, therefore, is 3:6:1, making the empirical formula C_3H_6O (in case you're wondering, molecular formulas of organic compounds are usually written carbon first, then hydrogen, followed by any other elements in alphabetical order).

There's an easy way to check your work in problems such as this. Simply find the mass percentage of one or more elements from your empirical formula. If your answer's correct, the percentages should match those given in the problem.

$$\frac{3 \times 12.01 \text{ g/mol}}{58.08 \text{ g/mol}} \times 100 = 62.04\% \text{ C}$$

Example: Determine the empirical formula of a compound that's 82.66% C and 17.34% H.

Following the same steps as before, we'll begin by converting percentages to masses using a 100.0g sample,

$$100.0 \text{ g} \times 0.8266 = 82.66 \text{ g C}$$
$$100.0 \text{ g} \times 0.1734 = 17.34 \text{ g H}$$

and then masses to moles

$$82.66 \text{ g C} \times \frac{1 \text{ mol C}}{12.01 \text{ g C}} = 6.883 \text{ mol C}$$

$$17.34 \; \cancel{g\,H} \times \frac{1 \; \text{mol H}}{1.008 \; \cancel{g\,H}} = 17.20 \; \text{mol H}$$

Finally, we determine our ratio, except this time we end up with a number that's actually closer to a fraction than a whole number.

$$\frac{17.20}{6.883} = 2.499 \approx 2.5 \; \text{or} \; 2\frac{1}{2} \; \text{H}$$

$$\frac{6.883}{6.883} = 1 \; \text{C}$$

If your ratio ends up with a fraction ($x.5$, $x.33$, etc.), don't round up to a whole number. Our ratio here isn't 3 carbons per hydrogen, it's 2½ carbons per hydrogen. Fractional subscripts aren't used in chemical formulas, however, so we'll get rid of the fraction by multiplying by its denominator (2, in this case), giving us a ratio of 5:2

$$CH_{2.5} \times 2 = C_2H_5$$

With most of the elemental analysis problems you encounter in a general chemistry course, it will be very apparent when you should simply round a number up or down (as it was with our first example) and when you have a fraction. In an actual laboratory situation, though, it may not be so easy.

Determining the Molecular Formula

In order to find the molecular formula of the compound, you need to know its molar mass. Like elemental analysis, experimentally determining a compound's molar mass is something that's routinely done by chemists. Once you have the molar mass, it's a simple matter of comparing that value to the molar mass of your empirical formula. In the previous example, the empirical formula was found to be C_2H_5, which has a molar mass of 29.06 g/mol. Let's say the compound's actual molar mass was 116 g/mol. These two molar masses differ by about a factor of four.

$$\frac{116}{29.06} = 3.99 \approx 4$$

If the compound's molar mass is four times higher than our empirical formula, then so is its molecular formula.

$$C_2H_5 \times 4 = C_8H_{20}$$

Again, there's an easy way to check your answer: the molar mass of C_8H_{20} is 116, the same molar mass given above.

Try It Yourself

P7. Calculate the percent composition in each of the following compounds: a) MgS, b) PBr_3, c) C_6H_{14}, d) C_2H_4O, e) $C_4H_8O_2$

P8. A compound was found to be 84.6% carbon and 14.4% hydrogen. Determine the compound's empirical formula.

P9. A compound with the empirical formula of CH_3O_2 has a molar mass of 235 g/mol. What is the molecular formula?

P10. A compound is found to be 40.64% carbon, 5.116% hydrogen, and 54.25% sulfur, with a molar mass of 354.68 g/mol.
a) What is the empirical formula of this compound?
b) What is the molecular formula of this compound?

Part 3: Chemical Equations

The purpose of an equation is to give you the basic "recipe" of a chemical reaction. It's similar to the pictures that go along with the directions of most food products: picture of an oven dial, picture of a pizza on the middle rack, then a picture of a clock showing you how long to cook it. It may not tell you *exactly* how to cook something, but it will at least give you the basic gist of it. Chemical equations aren't that much different.

For example, nitrogen and hydrogen can react to form ammonia, NH_3. An equation for this reaction would look something like this

$$N_2 + H_2 \rightarrow NH_3$$

The nitrogen and hydrogen on the left are called **reactants** (or reagents), and ammonia is the **product** of the reaction. Notice there's no real trick with the names: you react reactants and produce products. Chemical equations are always written "reactant to product," left to right, and are always written as additions.

You will often see the phase of each substance written in parentheses beside each substance. Commonly used phases include

(g)	gas
(l)	liquid
(s)	solid
(aq)	aqueous (dissolved in water)

In the ammonia reaction above, for example, everything is typically in the gas phase

$$N_2(g) + H_2(g) \rightarrow NH_3(g)$$

We'll discuss phases more in the next chapter.

Finally, if there's other information that might be of some importance—reaction temperature, pressure, solvent, etc.—it's common to place it above the arrow. For example, the reaction given above works best at around 500 °C, so you might include this as part of the equation.

$$N_2(g) + H_2(g) \xrightarrow{500\ °C} NH_3(g)$$

Balancing Equations

If you've already had some chemistry before, you might have already noticed that there's a problem with the above equation. On the reactant side, there are two atoms of nitrogen and two of hydrogen, but on the product side you only have one nitrogen and three hydrogens. Despite the fact that we still have four atoms on either side, some matter has been lost during the reaction (6 protons and 6 electrons, to be exact), which violates the law of conservation of mass. A **balanced** equation is one that does obey the law of conservation of mass, showing the same number of each element on both sides of an equation. One way to balance the above equation is to write it this way:

$$N_2 + 3H_2 \rightarrow 2NH_3$$

The 3 and 2 that was placed in front of H_2 and NH_3, respectively, are known as **coefficients**, which are simply numbers used to balance an equation. Similar to subscripts in formulas, coefficients of 1 aren't written (the 1 is implied). Now we have two nitrogen atoms and six hydrogens on each side of our equation, and the law of conservation of mass is obeyed.

There are no set rules for balancing an equation. For the most part, it's just a matter of doing a few to get the hang of it. However, there are a few tips that you can follow that will make balancing easier:

1) Balance one atom at a time. I usually just start with the first atom shown and work my way across. Occasionally, balancing one atom does unbalance one that was balanced earlier, but it doesn't happen as much as you'd think, especially if you use the other two tips below.

2) If an atom is in two or more reactants or two or more products, save that one for last.

3) If a polyatomic ion remains intact during the course of a reaction, you can treat the ion as a single unit.

Example: Balance the following equation

$$Ca(OH)_2 + HCl \rightarrow CaCl_2 + H_2O$$

Looking at the equation, we see that hydrogen is part of both reactants, so we'll follow tip 2 and save that atom for last. There's also a polyatomic ion in one of our reactants (hydroxide), but since it doesn't appear on the product side, tip 3 wouldn't be applicable here.

Starting with calcium, there is one on the left side of our equation and one on the right, so that atom's already balanced. Next up is oxygen. There are two on the left, but only one on the right. This atom can be balanced by placing a *2* in front of water.

$$Ca(OH)_2 + HCl \rightarrow CaCl_2 + \mathbf{2}H_2O$$

We're saving hydrogen for last, so we'll skip ahead to chlorine, where we have one on the left and two on the right. We'll make the Cl's equal by placing a *2* in front of HCl

$$Ca(OH)_2 + \mathbf{2}HCl \rightarrow CaCl_2 + \mathbf{2}H_2O$$

Finally, there's hydrogen, and here's why we saved it for last: notice that, at this point, we've looked at every substance in this equation and assigned a coefficient to it, even if the coefficient was *1*. If we haven't made any mistakes up to this point, that last atom should already be balanced, which it is: four hydrogens on the left and four on the right.

Example: Balance the following equation

$$Na_2SO_3 + H_3PO_4 \rightarrow Na_3PO_4 + H_2SO_3$$

Here, we have two polyatomic ions, sulfite and phosphate, and both remain intact during the reaction, so instead of balancing the sulfur, phosphorus and oxygen atoms individually, we'll balance each polyatomic ion as if it were a single atom (if you'd rather balance each atom individually, that's fine, but you might want to save the oxygens for last). Starting with sodium, there are two on the left and three on the right, so we'll balance it by putting a *3* in front of Na_2SO_3 and a *2* in front of Na_3PO_4, giving us six on each side.

$$\mathbf{3}Na_2SO_3 + H_3PO_4 \rightarrow \mathbf{2}Na_3PO_4 + H_2SO_3$$

Next up is sulfite. After putting a coefficient in front of sodium sulfite, we now have three sulfite ions on the left, but only one on the right, so we'll put a *3* in front of H_2SO_3

$$3Na_2SO_3 + H_3PO_4 \rightarrow 2Na_3PO_4 + \mathbf{3}H_2SO_3$$

Hydrogen is next, with three on the left and six on the right, so we'll put a *2* in front of H_3PO_4.

$$3Na_2SO_3 + \mathbf{2}H_3PO_4 \rightarrow 2Na_3PO_4 + 3H_2SO_3$$

The last thing to balance is phosphate ion, but since we've assigned a coefficient to every substance thus far, it's already balanced.

Example: Balance the following equation.

$$C_4H_{10} + O_2 \rightarrow CO_2 + H_2O$$

There are four carbons on the left and one on the right, so we'll put a *4* in front of CO_2.

$$C_4H_{10} + O_2 \rightarrow 4CO_2 + H_2O$$

Moving on to hydrogen, there are ten on the left and two on the right, so we'll put a *5* in front of water.

$$C_4H_{10} + O_2 \rightarrow 4CO_2 + 5H_2O$$

Finally, there's oxygen, which currently has two on the left and a total of *thirteen* on the right. Now, at this point, we've set a coefficient to every substance except O_2, and it would be nice if we could balance oxygen without screwing up anything we've already balanced. At first, that may not seem possible, since there isn't a number you can put in front of O_2 to give you thirteen oxygen atoms on the left. No *whole number*, that is. Another option is to use a coefficient of $\frac{13}{2}$

$$C_4H_{10} + \frac{13}{2}O_2 \rightarrow 4CO_2 + 5H_2O$$

In lower level chemistry courses, students are sometimes told that fractional coefficients are a no-no, since you can't have half an atom. While that may be true, in most cases chemists don't think of coefficients in terms of individual atoms and molecules, but as *moles* of elements and compounds. And remember that the mole is a counting unit, just like a dozen. It's possible to have half a dozen of something, right? Well, you can also have half a mole.

If you do want to get rid of the fraction (and there are times when it's more convenient to have all of your coefficients as whole numbers), you can multiply all the coefficients by the fraction's denominator—2, in this case.

$$2C_4H_{10} + 13O_2 \rightarrow 8CO_2 + 10H_2O$$

Keep in mind, though, that any set of whole number coefficients must be the simplest ratio possible. For example, if you somehow ended up with

$$4C_4H_{10} + 26O_2 \rightarrow 16CO_2 + 20H_2O$$

you would need simplify the equation by dividing the coefficients by 2.

Try It Yourself

P11. Balance the following equations.
a) $Al + ZnO \rightarrow Al_2O_3 + Zn$
b) $N_2O_5 \rightarrow NO_2 + O_2$
c) $Na + H_2O \rightarrow NaOH + H_2$
d) $Cr + Cl_2 \rightarrow CrCl_6$
e) $H_3PO_3 \rightarrow H_3PO_4 + PH_3$
f) $H_2S + O_2 \rightarrow H_2O + SO_2$
g) $KClO_4 \rightarrow KClO_3 + O_2$

Part 4: Stoichiometry

Recipes vs. Reactions

Stoichiometry calculations are by far the most common type of calculation you do as a first semester chemistry student. They can be intimidating for some, but as we'll soon see, it's essentially the same unit conversion problems we discussed in Chapter 1.

At the start of Part 3, we compared chemical equations to kitchen recipes. As you may know from experience (depending on how much you cook from scratch), it's very common to scale a recipe up or down to suit your needs. For example, let's say you and your buddies are craving one of those "monster-sized" burgers sold at many food restaurants (because you either hate your cardiovascular system or enjoy testing the limits of your arteries) so you decide to dust off the backyard grill to make a few. Condiments aside, the basic ingredients for each burger would be

Two patties of beef
Three slices of cheese
Four strips of bacon
One ~~defibrillator~~ hamburger bun

If you wanted to make eight burgers, how many slices of bacon would you need? You can probably do this one in your head and come up with thirty-two, but you could also find the answer by dimensional analysis.

$$8 \text{ burgers} \times \frac{4 \text{ bacon}}{1 \text{ burger}} = 32 \text{ bacon}$$

Now let's say you had twenty burger patties and needed to figure out how many slices of cheese you'd need? Using dimensional analysis, we get…

$$20 \text{ Patties} \times \frac{3 \text{ Cheese}}{2 \text{ Patties}} = 30 \text{ Cheese}$$

Believe it or not, stoichiometry isn't that different from the above examples. We're just scaling a chemical reaction instead of a cooking recipe.

One last question: if you have three pounds of cheese, does that mean you'd need two pounds of patties? Not really. Your preference for how thick you like your burgers aside, that 3:2 ratio shown in the ingredient list is a *numeric* ratio, not a mass ratio. While it's true that you'll often use mass and volume measurements in cooking recipes, in a chemical equation everything is related numerically (usually moles, as we'll see next).

Stoichiometry and Reactions

Now let's look at an actual chemical equation.

$$N_2 + 3H_2 \rightarrow 2NH_3$$

As we discussed in Part 3, it's better to think of coefficients in terms of moles instead of individual molecules and atoms. In other words, the recommended way to read the above equation is that one mole of N_2 reacts with three moles H_2 to produce two moles of NH_3.

If you start with 5 moles of nitrogen, how many moles of product can you make? Like our burger examples, we can solve the problem using dimensional analysis:

$$5 \text{ mol } \cancel{N_2} \times \frac{2 \text{ mol NH}_3}{1 \text{ mol } \cancel{N_2}} = 10 \text{ mol NH}_3$$

If you had 12 moles of hydrogen, how many moles of ammonia would you produce?

$$12 \text{ mol } \cancel{H_2} \times \frac{2 \text{ mol NH}_3}{3 \text{ mol } \cancel{H_2}} = 8 \text{ mol NH}_3$$

Compare these two calculations to the burger examples. Notice the similarities?

There is one significant difference between kitchen recipes and chemical reactions, however. Unlike in a kitchen, where one can easily count a couple dozen slices of cheese, it's not really practical (or probable) to count on a mole scale when working with chemical reactions. It's more common to start with some other measurement, such as mass, and convert that amount to moles. As we discussed in Part 1, we have an easy way to convert mass to moles or vice-versa: molar mass.

Example: Sodium and chlorine can combine to form sodium chloride (table salt).

$$2Na + Cl_2 \rightarrow 2NaCl$$

How many grams of sodium chloride can be made from 10.0 grams of chlorine?

Remember, in a chemical equation it's best to think of the coefficients in terms of moles, so the first step is to convert 10.0 g Cl_2 to mol Cl_2 using its molar mass.

$$10.0 \text{ g } \cancel{Cl_2} \times \frac{1 \text{ mol Cl}_2}{70.90 \text{ g } \cancel{Cl_2}}$$

From the chemical equation, we see that we need one mole of chlorine for every two moles of sodium chloride

$$10.0 \text{ g Cl}_2 \times \frac{1 \text{ mol Cl}_2}{70.90 \text{ g Cl}_2} \times \frac{2 \text{ mol NaCl}}{1 \text{ mol Cl}_2}$$

Finally, we use sodium chloride's molar mass to covert moles to grams

$$10.0 \text{ g Cl}_2 \times \frac{1 \text{ mol Cl}_2}{70.90 \text{ g Cl}_2} \times \frac{2 \text{ mol NaCl}}{1 \text{ mol Cl}_2} \times \frac{58.44 \text{ g NaCl}}{1 \text{ mol NaCl}} = 16.5 \text{ g NaCl}$$

Summing Up

To covert between...	Use...
moles and number	Avogadro's Number
grams and moles	molar mass
moles within a compound	the compound's formula
moles within an equation	the equation's coefficients

Yields

In our previous example, we calculated that 10.0 grams of chlorine would produce 16.5 grams of sodium chloride. This is known as a **theoretical yield** because that's how much should *theoretically* be produced from that amount of chlorine. However, there are several things that can prevent one from getting this amount. Sometimes it's things you can control (such as your lab technique), but there are also things that you can't completely control (side reactions, instrument accuracy, etc.) The amount you *actually* get after performing the reaction is called the **actual yield**. It's common to express the amount recovered as a percentage, which we call a **percent yield**.

124

$$\text{Percent yield} = \frac{\text{Actual yield}}{\text{Theoretical yield}} \times 100$$

For example, if you performed the reaction in the previous example and collect 12.6 g of sodium chloride, your percent yield would be

$$\frac{12.6 \text{ g}}{16.5 \text{ g}} \times 100 = 76.4\%$$

Many students will wonder if this is a good percent yield or not. Probably because getting a 76% at most U.S. colleges is a "C" grade. But just as a student's feeling on an earned grade is relative (some students are relieved to pass a course with a C, while others can't bear the thought of losing that 4.0 grade point average), so is the percent yield of a chemical reaction. In a general chemistry course, most of the reactions you perform in lab typically give pretty high yields. On the other hand, a chemist whose research involves making new compounds—or making known compounds in new ways—might only get yields in the teens or lower, but he or she is probably happy just to have made the stuff at all (though the next step in such cases is usually to find a way to improve your yields).

Try It Yourself

P12. If you have 32 slices of bacon and want to make some burgers using the recipe given at the beginning of this section, a) how many burgers could you make? b) how many patties, c) how many slices of cheese?

P13. Given the ammonia reaction shown earlier,

$$N_2 + 3H_2 \rightarrow 2NH_3$$

a) How many moles of hydrogen would be needed to produce 45.0 moles of ammonia?

b) How many moles of N_2 would be required to react with 4.50 mol H_2?

c) How many grams of NH_3 could be produced from 225 g H_2?

d) How many kilograms of nitrogen would be required to react with 3.4 kg of hydrogen?

P14. In the following reaction between phosphorus and oxygen

$$P_4 + 5O_2 \rightarrow P_4O_{10}$$

a) How many grams of phosphorus are required to produce 25.0 grams of tetraphosphorus decoxide?

b) How many grams of P_4O_{10} can be produced from 19.55 g O_2?

c) A student calculated that he would be able to produced 7.33 g P_2O_5, but only collected 5.82. What is his percent yield?

Part 5: Limiting Reagents

Let's begin this section with another food analogy: the great hot dog mystery. Franks typically come ten to a pack, but buns only have eight per pack. Why? Most of the time, you don't buy one without the other, so when you buy a pack of each, you end up with two franks left over. A similar thing can happen when you're preparing a chemical reaction, where you don't start with the amount of one reactant that's required to completely react with the other (often known as a *stoichiometric* amount). Sometimes a chemist will purposely use an excess amount of one reactant to ensure that the other one gets used up. For example, if one reactant is much more expensive than the other, you'd typically use a large excess of the cheaper chemical to ensure that the more expensive one reacts completely. In these instances, the reactant that's completely used is known as the **limiting reagent**, while the one that's in excess is the **excess reagent**. Applying these terms to our hot dog analogy, the pack of buns would be the limiting reagent and the franks would be the excess reagent.

Going back to our burger example from Part 4, let's say you had ten patties and ten slices of cheese. Assuming we had enough of the other ingredients, which of these two would be considered the "limiting reagent" and which would be in excess? This one's a little different than our hot dog example because our two ingredients aren't combining in a 1:1 ratio. Here, we need two patties for every three slices of cheese. If we wanted to use all ten patties, we would need...

$$10 \text{ \sout{patties}} \times \frac{3 \text{ cheese}}{2 \text{ \sout{patties}}} = 15 \text{ cheese}$$

Looks like we don't have enough cheese, making it our limiting reagent.

Now let's apply this concept to a chemical reaction...

Example: Hydrogen and oxygen can react to form water, as shown below.

$$2H_2 + O_2 \rightarrow 2H_2O$$

If 5.00 g of hydrogen are combined with 25.0 g of oxygen how many grams of water can be produced?

The first thing we have to do is determine which reactant is limiting and which is in excess. One way to do that is to pick either reactant and determine how much of the other you actually need, similar to what we did with the burger/cheese example above. Here, we'll see how much oxygen is actually required to react with 5.00 g of hydrogen.

$$5.00 \text{ g } H_2 \times \frac{1 \text{ mol } H_2}{2.016 \text{ g } H_2} \times \frac{1 \text{ mol } O_2}{2 \text{ mol } H_2} \times \frac{32.00 \text{ g } O_2}{1 \text{ mol } O_2} = 39.7 \text{ g } O_2$$

So we need 39.7 g of oxygen to completely react with all of the hydrogen, but we only have 25.0 g. If there isn't enough oxygen, it must be the limiting reagent.

Now that we know which reactant is limiting, we use it to determine how much water we can get from the reaction.

$$25.0 \text{ g } O_2 \times \frac{1 \text{ mol } O_2}{32.00 \text{ g } O_2} \times \frac{2 \text{ mol } H_2O}{1 \text{ mol } O_2} \times \frac{18.02 \text{ g } H_2O}{1 \text{ mol } H_2O} = 28.2 \text{ g } H_2O$$

Example: Zinc and silver nitrate react as follows

$$Zn + 2AgNO_3 \rightarrow Zn(NO_3)_2 + 2Ag$$

If you react 4.0 g of zinc with 6.0 g of silver nitrate how many grams of silver can be produced?

Again, we determine the limiting reagent by picking one reactant and seeing how much of the other you need. For this example, let's calculate how many grams of zinc we'd need to react with all 6.0 g of silver nitrate:

$$6.0 \text{ g AgNO}_3 \times \frac{1 \text{ mol AgNO}_3}{169.9 \text{ g AgNO}_3} \times \frac{1 \text{ mol Zn}}{2 \text{ mol AgNO}_3} \times \frac{65.39 \text{ g Zn}}{1 \text{ mol Zn}} = 1.1 \text{ g Zn}$$

This time, it appears that we have more than enough zinc to react with all of our silver nitrate (an *excess* amount, you might say), which means zinc is our excess reagent and silver nitrate the limiting reagent. Next, we use our limiting reagent to determine how much silver can be produced.

$$6.0 \text{ g AgNO}_3 \times \frac{1 \text{ mol AgNO}_3}{169.9 \text{ g AgNO}_3} \times \frac{2 \text{ mol Ag}}{2 \text{ mol AgNO}_3} \times \frac{107.9 \text{ g Ag}}{1 \text{ mol Ag}} = 3.8 \text{ g Ag}$$

Try It Yourself

P15. Given the following reaction between uranium and fluorine:

$$U + 3F_2 \rightarrow UF_6$$

a) If you started with 15 moles of each reactant, which would be the limiting reagent? How many moles of UF_6 could be produced?

b) If you started with 15.0 g of each reactant, which would be the limiting reagent? How many grams of UF_6 could be produced?

c) If 100.0 g of uranium was reacted with 50.0 g of fluorine, what is the theoretical yield of uranium (VI) fluoride?

Part 6: Combustion Reactions

A **combustion reaction** is any reaction between oxygen (O_2) and another substance. When you hear the word "combustion," you probably think of things burning. That's because when anything burns, it's undergoing a combustion reaction, which is why oxygen is one of the three things that are usually said to be required for a fire, (along with heat and a fuel source). For example, in Part 3 of this chapter we balanced an equation for the combustion of C_4H_{10}.

$$C_4H_{10} + \frac{13}{2}O_2 \rightarrow 4CO_2 + 5H_2O$$

C_4H_{10} is actually the molecular formula of butane, commonly known as lighter fluid. If you're a smoker, you probably perform this reaction several times a day (unless you're old fashioned and use matches). Another common example of a combustion reaction can be found in homes heated with a natural gas, which is primarily methane, CH_4.

$$CH_4 + 2O_2 \rightarrow CO_2 + 2H_2O$$

Finally, cellular respiration can be represented by the combustion of glucose, $C_6H_{12}O_6$.

$$C_6H_{12}O_6 + 6O_2 \rightarrow 6CO_2 + 6H_2O$$

You may have noticed that all three of these reactions form the same products: carbon dioxide and water. In a combustion reaction, oxygen combines with each element from the other reactant to form that element's primary oxide. All three substances contain carbon, whose primary oxide is carbon dioxide. Hydrogen is also present each time, and its primary oxide is water. The exception to this trend, as seen in the combustion of sugar, is when oxygen is present in the combusting substance. You don't form an "oxygen oxide" (which I suppose is really just a weird way to name O_2). That oxygen is used alongside O_2 to form the other elements' oxides.

Any other nonmetal will react to form its main oxide. For example, the form of phosphorus known as "white phosphorus" readily burns when exposed to air, producing tetraphosphorus decoxide.

$$P_4 + 5O_2 \rightarrow P_4O_{10}$$

Likewise, metals will undergo combustion to form metal oxides. One common example can be found in the "sparklers" used on Independence Day or other firework-related celebrations, whose intense, white light comes from the burning of magnesium:

$$2Mg + O_2 \rightarrow 2MgO$$

Summing up

If the reactant contains…	a combustion product is
carbon	CO_2
hydrogen	H_2O
another nonmetal	a nonmetal oxide
a metal	a metal oxide

Example: Ethanol (drinking alcohol) has the molecular formula C_2H_6O. Write an equation for the combustion of ethanol.

By definition, oxygen is the other reactant in a combustion reaction.

$$C_2H_6O + O_2 \rightarrow$$

The compound contains carbon, so CO_2 should be a product.

$$C_2H_6O + O_2 \rightarrow CO_2$$

And since hydrogen is present, another product will be water.

$$C_2H_6O + O_2 \rightarrow CO_2 + H_2O$$

There's also oxygen in the compound, but remember that element doesn't lead to a separate combustion product. Therefore, the only thing left to do is balance the equation.

$$C_2H_6O + 3O_2 \rightarrow 2CO_2 + 3H_2O$$

Combustion Analysis

In Part 2 of this chapter, we saw how the percent composition of a compound can be used to determine its empirical formula. You can also determine an empirical formula using a combustion reaction, using a technique known as combustion analysis. It's often used to determine the empirical formulas of organic compounds, which are primarily composed of carbon and hydrogen. The basic set-up for such a procedure is illustrated below

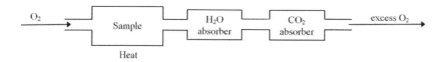

Pure oxygen is pumped through and the tube containing the sample is heated to the compound's combustion temperature. Any carbon is assumed to be converted to carbon dioxide and any hydrogen to water vapor. The oxygen being pumped in will push the gaseous products forward into another set of tubes, one containing a chemical known to absorb water, the other a chemical that will absorb carbon dioxide. If you know the initial weight of each absorbent/tube piece you can weigh it after the reaction to determine the mass of CO_2 and H_2O collected. Using the mass of the combustion products, you can determine the empirical formula in a manner similar to the one used in elemental analysis.

Example: A hydrocarbon (C_xH_y) underwent combustion to produce 0.379 g CO_2 and 0.1035 g H_2O. Determine the empirical formula of this compound.

Step 1: Calculate the number of moles of carbon in CO_2 and the number of moles of hydrogen in H_2O.

Remember, we're assuming that all of the carbon dioxide and water that was collected came from the combustion of our original sample.

$$C_xH_y + O_2 \rightarrow CO_2 + H_2O$$

If that's true, then the carbon in carbon dioxide and the hydrogen in water should equal the amounts found in our unknown compound. To determine the moles of each element present, we use the same type of calculations discussed in Part 1 of this chapter.

$$0.379 \text{ g CO}_2 \times \frac{1 \text{ mol CO}_2}{44.01 \text{ g CO}_2} \times \frac{1 \text{ mol C}}{1 \text{ mol CO}_2} = 0.00861 \text{ mol C}$$

$$0.1035 \text{ g H}_2O \times \frac{1 \text{ mol H}_2O}{18.02 \text{ g H}_2O} \times \frac{2 \text{ mol H}}{1 \text{ mol H}_2O} = 0.0115 \text{ mol H}$$

Step 2: Determine the element ratio of the compound.

Just as we did in our elemental analysis examples, once we know how many moles of each element were present in the original compound, we can find the ratio by dividing each number by the smallest.

$$\frac{0.0115}{0.00861} = 1.34 \text{ H}$$

$$\frac{0.00861}{0.00861} = 1 \text{ C}$$

Like before, we don't round when a number looks to be the decimal form of a fraction. Here, 1.34 is close to 1.33 (1⅓), so we multiple our ratio by 3 to get

$$CH_{1.34} \times 3 = C_3H_4$$

Example: A 0.500 g sample of a compound containing carbon, hydrogen, and oxygen ($C_xH_yO_z$) undergoes combustion to form 1.16 g CO_2 and 0.395 g H_2O. Determine the empirical formula of this compound.

Following the same steps as our previous example, we begin by finding the moles of each element in our sample. We find the moles of carbon in the compound using the mass of CO_2

$$1.16 \text{ g } CO_2 \times \frac{1 \text{ mol } CO_2}{44.01 \text{ g } CO_2} \times \frac{1 \text{ mol C}}{1 \text{ mol } CO_2} = 0.0264 \text{ mol C}$$

and the moles of hydrogen present using the mass of water,

$$0.395 \text{ g } H_2O \times \frac{1 \text{ mol } H_2O}{18.02 \text{ g } H_2O} \times \frac{2 \text{ mol H}}{1 \text{ mol } H_2O} = 0.0438 \text{ mol H}$$

What about oxygen, though? Remember, not all of the oxygen in our combustion products came from this compound. Some of it came from the oxygen being pumped in, but we're not told how much of that was used during the reaction (and it was probably an excess, anyway). However, we are given the mass of our sample

(0.500 g), and we can convert moles of C and H to grams, using their respective molar masses.

$$0.0264 \text{ mol C} \times \frac{12.01 \text{ g C}}{1 \text{ mol C}} = 0.317 \text{ g C}$$

$$0.0438 \text{ mol H} \times \frac{1.008 \text{ g H}}{1 \text{ mol H}} = 0.0442 \text{ g H}$$

There are three elements in this 0.500 g sample, and we know masses of two of them. Therefore, the mass of oxygen must be

$$
\begin{array}{rl}
0.500 & \text{g } C_xH_yO_z \\
- \ 0.317 & \text{g carbon} \\
- \ 0.0442 & \text{g hydrogen} \\
\hline
0.139 & \text{g oxygen}
\end{array}
$$

which we can convert to moles

$$0.139 \text{ g O} \times \frac{1 \text{ mol O}}{16.00 \text{ g O}} = 0.00869 \text{ mol O}$$

Now that we have the moles of all three elements in our compound, we can find our ratio.

$$\frac{0.0264}{0.00869} = 3.04 \approx 3 \text{ C}$$

$$\frac{0.0438}{0.00869} = 5.04 \approx 5 \text{ H}$$

$$\frac{0.00869}{0.00869} = 1 \text{ O}$$

Our empirical formula, therefore, is C_3H_5O.

Try It Yourself

P16. Write balanced equations showing the combustion of each of the following: a) Ca_2C, b) $C_8H_{10}O_3$, c) KH

P17. A hydrocarbon underwent combustion, forming 3.14 g carbon dioxide and 1.28 g water. The molar mass was found to be 84.12 g/mol. Determine the molecular formula of this compound.

P18. A 1.00 g sample of a compound containing carbon, hydrogen, and oxygen underwent combustion, producing 1.76 g CO_2 and 0.839 g H_2O. Determine the empirical formula of this compound.

Learning Beyond

Now that you know how to read chemical equations, why not learn about some of the chemical reactions and processes that have helped shape our lives, such as…
- The Haber-Bosch process of ammonia production
- The Hall–Héroult process of aluminum production
- Fluorinating you teeth to prevent tooth decay.

Test Your Skills

★ DeCaf

1. Convert each of the following to units of grams:
a) 9.80 mol Ca, b) 0.00489 mol Si, c) 45.01 mol F_2, d) 0.305 mol NaI, e) 6.2 mol CF_2Cl_2

XP: +4 each

2. Convert each of the following to units of moles.
a) 13.1 g Fe, b) 8.0 g Mg, c) 0.558 g PCl_3, d) 3.099 g $CuCl_2$

XP: +4 each

3. How many moles of chlorine (Cl) are in each of the following?
a) 5.00 mol NaCl, b) 0.44 mol CCl_4, c) 10.22 mol $Ti(ClO_4)_3$

XP: +4 each

4. How many grams of carbon are in each of the following?
a) 55.0 g CO_2, b) 37.43 g C_4H_8, c) 128.5 g $Ca(CO_3)_2$

XP: +4 each

5. What is the mass (in grams) of each of the following?
a) 8.90×10^{24} nickel atoms, b) 2.7×10^{23} I_2 molecules, c) 7.004×10^{22} SF_6 molecules

XP: +4 each

6. Determine the percent composition of each of the following compounds: a) Fe_2O_3, b) N_2O_3, c) CF_3Cl, d) Cu_3PO_4

XP: +4 each

7. Determine the empirical formulas of each of the following compounds:
a) 23.7% manganese, 76.3% chlorine
b) 79.9% carbon, 20.1% hydrogen
c) 25.94% nitrogen, 74.06% oxygen

XP: +4 each

8. Determine the molecular formula of each of the following compounds.
a) Empirical formula = C_3H_7, molar mass = 172.34 g/mol
b) Empirical formula = CH_3O_2, molar mass = 192.0 g/mol
c) Empirical formula = $C_5H_{12}P$, molar mass = 103.1 g/mol

XP: +4 each

9. Balance the following equations
a) $CS_2 + Cl_2 \rightarrow S_2Cl_2 + CCl_4$
b) $CS_2 + O_2 \rightarrow CO_2 + SO_2$
c) $P_4O_6 + H_2O \rightarrow H_3PO_3$
d) $Fe(OH)_3 + HNO_3 \rightarrow Fe(NO_3)_3 + H_2O$
e) $Ca + H_2O \rightarrow Ca(OH)_2 + H_2$

XP: +4 each

10. Calcium carbide can be prepared by reacting calcium oxide with carbon.

$$CaO + 3C \rightarrow CaC_2 + CO$$

a) How many moles of carbon are required to react with 14.5 moles of calcium oxide?
b) How many grams of CaC_2 can be produced from 55.0 g CaO?
c) How many grams of carbon are required to produce 427 g of calcium carbide?
d) A chemist calculates a theoretical yield of 395 g CaC_2, but is only able to collect 275 g. What is the percent yield of this reaction?

XP: +4 each

11. Write equations showing the combustion of each of the following compounds.
a) Li, b) AlH_3, c) C_5H_{10}, d) $C_{10}H_{14}O_3$

XP: +4 each

138

12. A hydrocarbon (C_xH_y) undergoes combustion to produce 9.09 g CO_2 and 4.65 g H_2O. Determine the empirical formula of this compound.

XP: +4

13. A hydrocarbon undergoes combustion to produce 3.14 g CO_2 and 1.29 g H_2O. In a separate experiment, the molar mass was found to be 140.3 g/mol. Determine the molecular formula of this compound.

XP: +5 each

★XP: _____

If your XP is 133 or higher, maybe you'd like to try a...

★★Latte

14. Perform the following calculations.
a) How many moles of sodium are in 9.4 g Na_2SO_4?
b) How many moles of water are in 31.75 g $NiCl_2 \cdot 6H_2O$?
c) How many grams of $Fe(NO_3)_3$ contain 14.2 mol nitrate?
d) How many grams of $Cr(PO_4)_3$ contain 239.2 mol oxygen?

XP: +5 each

15. Perform the following calculations.
a) What is the mass (in grams) of 5.33 x 10^{24} neon atoms?
b) How many grams of $SrI_2 \cdot 6H_2O$ contain 8.330 x 10^{24} water molecules?
c) How many chlorine atoms are in 22.0 g PCl_3?
d) How many perchlorate ions are in 90.8 g $Ti(ClO_4)_4$?

XP: +5 each

16. Determine the empirical formulas of each of the following compounds.
a) 58.5% carbon, 7.37% hydrogen, 34.13% nitrogen

b) 53.3% carbon, 11.2% hydrogen, 35.5% oxygen

XP: +5 each

17. A 5.00 g sample of a chromium oxide (Cr_xO_y) was reacted with aluminum, forming aluminum oxide and chromium metal. The chromium was collected and had a mass of 3.42 g.
a) What is the percent composition of the chromium oxide?
b) What is the empirical formula of this compound?

XP: +5 each

18. Write balanced equations for each of following:
a) Calcium chloride and sodium carbonate react to produce calcium carbonate and sodium chloride.
b) Copper (II) sulfate reacts with iron to produce iron (II) sulfate and copper.
c) Uranium and oxygen react to form uranium (VI) oxide.
d) Potassium chlorate decomposes into potassium chloride and elemental oxygen.

XP: +5 each

19. Tarnished silver is actually silver sulfide that forms when silver reacts with hydrogen sulfide (which is found, among other places, in human flatulence). A common method of restoring tarnished silver involves wrapping it in aluminum foil, which converts the silver sulfide back to silver metal.

$$3Ag_2S + 2Al \rightarrow 6Ag + Al_2S_3$$

a) How many grams of silver sulfide can be treated with a 3.00 g Al?
b) How many grams of silver can be formed from 30.0 g Ag_2S?
c) If you start with 10.00 g of each reactant, how many grams of aluminum sulfide will form?

XP: +5 each

20. A generalized way to show how aluminum is extracted from its ore is shown below.

$$2Al_2O_3 + 3C \rightarrow 3CO_2 + 4Al$$

a) How many grams of carbon are required to produce 3.00×10^6 kg of aluminum?
b) How many grams of carbon dioxide are produced from the reaction of 873 g aluminum oxide?
c) If you start with 525 g Al_2O_3 and 842 g carbon, which reactant is the limiting reagent?

XP: +5 each

21. During a combustion reaction, carbon can also undergo incomplete combustion, forming carbon monoxide. This is why people that use natural gas to cook or heat their homes are often cautioned that using older or poorly maintained appliances can increase the risk of carbon monoxide poisoning. Write an equation for the combustion of methane (CH_4, the primary component of natural gas) showing carbon undergoing incomplete combustion.

XP: +5

22. A compound containing carbon, hydrogen, and oxygen was analyzed by combustion analysis. A 2.00 g sample of the compound produced 3.56 g of carbon dioxide and 1.46 g of water. In a separate experiment, the molar mass was found to be 296.3 g/mol. Determine the molecular formula of this compound.

XP: +5

★★XP: _____   Total XP: _____

If your total XP is 223 or higher, maybe you'd like to try an...

★★★Espresso

23. A cube of titanium (d = 4.52 g/mL) contains 7.50×10^{24} atoms. Calculate the dimensions of the cube.

XP: +10

24. A 3.500 g sample of hydrated bismuth (III) nitrate, $Bi(NO_3)_3 \cdot xH_2O$, was heated to remove the water. The mass of the anhydrous $Bi(NO_3)_3$ was 3.079 g.
a) What is x in this hydrated compound?
b) What is the name of the hydrated compound?

XP: +5 each

25. If an automobile travels 225 mi with a gas mileage of 20.5 mi/gal (1 gal = 3.78L), how many kilograms of CO_2 are produced? Although gasoline is a mixture, assume an average molecular formula of C_8H_{18} and a density of 0.69 g/mL.

XP: +10

26. Write equations, with phases, for each of the following reactions.
a) Solid nitrogen triiodide will decompose to nitrogen and iodine, both of which are gases.
b) When a solid mixture of calcium oxide and carbon is heated, solid calcium carbide and oxygen gas are produced.
c) Solid lead (II) sulfide reacts with oxygen gas to produce solid lead (II) oxide and gaseous sulfur dioixde.
d) Barium nitrate and sodium phosphate are dissolved in water, producing produce barium phosphate and sodium nitrate. Barium phosphate forms as a solid, but sodium nitrate remains dissolved.

XP: +10 each

27. Chromium (VI) oxide, a material used for chrome plating can be produced by reacting sulfuric acid (H_2SO_4) with sodium chromate.

$$H_2SO_4 + Na_2CrO_4 \rightarrow CrO_3 + Na_2SO_4 + H_2O$$

a) How many grams of CrO_3 can be made from 50.0 kg Na_2CrO_4?

b) 500.0 g of sodium chromate is mixed with 400.0 g of an 80.0 % (by mass) solution of sulfuric acid. Calculate the theoretical yield, in grams, of chromium (VI) oxide.

c) If someone collected 56.3 g CrO_3 and reported an 88.3% yield, how much Na_2CrO_4 was used in the reaction?

XP: +10 each

★★★ XP: _____   Total XP: _____

If your total XP is 275 or greater: Level up!

Achievement Unlocked: Holy Moley!
Completed Chapter 4

You're now ready to learn about aqueous reactions

Chapter 5
Aqueous Chemistry

Part 1: Solutions

Essentially, a **solution** is defined as a homogeneous mixture. Heterogeneous "solutions," such as milk, are technically known as *suspensions*, which we'll discuss in Chapter 13. We typically think of solutions as a solid being dissolved in a liquid, and many of the solutions you encounter are just that, but they aren't limited to such mixtures. Carbonated beverages, for example, contain dissolved carbon dioxide, while alcoholic beverages are primarily composed of two liquids: ethanol (the chemical name for drinking alcohol) and water.

A solution is composed of two parts: the solute and the solvent. In general terms, the **solute** is the substance being dissolved while the **solvent** is the substance (usually a liquid) that's dissolving the solute. An alternate, broader, set of definitions defines the solute as the substance in lesser amount while the solvent is the one in greater amount. For example, alcoholic beverages that are 80 proof are 40% alcohol and approximately 60% water, making alcohol the solute and water the solvent. On the other hand, Everclear is 190 proof, meaning it's 95% alcohol and 5% water. In that case water is the solute and alcohol is the solvent (and yes, there is such a thing as 200 proof; it's simply pure ethanol).

In this chapter, we'll discuss many of the common types of reactions performed under **aqueous** conditions, which means water is the solvent. Most or all of the chemical reactions you encounter in a general chemistry course—including labs—will be aqueous. One reason is that water has an almost unique ability to dissolve a wide variety of compounds, including many of the types of compounds introduced in Chapter 3. Plus, from an environmental standpoint, water is usually a "greener" solvent to use in an instructional lab. Before we discuss reactions, however, we need to first say a few words about...

How Things Dissolve

How a solute dissolves depends on what type of substance it is. Most covalent compounds dissolve by simply breaking up into individual molecules (except acids, which we'll discuss later). When sugar is dissolved in water, the solution primarily consists of individual sugar molecules that are floating around in water. Using the phases introduced in Chapter 4 (Part 3), the process can be shown as

$$C_6H_{12}O_6(s) \xrightarrow{H_2O} C_6H_{12}O_6(aq)$$

If the solute is an ionic compound, it will usually dissolve by breaking up into ions, a process known as **dissociation**. Sodium chloride (table salt), for example, will dissociate into sodium ions and chloride ions when dissolved in water.

$$NaCl(s) \xrightarrow{H_2O} Na^+(aq) + Cl^-(aq)$$

Something similar happens with magnesium chloride and potassium nitrate:

$$MgCl_2(s) \xrightarrow{H_2O} Mg^{2+}(aq) + 2Cl^-(aq)$$

$$KNO_3(s) \xrightarrow{H_2O} K^+(aq) + NO_3^-(aq)$$

Notice that for the dissociation of potassium nitrate, the nitrate ion stays intact. As we discussed in Chapter 3, polyatomic ions aren't composed of monatomic ions, but are covalent compounds that happen to have an overall charge.

Compounds that dissociate when they're dissolved in water are often referred to as **electrolytes** because solutions of these compounds are strong conductors of electricity. Pure water is actually a poor conductor. It's the dissociated ions of electrolytes that allow current to flow through it so well. Most covalent compounds are **nonelectrolytes** because they don't dissociate into solution, and such solutions are generally poor conductors.

(Before you get any ideas involving electricity and water, know that you *rarely* encounter pure water in life. No, not even the stuff you buy in bottles. And pure water becomes ionized quite easily when exposed to the air—or your skin, for that matter. Don't be a moron, is what I'm basically trying to say.)

The Solubility of Ionic Compounds

To say a compound is soluble means that it dissolves to a significant degree. Generally speaking, every compound will dissolve to *some* degree, but if only 0.01% of a compound dissolves as the other 99.99% just sinks to the bottom of the beaker, that isn't very significant. Most of the compounds you encounter in a general chemistry lab are "all or nothing" in terms of solubility, meaning all of it will dissolve or essentially none of it will. Eventually, though, you will reach the solubility limit of your solvent and form a **saturated** solution, at which point no more solute will dissolve.

Solubility Trends

One way to predict whether or not a given compound will be soluble in water is to use the following trends. They are listed in decreasing priority, meaning rule 1 has the highest priority and rule 7 the lowest.

1. Group 1A compounds, ammonium compounds, and acids are soluble.
2. Nitrates, acetates, chlorates, and perchlorates are soluble.
3. Silver, lead, mercury (I), and copper (I) compounds are insoluble.

148

4. Chlorides, bromides, and iodides are soluble.
5. Sulfates are soluble except for calcium and barium sulfate.
6. Compounds with a 2- or 3- anion are insoluble.
7. Hydroxides are insoluble except for calcium hydroxide and barium hydroxide.

To use these trends, you begin with #1 and work your way down the list until you find one that's applicable to the compound in question.

Examples: Predict the solubility of each of the following compounds:

a) NaCl

Sodium is a group 1A compound, which is covered in trend #1, so there's no need to go any further down the list. According to trend #1, sodium chloride should be **soluble** in water. If you do look further down you'll notice a rule that mentions chlorides, but you don't use these trends by finding a match for *both* ions. You only need to find a match for one.

b) $AgNO_3$

Trend #1 doesn't apply to this compound, so we move on to #2, which mentions nitrates. Again, we don't bother going any further down the list. There is a later trend (#3) that mentions silver, and this one seems to contradict trend #2, but remember that these are given in a priority sequence. Only the one with the highest priority is used to predict solubility, so we predict silver nitrate to be **soluble**.

c) AgCl

This time, trend #3 is the first one that's relevant to the compound in question, so we use it to predict that AgCl is **insoluble**. The trend that mentions chlorides (#4) has a lower priority and is therefore ignored.

d) $FeCl_2$

The first applicable trend is #4, so we predict this compound to be **soluble** in water.

e) $MgSO_4$

Soluble by trend #5

f) CaS

Insoluble by trend #6

g) $Ba(OH)_2$

Soluble by trend #7

It should be mentioned that these rules can't be used for *every* ionic compound out there, but it should cover the vast majority (maybe even all) of the ionic compounds you'll encounter in a general chemistry course.

Solubility and Chemical Equations

In chemical equations for an aqueous reaction, compounds that are soluble in water are designated as being in the aqueous phase, since they're predicted to dissolve in water, while insoluble compounds remain in the solid phase. For example, the seven compounds in the previous example would be assigned the following phases in a chemical equation.

a) NaCl(aq)
b) $AgNO_3$(aq)
c) AgCl(s)
d) $FeCl_2$(aq)
e) $MgSO_4$(aq)
f) CaS(s)
g) $Ba(OH)_2$(aq)

It's not always necessary to include phases in every equation (as you may have noticed in the previous chapter), but they should be included when it will help the reader have a better understanding of the reaction being discussed.

Try It Yourself

P1. Write equations, with phases, showing the dissociation of each of the following solids in water: a) CaI_2, b) $CuSO_4$, c) $FeBr_3$, d) NH_4NO_3, e) $Mg(ClO_4)_2$, f) K_3PO_4

P2. Which of the following compounds are predicted to be soluble?
a) Li_2S, b) NH_4CN, c) $FePO_4$, d) $Pb(NO_3)_4$, e) $CaCO_3$, f) CuS, g) AlI_3

Part 2: Precipitation Reactions

Precipitation reactions are reactions that produce a solid. The solid produced is often referred to as a *precipitate* (sometimes abbreviated "ppt"). While any reaction that forms a solid can be classified as a precipitation reaction, those involving two ionic compounds usually undergo a *double displacement* reaction, where the two compounds simply "swap" ions, with one of the products being insoluble in water.

$$AB + XY \rightarrow AY + XB$$

For example, sodium chloride and silver nitrate react to produce aqueous sodium nitrate and solid silver chloride.

$$NaCl(aq) + AgNO_3(aq) \rightarrow NaNO_3(aq) + AgCl(s)$$

Example: Write an equation, with phases, for the reaction between barium perchlorate and lithium phosphate.

We begin by recalling how to write the formulas for these two compounds (see Chapter 3): $Ba(ClO_4)_2$ and Li_3PO_4, respectively. These are our reactants.

$$Ba(ClO_4)_2 + Li_3PO_4 \rightarrow$$

Since the two compounds are ionic, we assume a double displacement reaction will occur, meaning barium and lithium will swap anions to form barium phosphate and lithium perchlorate. But remember our discussion on ionic formulas from Chapter 3. While barium and perchlorate form a compound in a 1:2 ratio, when barium and phosphate combine, the ratio is 3:2.

$$Ba(ClO_4)_2 + Li_3PO_4 \rightarrow \textbf{Ba}_3\textbf{(PO}_4\textbf{)}_2$$

152

Similarly, lithium forms a 3:1 ratio with phosphate, but a 1:1 ratio with perchlorate.

$$Ba(ClO_4)_2 + Li_3PO_4 \rightarrow Ba_3(PO_4)_2 + \mathbf{LiClO_4}$$

Once we have a complete equation, we balance it

$$3Ba(ClO_4)_2 + 2Li_3PO_4 \rightarrow Ba_3(PO_4)_2 + 6LiClO_4$$

Finally, we can assign phases using the solubility trends discussed in Part 1. Both lithium compounds are soluble by trend #1 (lithium is a group 1A element) and barium perchlorate is soluble by trend #2. Barium phosphate, however, is insoluble (#6), making it our precipitate.

$$3Ba(ClO_4)_2(aq) + 2Li_3PO_4(aq) \rightarrow Ba_3(PO_4)_2(s) + 6LiClO_4(aq)$$

Net Ionic Equations

Looking back at the reaction between sodium chloride and silver nitrate,

$$NaCl(aq) + AgNO_3(aq) \rightarrow NaNO_3(aq) + AgCl(s)$$

let's try to imagine what's really going on during this reaction, using the following (admittedly crude) figures. We'll begin with the two aqueous reactants, each in their own beaker (or whatever you prefer keeping your solutions in).

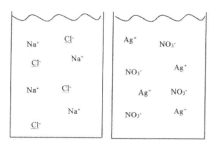

When you mix the two, aqueous sodium nitrate and solid silver chloride are formed as products.

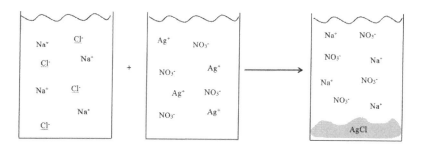

Now, look carefully at sodium and nitrate in this picture. They aren't *really* undergoing any chemical change, are they? They were aqueous ions before the reaction and they're aqueous ions afterwards. Such ions are known as **spectator ions**. Another way to see this is to rewrite the equation showing each soluble compound as the dissociated ions they actually are.

$$Na^+(aq) + Cl^-(aq) + Ag^+(aq) + NO_3^-(aq) \rightarrow Na^+(aq) + NO_3^-(aq) + AgCl(s)$$

In algebra, equations can be simplified when the same term appears on either side of the equation. For example,

$$x + y + 2 = 3 + x + z$$

can be simplified to

$$y + 2 = 3 + z$$

Likewise, chemical equations can be simplified by removing the spectator ions. Removing sodium and nitrate from the previous chemical equation, we're left with

$$Ag^+(aq) + Cl^-(aq) \rightarrow AgCl(s)$$

This type of chemical equation is called a **net ionic equation**. Sometimes a net ionic equation is more useful than the complete equation as it clears away the "clutter" and allows you to see what chemical changes are actually occurring during a given reaction.

Example: Write the net ionic equation for the reaction between barium perchlorate and lithium phosphate.

$$3Ba(ClO_4)_2(aq) + 2Li_3PO_4(aq) \rightarrow Ba_3(PO_4)_2(s) + 6LiClO_4(aq)$$

We'll start by rewriting the equation, showing each dissociated compound as separate ions (you can also sketch out a figure, as we did earlier, if that helps; or if you're more of the artistic type). Both reactants are aqueous, so the three barium perchlorates will dissociate into three barium ions and six perchlorate ions.

$$3Ba^{2+}(aq) + 6ClO_4^-(aq)$$

and the two lithium phosphates shown will dissociate into six lithium and two phosphate ions

$$3Ba^{2+}(aq) + 6ClO_4^-(aq) + \mathbf{6Li^+(aq) + 2PO_4^{3-}} \rightarrow$$

On the product side, barium phosphate is an insoluble solid, which means it's *not* dissociated and therefore isn't split up into ions. The same would be true for any substances in the liquid or gas phase (more on that later).

$$3Ba^{2+}(aq) + 6ClO_4^-(aq) + 6Li^+(aq) + 2PO_4^{3-} \rightarrow \textbf{Ba}_3\textbf{(PO}_4\textbf{)}_2\textbf{(s)}$$

Lithium perchlorate is aqueous, so it will dissociate.

$$3Ba^{2+}(aq) + 6ClO_4^-(aq) + 6Li^+(aq) + 2PO_4^{3-} \rightarrow$$
$$Ba_3(PO_4)_2(s) + \textbf{6Li}^+\textbf{(aq)} + \textbf{6ClO}_4^-\textbf{(aq)}$$

Looking at our dissociated equation, we see that lithium and perchlorate haven't changed during the course of the reaction, being aqueous ions on both sides of the equation, so they're our spectator ions. Removing them gives us the net ionic equation:

$$3Ba^{2+}(aq) + 2PO_4^{3-} \rightarrow Ba_3(PO_4)_2(s)$$

At this point, it should be noted that while our last two examples contained two spectator ions, that certainly isn't the case for every reaction (or chemical system in general). You can have more than two, just one, or none at all.

When a Reaction isn't Really a Reaction

Finally, let's imagine the reaction between sodium chloride and magnesium nitrate. The chemical equation would be

$$2NaCl(aq) + Mg(NO_3)_2(aq) \rightarrow 2NaNO_3(aq) + MgCl_2(aq)$$

The dissociated form of the equation would be

$$2Na^+(aq) + 2Cl^-(aq) + Mg^{2+}(aq) + 2NO_3^- \rightarrow$$
$$2Na^+(aq) + 2NO_3^-(aq) + Mg^{2+}(aq) + 2Cl^-(aq)$$

So what are our spectators? Well, it appears that the answer is *all of them*. If that's true, though, is there *really* a reaction occurring? Remember, for a reaction to occur, something must undergo a *chemical* change, such as an aqueous ion becoming part of a precipitate.

Try It Yourself

P3. Write equations, with phases, showing the reaction between each of the following:
a) LiBr and $Pb(NO_3)_4$
b) $FeSO_4$ and NaOH
c) $CaCl_2$ and $CuClO_4$
d) K_3PO_4 and $CrBr_3$

P4. Write net ion equations, with phases, for each of the reactions in P3.

Part 3: Acids & Bases

There are various ways to define acids and bases. In this chapter, we'll use the simplest definition, but in Chapter 17 we'll discuss a couple of others.

Acids

An **acid** can be defined as a substance that dissolves in water to produce hydrogen ion (H^+). Hydrogen ion is sometimes referred to as a *proton* because 99.99% of hydrogen is ^1H. When you remove its one electron, all that's left is a proton. In general, any substance with the general formula HA is assumed to be an acid in aqueous solution and will dissociate into H^+ and its respective anion. For now, we'll assume all acids dissociate completely, but we'll revisit this idea in a later chapter to discuss how that's not always the case.

$$HA \xrightarrow{H_2O} H^+ + A^-$$

$$HCl(g) \xrightarrow{H_2O} H^+(aq) + Cl^-(aq)$$

$$HNO_3(l) \xrightarrow{H_2O} H^+(aq) + NO_3^-(aq)$$

Again, this is actually a simplified way to describe what happens when an acid is dissolved in water, but it'll be good enough for the things we'll be discussing in this chapter.

Naming Acids

How you name an acid depends on the identity of the anion that forms during the dissociation (A^-), which is summarized in the following table:

Anion suffix	Acid name
"-ide"	add "hydro-" and replace suffix with "-ic"
"-ate"	replace suffix with "-ic"
"-ite"	replace suffix with "-ous"

An exception occurs with sulfur based compounds, where we actually use the element name ("sulfur") followed by the appropriate suffix.

Examples: HCl is Hydrochloric acid, HNO_3 is Nitric acid, H_2SO_3 is Sulfurous acid

As a pure substance, acids with a monatomic anion are usually named as any other covalent compound (see Chapter 3). Pure HCl, for instance, would be called "hydrogen chloride," but when you dissolve it in water, the resulting solution is "hydrochloric acid." This doesn't work as well when the anion is polyatomic, so they're usually referred to as an "anhydrous" acid in its pure form. For example, pure HNO_3 would simply be called "anhydrous nitric acid."

Bases

Bases can be defined as a substance that dissolves in water to produce hydroxide ion (OH^-). In general chemistry, most of the bases you encounter will be metal hydroxides, which can dissociate to produce a metal ion and hydroxide.

$$NaOH(s) \xrightarrow{H_2O} Na^+(aq) + OH^-(aq)$$

$$Ca(OH)_2(s) \xrightarrow{H_2O} Ca^{2+}(aq) + 2OH^-(aq)$$

However, another common base is ammonia (NH_3). When ammonia dissolves in water, it will react with water to produce ammonium hydroxide, which according to the solubility trends is soluble.

$$NH_3(g) + H_2O(l) \rightarrow NH_4^+(aq) + OH^-(aq)$$

Hydroxide is produced, which by definition makes it a base.

Acid-Base Reactions

An **acid-base reaction**, as the name implies, is a reaction between an acid and a base. As it was with precipitation reactions, acids and bases will usually react via a double displacement reaction in aqueous solution. For example, when nitric acid and sodium hydroxide react, they'll swap ions to produce sodium nitrate and water ("HOH").

$$HNO_3(aq) + NaOH(aq) \rightarrow NaNO_3(aq) + H_2O(l)$$

Because acids usually have the general formula HA and bases have the general formula BOH (B being either a metal ion or ammonium), the resulting products from the ion swap will be water (from the hydrogen and hydroxide ions) and a salt composed of the other two ions.

$$HA + BOH \rightarrow BA + H_2O$$

$$ACID + BASE \rightarrow SALT + WATER$$

Technically, a *salt* is defined as an ionic compound produced from an acid-base reaction, but the term is often used to describe any generic ionic compound.

Because the resulting solution is often neutral, meaning it's neither acidic nor basic (though not always, as we'll see in

Chapter 18), acid-base reactions are also known as *neutralization reactions*, though the term can be applied to any reaction where one chemical is completely reacted (*neutralized*) by another.

Example: Antacids work by neutralizing excess stomach acid (gastric acid), which is primarily hydrochloric acid. As such, the active ingredient for many antacids is a base. One such example is Philips' Milk of Magnesia, whose name comes from its active ingredient, magnesium hydroxide.

a) Write an equation, with phases, showing the neutralization of hydrochloric acid with magnesium hydroxide.

We approach this problem the same way we did with precipitation reactions in Part 2. The reactants are

$$Mg(OH)_2 + HCl \rightarrow$$

When the two compounds swap ions, magnesium ion will combine with chloride to form magnesium chloride,

$$Mg(OH)_2 + HCl \rightarrow \mathbf{MgCl_2}$$

while hydrogen ion and hydroxide will form water.

$$Mg(OH)_2 + HCl \rightarrow MgCl_2 + \mathbf{H_2O}$$

Next, we balance the equation

$$Mg(OH)_2 + 2HCl \rightarrow 2H_2O + MgCl_2$$

then add phases using our solubility trends.

$$Mg(OH)_2(s) + 2HCl(aq) \rightarrow 2H_2O(l) + MgCl_2(aq)$$

b) Write the net ionic equation for this reaction.

Hydrochloric acid and magnesium chloride are aqueous, so they can be broken up into dissociated ions. Magnesium hydroxide is a solid and water is a liquid, so those are left alone.

$$Mg(OH)_2(s) + 2H^+(aq) + 2Cl^-(aq) \rightarrow 2H_2O(l) + Mg^{2+}(aq) + 2Cl^-(aq)$$

Chloride appears to be the lone spectator ion. Removing it gives us the net ion equation.

$$Mg(OH)_2(s) + 2H^+(aq) \rightarrow 2H_2O(l) + Mg^{2+}(aq)$$

Try It Yourself

P5. Name each of the following as acids:
a) HI, b) H_3PO_4, c) $HC_2H_3O_2$, d) HF, e) HNO_2, f) H_2CrO_4

P6. Write formulas for each of the following acids:
a) carbonic acid, b) hydrobromic acid, c) chlorous acid

P7. Write equations, with phases, showing the reaction between each of the following:
a) LiOH and HBr
b) H_3PO_4 and NaOH
c) hydrofluoric acid and ammonium hydroxide
d) iron (II) hydroxide and sulfuric acid

P8. Write net ionic equations, with phases, for each of the reactions in P7.

Part 4: Gas-forming Reactions

Any reaction that produces a gas can be labeled as a gas-forming reaction. Here, we'll discuss four common examples.

Reactions That Produce Carbonic Acid

Aqueous carbonic acid, H_2CO_3, is unstable and will decompose to form water and carbon dioxide.

$$H_2CO_3(aq) \rightarrow H_2O(l) + CO_2(g)$$

For example, the reaction between hydrochloric acid and sodium bicarbonate begins like any other double displacement we've discussed so far.

$$HCl(aq) + NaHCO_3(aq) \rightarrow NaCl(aq) + H_2CO_3(aq)$$

Here, however, as soon as carbonic acid forms it's immediately converted to water and carbon dioxide.

$$HCl(aq) + NaHCO_3(aq) \rightarrow NaCl(aq) + H_2O(l) + CO_2(g)$$

or, as a net ionic equation

$$H^+(aq) + HCO_3^-(aq) \rightarrow H_2O(l) + CO_2(g)$$

As new as this might look to you, odds are you're not only familiar with this type of reaction, but you might have even done it yourself at one point in your life. It's the "volcano reaction" between baking soda (the common name for sodium bicarbonate) and vinegar, which is really nothing more than a dilute solution of acetic acid ($HC_2H_3O_2$).

$$HC_2H_3O_2(aq) + NaHCO_3(aq) \rightarrow NaC_2H_3O_2(aq) + H_2O(l) + CO_2(g)$$

Reactions That Produce Sulfurous Acid

Like carbonic acid, aqueous sulfurous acid (H_2SO_3) will decompose, forming water and sulfur dioxide.

$$H_2SO_3(aq) \rightarrow H_2O(l) + SO_2(g)$$

In the reaction between nitric acid and calcium sulfite, for example, it starts out as a double displacement

$$2HNO_3(aq) + CaSO_3(s) \rightarrow H_2SO_3(aq) + Ca(NO_3)_2(aq)$$

but as soon as sulfurous acids forms in solution, it breaks down into SO_2 and H_2O.

$$2HNO_3(aq) + CaSO_3(s) \rightarrow H_2O(l) + SO_2(g) + Ca(NO_3)_2(aq)$$

Reactions That Produce Hydrogen Sulfide

Acids are generally assumed to be soluble (trend #1 of our solubility trends), but hydrogen sulfide (H_2S) is an exception, existing as an insoluble gas at room temperature. For example, the reaction between sodium sulfide and hydrochloric acid is

$$Na_2S(aq) + 2HCl(aq) \rightarrow 2NaCl(aq) + H_2S(g)$$

It's a good idea to know if hydrogen sulfide's going to form during a reaction for several reasons. First, at low concentrations it smells incredibly bad (it's what gives rotten eggs and flatulence their trademark fragrances). Higher concentrations will deaden your sense of smell, which at first may seem like a good thing, given its odor. But if the concentration climbs a little higher, the gas becomes quite toxic and inhaling the compound can be fatal.

Reactions between Metals and Acids

Not all metals react with acids (more on that in Chapter 20), but when they do, they usually do so by the following general equation.

$$METAL + ACID \rightarrow SALT + H_2(g)$$

The salt will be composed of the metal and the anion of the acid. For example, zinc and hydrochloric acid react by the following equation

$$Zn(s) + 2HCl(aq) \rightarrow ZnCl_2(aq) + H_2(g)$$

Notice that, unlike other reactions we've seen in this chapter so far, this reaction isn't a double displace, but a *single* displacement, where the anion essentially replaces hydrogen with the metal.

One exception worth noting, however, occurs with nitric acid, as seen in the following reaction with copper.

$$Cu(s) + 4HNO_3(aq) \rightarrow Cu(NO_3)_2(aq) + 2NO_2(g) + 2H_2O(l)$$

In this instance, the metal reacts more readily with nitrate ion instead of hydrogen ion, though the reaction is still gas forming (NO_2).

Try It Yourself

P9. Write equations, with phases, for each of the following reactions:
a) $KHSO_3$ and HBr
b) $FeCO_3$ and H_2SO_4
c) Aluminum and perchloric acid
d) Copper (I) sulfide and phosphoric acid

P10. Write net ionic equations, with phases, for each of the reactions in P9

P11. Write net ionic equations, with phases, for the following reactions.
a) $2HNO_3(aq) + CaSO_3(s) \rightarrow H_2O(l) + SO_2(g) + Ca(NO_3)_2(aq)$
b) $Na_2S(aq) + 2HCl(aq) \rightarrow 2NaCl(aq) + H_2S(g)$
c) $Zn(s) + 2HCl(aq) \rightarrow ZnCl_2(aq) + H_2(g)$
d) $Cu(s) + 4HNO_3(aq) \rightarrow Cu(NO_3)_2(aq) + 2NO_2(g) + 2H_2O(l)$

Part 5: Oxidation-Reduction Reactions

Oxidation-reduction reactions (or *redox* reactions, for short) are reactions that involve a transfer of electrons between reactants. The name derives from the two processes that occur: a substance that undergoes **oxidation** is *losing electrons* while the one undergoing **reduction** is *gaining electrons*. It might sound weird that the one being "reduced" is the one doing the gaining, but these names predate our knowledge of electrons.

There are a couple of popular mnemonics that students often use to help remember which process does what: *OIL RIG*

OIL = Oxidation Is Loss
RIG = Reduction Is Gain

and *LEO goes GER*

LEO = Loss of Electrons is Oxidation
GER = Gain of Electrons is Reduction

One of the simplest types of redox reactions is the combining of elements into compounds, such the reaction between sodium and chlorine to form sodium chloride.

$$2Na + Cl_2 \rightarrow 2NaCl$$

Sodium originally had 11 electrons, but after reacting with chlorine it was converted to sodium ion, which has 10. Each chlorine atom, meanwhile, began with 17 electron, but during the conversion to chloride ion, it picked up an electron (the one sodium lost), for a total of 18. Therefore, during this reaction sodium is oxidized while chlorine is reduced.

Oxidation Numbers

With many redox reactions, it's not as easy to identify which reactant is being oxidized and which is being reduced. For example, phosphorus and oxygen can react to form tetraphosphorus pentoxide.

$$P_4 + 5O_2 \rightarrow P_4O_{10}$$

Like the reaction between sodium and chlorine, this reaction is also a redox reaction, which might seem confusing at first, since all three substances are covalent compounds, and in Chapter 3 we said that such compounds share electrons. However, one thing we've yet to discuss is that not all covalent compounds share their electrons *equally*, but that's a discussion we'll save for a later chapter. For now, just take it as a given that electrons are being transferred between the two reactants. That being said, unlike our previous example, we can't simply count electrons to determine which element is being oxidized and which is reduced.

Oxidation numbers are a useful way to keep track of electrons in a redox reaction, especially those like the one above. They can either be real charges or merely fake ones that we've systematically assigned to each element. We can assign oxidation numbers using the following set of rules:

1. Substances in their elemental state have an oxidation number (ON) of zero. This is true regardless of whether the elemental state is monatomic, diatomic, or polyatomic. For example, Na, Cl_2, P_4 all have an oxidation number of zero.
2. Monatomic ions have an oxidation number that's equal to their actual charge. For example, Na^+ has an ON of +1, Fe^{2+} has an ON of +2, and N^{3-} has an ON of -3.
3. For many covalent compounds, the following oxidation numbers are used in decreasing priority (3a has priority over 3b, etc).

a) Fluorine has an ON of -1
b) Hydrogen has an ON of +1
c) Oxygen has an ON of -2
d) Other halogens (besides fluorine) have an ON of -1

4. The sum of the oxidation numbers must equal the overall charge. This is known as the **algebraic sum rule**.

Example: Determine the oxidation numbers in each of the following compounds:

a) PCl_3

According to rule 3d, the oxidation number of chlorine is -1. There's no rule for phosphorus, but we can find its oxidation number using the algebraic sum rule, which says that the sum of the oxidation numbers must equal the compound's overall charge (zero, in this case)

$$P + 3Cl = 0$$
$$P + 3(-1) = 0$$
$$P = +3$$

If you remember the charge trend discussed in Chapter 2, you might find it odd to see phosphorus assigned a charge of +3 instead of -3, but remember that this is a covalent compound. Any charges we assign to these atoms are fake, even in cases such as chlorine where they resemble the atom's "normal" charge.

b) OF_2

Rule 3c says that oxygen usually has an oxidation number of -2 and rule 3a says fluorine has an oxidation number of -1. However, using both of these oxidation numbers will violate the algebraic sum rule.

$$-2 + 2(-1) \neq 0$$

This is when you have to remember the priority sequence of rule 3. Fluorine has the higher priority, so it keeps its assigned oxidation number and we find oxygen's using the sum rule

$$O + 2(-1) = 0$$
$$O = +2$$

c) SO_4^{2-}

Rule 3c says oxygen has an oxidation number of -2, and we can find sulfur's oxidation number using the algebraic sum rule. This time, though, the compound is a polyatomic ion, and the overall charge is -2.

$$S + 4O = -2$$
$$S + 4(-2) = -2$$
$$S = +6$$

d) $Ca(OH)_2$

With ionic compounds, it's best to look at each ion individually. In this example, the two ions are Ca^{2+} and OH^-. Monatomic ions have an oxidation number equal to its charge, so calcium's oxidation number will be +2.

Looking at hydroxide, hydrogen is initially assigned an oxidation number of +1 (rule 3b) and oxygen's will be -2 (rule 3c). As we did with OF_2, we need to check and see if the sum rule is being obeyed. This time, however, there's no conflict, so the two atoms can keep their assigned oxidation numbers.

$$-2 + (+1) = -1$$

e) C_3H_6O

As before, hydrogen's oxidation number is +1 and oxygen's is -2 (and by this point, you can see why out these two atoms and the halogens were picked for rule 3, as they show up in the vast majority of the compounds we encounter in a general chemistry class; just look back at the first four chapters and see). We'll find carbon's oxidation number using the sum rule.

$$3C + 6H + O = 0$$
$$3C + 6(+1) + (-2) = 0$$
$$3C = -4$$
$$C = -\frac{4}{3}$$

Though it may look odd, there's nothing wrong with a fractional oxidation number. It usually means the atoms in question don't have the same oxidation number, and the average just happens to be a fraction. If we knew more about the structure of this compound, we could determine the individual oxidation numbers of each carbon, but in this chapter just knowing the average value will be fine.

Using Oxidation Numbers

Now that we've discussed how to determine the oxidation numbers in a given compound, let's see how they can be used to figure out what's being oxidized and reduced in a redox reaction, starting with the aforementioned reaction between phosphorus and oxygen

$$P_4 + 5O_2 \rightarrow P_4O_{10}$$

On the reactant side, both atoms are in their elemental state, so both phosphorus and oxygen will be assigned oxidation numbers of zero (rule 1).

$$\begin{array}{ccc} P_4 + & 5O_2 \rightarrow & P_4O_{10} \\ \mathbf{0} & \mathbf{0} & \end{array}$$

As for the product, rule 3 says oxygen will have an oxidation number of -2

$$P_4 + 5O_2 \rightarrow P_4O_{10}$$
$$ 0 \quad\quad 0 \quad\quad -2$$

and we can use the sum rule to figure out the oxidation number of phosphorus.

$$4P + 10O = 0$$
$$4P + 10(-2) = 0$$
$$P = +5$$

We now have the oxidation numbers for each atom, on both sides of our equation:

$$P_4 + 5O_2 \rightarrow P_4O_{10}$$
$$ 0 \quad\quad 0 \quad\quad +5 \ -2$$

Even though it's been emphasized that oxidation numbers in compounds like these are fake charges, let's *pretend* that they're real. If you were to actually convert a phosphorus atom to a +5 ion, electrons would need to be removed. Therefore, phosphorus must be the one undergoing oxidation in this reaction. Likewise, converting a neutral oxygen atom to a -2 ion would require a gain of electrons, so oxygen must be the one being reduced.

Example: Identify the elements being oxidized and reduced in the following reaction.

$$Cu + 2NO_3^- + 4H^+ \rightarrow Cu^{2+} + 2NO_2 + 2H_2O$$

Regardless of how many are present, in most redox reactions the transfer is only occurring between two elements. In fact, if you have a reaction with hydrogen, oxygen and two other elements, usually it's the other two elements that are swapping electrons.

Starting with copper, we see that it's going from a neutral element (ON = 0) to a +2 cation (ON = +2).

$$Cu + 2NO_3^- + 4H^+ \rightarrow Cu^{2+} + 2NO_2 + 2H_2O$$
$$\mathbf{0} \qquad\qquad\qquad\qquad \mathbf{+2}$$

For this to happen, electrons have to be removed (similar to sodium and phosphorus in our earlier examples) so copper is being oxidize in this reaction.

Using our rules for oxidation numbers, nitrogen has an oxidation number of +5 in NO_3^-

$$N + 3(-2) = -1$$
$$N = +5$$

and +4 in NO_2

$$N + 2(-2) = 0$$
$$N = +4$$

which means nitrogen is undergoing reduction.

$$Cu + 2NO_3^- + 4H^+ \rightarrow Cu^{2+} + 2NO_2 + 2H_2O$$
$$\mathbf{+5} \qquad\qquad\qquad\qquad \mathbf{+4}$$

Back to what was said earlier about hydrogen and oxygen in these types of reactions, notice that their oxidations numbers don't change during the course of the reaction.

$$Cu + 2NO_3^- + 4H^+ \rightarrow Cu^{2+} + 2NO_2 + 2H_2O$$
$$\mathbf{-2} \quad \mathbf{+1} \qquad\qquad\qquad \mathbf{-2} \quad \mathbf{+1} \ \mathbf{-2}$$

As expected, only one transfer is occurring, and it's between the other two elements (copper and nitrogen).

Oxidizing & Reducing Agents

In redox reactions, the **oxidizing agent** is the reactant that's oxidizing another substance, while a **reducing agent** is the reactant that's reducing another substance. Now, imagine a redox reaction between two reactants, A and B, where A is being oxidized and B reduced.

Since A is reducing B, A is the reducing agent. But in order for A to reduce B, A has to *lose* electrons and undergo oxidation. Looking at it from B's point of view, it underwent reduction by *oxidizing* A, making it the oxidizing agent in this reaction. In other words, the oxidizing agent is the reactant undergoing reduction while reducing agent is the one undergoing oxidation.

Looking back in our previous two examples, in the reaction between phosphorus and oxygen, phosphorus is the reducing agent and oxygen is the oxidizing agent.

$$P_4 \quad + \quad 5O_2 \quad \rightarrow \quad 2P_2O_5$$

Oxidized   Reduced,
(Red. agent)   (Ox. agent)

We typically refer to the entire reactant as the "agent," so in the reaction between copper and nitrate, nitrate is said to be the oxidizing agent because the nitrogen in that ion is undergoing reduction. Copper, in turn, is said to be the reducing agent.

$$Cu + 2NO_3^- + 4H^+ \rightarrow Cu^{2+} + 2NO_2 + 2H_2O$$

Oxidized   Reduced,
(Red. agent)   (Ox. agent)

Many chemicals are known for their ability to act as either oxidizing or reducing agents, both in the laboratory as well as the home. If you want to remove a stain from clothing or a counter top, you'll most likely grab a cleaner that contains bleach. That's because the active ingredient of many bleaches is sodium hypochlorite (NaClO), a very strong oxidizing agent. In the case of fabrics, it will oxidize the stain (or the fabric dye, if you're not careful) and convert them into colorless chemicals. Another oxidizing agent you're probably familiar with is hydrogen peroxide (H_2O_2), which is commonly used as a disinfectant, killing those microorganisms we call "germs" by oxidizing them.

A common example of a reducing agent is Vitamin C (L-ascorbic acid). Just as germs can be damaged or killed by peroxides and other forms of oxygen (known in biology as "reactive oxygen species" or ROS, for short), so can the cells in our bodies. Vitamin C and similar types of compounds will react with these substances, reducing them before they have a chance to oxidize our cells, hence the name "antioxidants."

Try It Yourself

P12. Determine the oxidation numbers of the atoms in each of the following compounds:
a) AlF_3, b) NO_2, c) NO_2^-, d) IO_3^-, e) Na_3PO_4, f) $C_6H_{12}O_6$

P13. Identify the atoms undergoing oxidation and reduction in each of the following reactions:
a) $FeCl_2 + Zn \rightarrow Fe + ZnCl_2$
b) $CH_4 + O_2 \rightarrow CO_2 + H_2O$
c) $6Fe^{2+} + Cr_2O_7^{2-} + 14H^+ \rightarrow 6Fe^{3+} + 2Cr^{3+} + 7H_2O$

P14. Identify the oxidizing and reducing agents in P13.

Part 6: Molarity

Molarity

There are different ways to express how concentrated a solution is (how much solute you have in a given amount of solvent). Many household solutions use percent volume. If you look on a bottle of household hydrogen peroxide, for example, you'll see its concentration is given as 3% by volume. For a chemist, the most commonly used unit of concentration is **molarity**, which expresses concentration in moles of solute per liter of solution

$$\text{Molarity} = \frac{\text{moles solute}}{\text{liters solution}}$$

Suppose you have a 200.0 mL solution that contains 4.0 g of NaOH. We can use the solute's molar mass to find the number of moles present.

$$4.0 \text{ g NaOH} \times \frac{1 \text{ mol NaOH}}{40.00 \text{ g NaOH}} = 0.10 \text{ mol NaOH}$$

and since molarity is defined as being per liter,

$$200.0 \text{ mL} \times \frac{10^{-3} \text{ L}}{1 \text{ mL}} = 0.2000 \text{ L}$$

The molarity of our solution would be

$$\text{Molarity} = \frac{0.10 \text{ mol}}{0.2000 \text{ L}} = 0.50 \text{ mol/L}$$

It's common to symbolize the units of molarity, mol/L, with the letter "M," which stands for "molar."

Example: You wish to make 4.0 L of a 2.0 M ("two molar") potassium bromide solution. How many grams of KBr are required?

Remember that 2.0 M is the same as 2.0 mol/L, so we can convert L to mol using dimensional analysis

$$4.0 \ \cancel{\text{L KBr}} \times \frac{2.0 \text{ mol KBr}}{1 \ \cancel{\text{L KBr}}}$$

Now that we're in units of mol KBr, we can use its molar mass (119.0 g/mol) to convert mol to grams (see Ch. 4, Part 1)

$$4.0 \ \cancel{\text{L KBr}} \times \frac{2.0 \ \cancel{\text{mol KBr}}}{1 \ \cancel{\text{L KBr}}} \times \frac{119.0 \text{ g KBr}}{1 \ \cancel{\text{mol KBr}}} = 950 \text{ g KBr}$$

Therefore, if you dissolve 950 g of potassium bromide in enough water to make a 4.0 L solution, the concentration should be 2.0 M.

From the previous example, you can see that one of the benefits of using the molarity unit is it allows you to easily convert between moles and liters, similar to how molar mass allows us to convert between moles and grams. This means our list of common conversion factors is now up to five:

To covert between...	Use...
moles and number	Avogadro's Number
grams and moles	molar mass
moles within a compound	the compound's formula
moles within an equation	the equation's coefficients
moles to liters	molarity

Example: Silver nitrate and sodium chloride react by the following equation.

$$AgNO_3(aq) + NaCl(aq) \rightarrow AgCl(s) + NaNO_3(aq)$$

How many grams of precipitate can be produced from 0.500 L of 1.25 M $AgNO_3$?

As we discussed in the previous chapter, the first step of a stoichiometry problem is to convert the given measurement to units of moles. The same is true here, only we're given a volume instead of a mass, but since we have the molarity of this solution we can use that to convert L $AgNO_3$ to mol $AgNO_3$

$$0.500 \text{ L AgNO}_3 \times \frac{1.25 \text{ mol AgNO}_3}{1 \text{ L AgNO}_3}$$

From here, it's just like the stoichiometry problems from Chapter 4. We convert mol $AgNO_3$ to mol $AgCl$.

$$0.500 \text{ L AgNO}_3 \times \frac{1.25 \text{ mol AgNO}_3}{1 \text{ L AgNO}_3} \times \frac{1 \text{ mol AgCl}}{1 \text{ mol AgNO}_3}$$

then mol $AgCl$ to g $AgCl$

$$0.500 \text{ L AgNO}_3 \times \frac{1.25 \text{ mol AgNO}_3}{1 \text{ L AgNO}_3} \times \frac{1 \text{ mol AgCl}}{1 \text{ mol AgNO}_3} \times \frac{143.35 \text{ g AgCL}}{1 \text{ mol AgCl}}$$

$$= 89.6 \text{ g AgCl}$$

Titrations

A titration is a common method for determining the concentration of an unknown solution, using another solution whose concentration you do know. The known solution is often referred to as the *standard*. If your unknown were an acid, you would most likely choose a base as your standard. A typical set-up for a titration is shown below

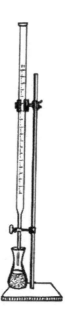

That long, skinny piece of glassware is a **buret**. The solution that's placed in the buret is known as the **titrant**. The benefit of using a buret is that it allows you to control how much titrant is added to other solution (dropwise or in a slow stream) while at the same time measuring the amount being added with a high degree of accuracy.

If the reaction doesn't result in a visible change (color change, formation of a precipitate, etc), you can add small amount of an **indicator** to let you know when the reaction is complete. For example, phenolphthalein is a commonly used indicator for acid-base titrations, since all reactants and products are usually colorless in aqueous solution. The chemistry behind acid-base indicators will be discussed in Chapter 18. Until then, if you're currently taking a general chemistry course with a laboratory component, you'll probably learn more about titrations in a future lab (if you haven't already).

Example: 100.0 mL of 1.0 M H_2SO_4 is used to titrate 25.0 mL of a NaOH solution. Determine the concentration of NaOH in units of molarity

A titration problem is really nothing more than a stoichiometry problem. We know the volume of our NaOH solution, but we need to find the amount in moles. Before we can do the stoichiometry calculation, however, we need the chemical equation for this reaction. Since H_2SO_4 is an acid (sulfuric acid) and NaOH is a base, we should be able to do that after our discussion of acid-base reactions in Part 3.

$$H_2SO_4 + 2NaOH \rightarrow Na_2SO_4 + 2H_2O$$

Now we can begin our calculation, first by converting the volume of sulfuric acid to moles

$$100.0 \ \cancel{mL \ H_2SO_4} \times \frac{10^{-3} \ \cancel{L \ H_2SO_4}}{1 \ \cancel{mL \ H_2SO_4}} \times \frac{1.0 \ mol \ H_2SO_4}{1 \ \cancel{L \ H_2SO_4}}$$

and then mol H_2SO_4 to mol NaOH

$$100.0 \ \cancel{mL \ H_2SO_4} \times \frac{10^{-3} \ \cancel{L \ H_2SO_4}}{1 \ \cancel{mL \ H_2SO_4}} \times \frac{1.0 \ \cancel{mol \ H_2SO_4}}{1 \ \cancel{L \ H_2SO_4}} \times \frac{2 \ mol \ NaOH}{1 \ \cancel{mol \ H_2SO_4}}$$

$$= 0.20 \ mol \ NaOH$$

Now that we know how many moles are present, we can find the molarity of the solution.

$$\frac{0.20 \ mol}{0.025 \ L} = 8.0 \ M$$

Dilutions

There are many instances where a chemist will need to dilute a solution to a lower concentration. While it is possible to use dimensional analysis to find the concentration of the diluted solution, most chemist use the following equation (sometimes called the *dilution equation*):

$$M_1V_1 = M_2V_2$$

In this equations, M represents the initial and final concentrations while V represents the initial and final volumes (it doesn't matter which you designate as *1* and which is *2*). Also, despite our use of M for molarity, this equation can be used for most other units of concentration, as well.

Example: Nitric acid is usually purchased as a 16 M stock solution. If you wanted to make 800.0 mL of 0.50 M nitric acid, how many mL of stock solution would be required?

For this example, we'll make 800.0 mL and 0.50 M V_1 and M_1, respectively, which means 16 M will be M_2.

$$M_1 = 0.50M \qquad M_2 = 16 \text{ M}$$
$$V_1 = 800.0\text{mL} \qquad V_2 = ?$$

From this point, it's a simple matter of plugging these into our dilution equation and solving for the unknown

$$(0.50 \text{ M})(800.0 \text{ mL}) = (16 \text{ M})V_2$$

$$V_2 = \frac{(0.50 \text{ M})(800.0 \text{ mL})}{16 \text{ M}} = 25 \text{ mL}$$

So if we take 25 mL of stock solution and dilute it to 800 mL, the new concentration should be 0.50 M.

You might have noticed that I didn't bother converting milliliters to liters. Since the molarity unit cancels out during the calculation, whatever unit of volume we use for V_1 will be the unit of V_2. This is also why other units of concentration can usually be used in place of molarity.

Try It Yourself

P15. Calculate the molarity of the following solutions:
a) 2.0 mol HCl in a 2.00 L solution
b) 33.2 g $CuBr_2$ in a 874 mL solution
c) 100.0 g NH_4NO_3 in a 10.0 L solution
d) 3.50 g KOH in a 550.0 mL solution

P16. For each of the following solutions, calculate mass (in grams) of solute required.
a) 3.0 L of 1.5 M KBr
b) 1.00 L of 5.0 M H_2SO_4
c) 250.0 mL of 2.00 M $Ca(OH_2)_2$

P17. In the reaction between iron (II) bromide and aluminum

$$3FeBr_2(aq) + 2Al(s) \rightarrow 2AlBr_3(aq) + 3Fe(s)$$

a) How many grams of aluminum are needed to react with 100.0 mL of 2.20 M $FeBr_2$?
b) How many milliliters of 3.50 M $FeBr_2$ is required to produce 8.50 g Fe?
c) A 25.0 mL solution of 4.00 M iron (II) bromide reacts with an excess amount of aluminum. Assuming the volume stays the same, what is the concentration of the resulting aluminum bromide solution?

P18. Perform the following calculations.

a) A 1.25 L, 10.0 M solution is diluted to a volume of 5.00 L. What is the new concentration?

b) You have a 255 mL solution of 8.0 M HCl that you wish to dilute to 2.5 M. How much water should you add?

Learning Beyond

There are numerous interesting (and—dare I say—cool) aqueous reactions that have become mainstays as teaching demos, many of which you can find online. Here's a few to check out:

- The reaction between sugar (sucrose) and sulfuric acid.
- The "silver mirror" test
- The reaction between sodium and water.
- The iodine "clock reaction."

Test Your Skills

★ Try Hard

1. Which of the following compounds are predicted to be soluble in water? a) ZnS, b) Li_3PO_4, c) $Cu(NO_3)_2$, d) $HgSO_4$, e) $Co(OH)_3$

XP: +4 each

2. Write equations, with phases, showing the reaction between each of the following:
a) $CaCl_2$ and KOH
b) $Pb(ClO_4)_4$ and H_3PO_4
c) Na_2SO_4 and $BaBr_2$

XP: +4 each

3. Write equations, with phases, showing the reaction between each of the following: a) H_2SO_4 and KOH, b) HI and $Al(OH)_3$

XP: +4 each

4. Write equations, with phases, showing the reaction between each of the following:
a) $KHCO_3$ and HBr, b) CuS and HNO_3, c) HCl and Mg

XP: +4 each

5. Determine the oxidation numbers of each element in the following: a) Cu_3N, b) $CaCO_3$, c) N_2O_3, d) $C_2H_3O_2^-$, e) H_2O_2

XP: +4 each

6. In each of the following reactions, determine which element is undergoing oxidation and which is undergoing reduction.
a) $2Ce^{4+} + 2F^- \rightarrow F_2 + 2Ce^{3+}$
b) $N_2 + 3H_2 \rightarrow 2NH_3$
c) $Cl_2 + 2KBr \rightarrow 2KCl + Br_2$

XP: +4 each

7. Calculate the molarity of each of the following solutions:
a) 2.00 g HNO_3 in a 1.3 L solution
b) 13.2 g $PbCl_4$ in a 3.00 L solution
c) 0.590 g KOH in a 250.0 mL solution

XP: +4 each

8. Ammonium sulfate and sodium hydroxide can reaction by the following equation:

$$(NH_4)_2SO_4(aq) + 2NaOH(aq) \rightarrow$$
$$Na_2SO_4(aq) + 2H_2O(l) + 2NH_3(g)$$

a) Write the net ionic equation for this reaction.
b) How grams of ammonium sulfate is required to react with 75.0 mL of 1.50 M sodium hydroxide?
c) How many milliliters of 2.0 M sodium hydroxide is needed to react with 50.0 g ammonium sulfate?

XP: +4 each

9. Sodium carbonate and silver bromide can react as follows:

$$Na_2CO_3(aq) + 2AgBr(aq) \rightarrow 2NaBr(aq) + Ag_2CO_3(s)$$

a) What is the net ionic equation for this reaction?
b) How many grams of silver carbonate can be produced from 135 mL of 4.50 M AgBr?
c) How many milliliters of 3.00 M silver bromide is required to react with 240.0 mL of 2.8 M sodium carbonate?

XP: +4 each

10. Suppose you have a 2.00 L solution of 4.25 M NaOH.
a) How much of the solution (in mL) would be required to make a 1.0 L, 1.5 M solution of NaOH?
b) What would be the new concentration if you added more water to the solution, increasing its volume from 2.00 L to 10.0 L?

XP: +4 each

★XP: _____

If your XP is 96 or higher, let's see if you can...

★★Try Harder

11. Suppose you have a set of solutions, each with one of the following mixture of ions:

a) S^{2-} and SO_4^{2-}, b) K^+ and Mg^{2+}, c) OH^- and SO_4^{2-}

You also have the following reagents available: $Fe(NO_3)_2$, Na_2CO_3, and Na_2SO_4. For each solution, which reagent will allow you to precipitate one ion while leaving the other dissolved?

XP: +5 each

12. Write net ionic equations, with phases, showing the precipitation reaction for each of your answers in question 11.

XP: +5 each

13. Write equations, with phases, showing the reaction between hydrochloric acid and each of the following: a) calcium, b) mercury (I) nitrate, c) nickel (III) carbonate, d) potassium sulfite, e) barium hydroxide, f) ammonium sulfide

XP: +5 each

14. Write net ionic equations, with phases, for each reaction in question 13.

XP: +5 each

15. Identify the oxidizing and reducing agents in each of the following reactions:
a) $2S_2O_3^{2-} + I_2 \rightarrow S_4O_6^{2-} + 2I^-$
b) $4H^+ + O_2 + 4Fe^{2+} \rightarrow 4Fe^{3+} + 2H_2O$

c) $5Fe^{2+} + MnO_4^- + 8H^+ \rightarrow 5Fe^{3+} + Mn^{2+} + 4H_2O$

XP: +5 each

16. Identify the oxidizing and reducing agents in each of the following reactions:
a) The reaction between a metal and an acid.
b) The combustion of a hydrocarbon (C_xH_y).

XP: +5 each

17. A 2.0 L solution contains 32.5 g $Co(NO_3)_6$.
a) Calculate the $Co(NO_3)_6$ concentration of this solution (in units of molarity).
b) Calculate the concentration (in M) of Co^{6+} ion in this solution.
c) Calculate the concentration (in M) of nitrate ion in this solution.

XP: +5 each

★★XP: _____   Total XP: _____

If your total XP is 197 or higher...

★★★Try Hard: With a Vengeance

18. You have a solution containing three anions: bromide, sulfate, and phosphate. Suggest a method for separating the three ions.

XP: +10

19. The solubility of a compound refers to the maximum amount that can be dissolved in a given solute (at which point to solution becomes saturated). For example, the solubility of iron (II) sulfate (d = 2.84 g/mL) is 25.6 g per 100.0 mL H_2O. Using this information, determine the maximum molarity possible for an aqueous solution of this compound (assuming volumes are additive).

XP: +10

20. A piece of zinc was mixed with just enough hydrochloric acid to completely "dissolve" the metal (technically, it reacted, but it's commonplace to use the term here as well). Next, a solution of copper (I) nitrate was slowly added, causing a precipitate to form. Once precipitation stopped, the solid was separated from the solution by filtration. Sodium sulfide was then added to the solution, forming a second precipitate, which was again separated from the solution. This second precipitate was mixed with a solution of sulfuric acid. The solid dissolved and gas bubbles were observed. Finally, once the bubbling stopped, the solution was mixed was a solution of potassium phosphate, forming a third precipitate. What is the identity of the third solid?

XP: +10

21. Besides electrons, many oxidations and reductions can be identified by the loss or gain of oxygen and/or the loss or gain of hydrogen (it works particularly well with organic reactions). Looking back at the reactions shown in this chapter, what's the connection between redox and these two elements?

XP: +10 each

22. A stock solution of sodium hydroxide was prepared by dissolve 50.00 g of the compound in enough water to make a 1.00 L solution. Later, a second solution was prepared by taking 25.0 mL of the stock solution and diluting it to a volume of 200.0 mL, which was used in a titration to determine the concentration of a phosphoric acid solution. It took 33.0 mL of this second solution to neutralize a 30.0 mL sample of the acid. What was the molarity of the phosphoric acid solution?

XP: +10

23. Silver ion is present in seawater in concentrations of around 55 parts per billion (ppb), which means there's 55 gram Ag^+ per billion grams of seawater. The density of seawater is 1.029 g/mL.
a) Calculate the concentration of silver ion in units of molarity.

b) How many liters of seawater would be required to get 1.00 g of silver?

XP: +10 each

24. A 20.0 mL, 2.0 M NaCl solution was mixed with a 30.0 mL, 1.5 M $Pb(NO_3)_2$ solution.
a) Write an equation, with phases, for the reaction that occurred.
b) How many grams of precipitate can be produced by this reaction?
c) What is the concentration (in M) of the other product, which is still part of the solution?

XP: +5 each

25. An unknown compound was believed to be an alkali metal hydroxide (MOH). A 1.22 g sample was dissolved in water and titrated with 1.01 M sulfuric acid. It took 10.8 mL of the acid to neutralize the base. Identify the base.

XP: +10

26. An organic acid was found to be 54.53% C, 9.15% H, and 36.32% O. It was believed to be monoprotic, meaning only one hydrogen dissociates in water (HA). A 2.00 g sample was titrated with 0.502 M sodium hydroxide and 13.0 mL of the base was required to neutralize the acid. a) What is the molar mass of the acid? b) What is its molecular formula?

XP: +10 each

★★★ XP: _____   Total XP: _____

If your total XP is 283 or greater: Level up!

Achievement Unlocked: If you're not part of the solution...
Completed Chapter 5

You're now ready to learn about gas behavior.

Chapter 6
Properties of Gases

Part 1: Units of Pressure

Pressure can be defined as the application of a force over a given area. For a gas in a container, the pressure comes from the gas particles colliding against the container walls. For example, tire pressure is typically measured in units of psi, pounds per square inch. In other words, it's a measure of the pounds of force per square inch of area inside that tire. There's also an **atmospheric pressure** from the gases that make up our atmosphere as they collide with the ground, buildings, people, etc. At higher altitudes, the air gets "thinner" (fewer gas particles), which causes atmospheric pressure to decrease. In this chapter, though, we'll primarily deal with *standard atmospheric pressure*, meaning the atmospheric pressure at sea level.

There are several other ways to measure pressure besides psi. The ones often used by chemists include…

mmHg (millimeters mercury)

The **mmHg** unit originates from the early designs of barometers, which were simply a glass tube in a dish of mercury.

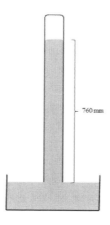

760 mm

The tube is under vacuum, which draws the mercury up the tube, just like when you drink with a straw. Why does this happen? Because on the other side of that tube, atmospheric pressure is pressing down on the surface of the liquid in the dish, effectively "pushing" it up the tube. As with any force, though, there's a limit to how far atmospheric pressure can push up a liquid, whether it's a dish of mercury or a glass of your favorite beverage. In the case of mercury this limit is 76 cm or 760 mm. As such, standard atmospheric pressure is often defined as 760 mmHg.

Torr

Admittedly, the mmHg unit is rather odd looking, especially if you aren't familiar with a) the metric system or b) the periodic table. Also, *millimeter mercury* can be a bit of a tongue twister (try it; say it three times, as fast as you can). As an alternative, some prefer to use the **torr** unit, named after Evangelista Torricelli (1608-1647), inventor of the aforementioned barometer. There's no conversion required to switch between the two, as 1 mmHg = 1 torr.

Atmospheres

Remember how the atomic mass unit was devised? We basically took the mass of a proton and gave it a relative value of 1. The **atmosphere (atm)** unit was developed along those same lines. Since our typical reference for pressure is standard atmospheric pressure, we assign it a relative value of 1 atmosphere, or 1 atm. Therefore, the relationship between atmospheres, mmHg, and torr is

$$1 \text{ atm} = 760 \text{ mmHg} = 760 \text{ torr (exactly)}$$

Try It Yourself

P1. Perform the following conversions:
a) 1.3 atm to mmHg
b) 815 mmHg to torr
c) 1,029 torr to atm

Part 2: Gas Laws

It wasn't until the 17th century that scientists really understood that gases were actually a third phase of matter. Once they did, they began to study and observe its behavior, which led to the formation of several scientific laws, including the following:

Boyle's Law: Volume vs. Pressure

Though he started out as an alchemist, Robert Boyle (1627-1691) is regarded by many to be the first modern chemist. Among his many contributions is **Boyle's law**, which states that at constant temperature, the volume and pressure of a gas are inversely proportional. *Inversely proportional* means that as one goes up, the other goes down (and vice versa). The reason temperature is held constant is that it can also affect the volume and pressure of a gas, which we'll see momentarily.

In mathematical equations, proportional relationships are shown using a lower case, Greek letter alpha (α). The inverse relationship between volume and pressure, for example, can be written as

$$V \, \alpha \, \frac{1}{P}$$

To change this equation from a proportionality (α) equation to an equality ($=$), you have to factor in a constant, which we'll represent with the letter b (for Boyle).

$$V = b \cdot \frac{1}{P}$$

The actual value of b will vary with temperature, but suppose you have two sets of pressure and volume, V_1 & P_1 and V_2 & P_2. They should both follow the above equation.

$$V_1 = b \cdot \frac{1}{P_1}$$

$$V_2 = b \cdot \frac{1}{P_2}$$

Remember, b is a constant, so its value is the same in both equations. If we rewrite the equations where the constant is by itself, we get

$$P_1 V_1 = b$$

$$P_2 V_2 = b$$

If P_1V_1 and P_2V_2 are both equal to b, then they're equal to each other. Combining these two equations gives us the most common way of expressing Boyle's Law mathematically.

$$P_1 V_1 = P_2 V_2$$

Example: A gas has a pressure of 1.0 atm at a volume of 200.0mL. What will be the pressure if the volume is expanded to 500.0mL at a constant temperature?

Like the dilution equation from Chapter 5, it doesn't matter which values are assigned as 1's and which are 2's, just make sure you keep each set of P and V together. Here, if we assign P_1 as 1.0 atm, V_1 will be 200.0mL, leaving the second volume—and the pressure we're trying to determine—as V_2 and P_2, respectively.

$$P_1 = 1.0 \text{ atm} \qquad P_2 = ?$$
$$V_1 = 200.0 \text{ mL} \qquad V_2 = 500.0 \text{ mL}$$

Plugging this into our expression of Boyle's law gives us

$$(1.0 \text{ atm})(200.0 \text{ mL}) = P_2(500.0 \text{ mL})$$

which allows us solve for P_2

$$P_2 = \frac{(1.0 \text{ atm})(200.0 \text{ mL})}{500.0 \text{ mL}} = 0.40 \text{ atm}$$

Notice that, as expected, volume increased as the pressure decreased.

Charles's Law: Volume vs. Temperature.

Charles's law, named after 18th century chemist Jacques Charles, states that at constant pressure, the volume and temperature of a gas are directly proportional. In other words, if one goes up, the other goes up (and vice versa). The way to write this mathematically is

$$V \,\alpha\, T$$

As before, we can turn this equation into an equality by factoring in a constant (in this case, c for Charles).

$$V = cT$$

And like before, for two sets of conditions, V_1 & T_1 and V_2 & T_2, we get

$$V_1 = cT_1$$
$$V_2 = cT_2$$

which can be rewritten as

$$\frac{V_1}{T_1} = c$$

$$\frac{V_2}{T_2} = c$$

Combining the two equations gives the most common way to show Charles' Law mathematically.

$$\frac{V_1}{T_1} = \frac{V_2}{T_2}$$

Example: A gas has a volume of 3.5L at 80°C. What will the volume be if the temperature is raised to 130°C?

As we did in the Boyle's law example, we begin by sorting out the data given in the problem

$$V_1 = 3.5 \text{ L} \qquad V_2 = ?$$
$$T_1 = 80 \text{ °C} \qquad T_2 = 130 \text{ °C}$$

Before you start plugging numbers into our Charles' law equation, however, we must first address an issue concerning the units of temperature. With Boyle's law, the values of pressure and volume weren't required to be in any particular unit. Looking back at that example, having the volume in liters instead of mL would have given the exact same answer.

$$(1.0 \text{ atm})(0.2000 \text{ L}) = P_2(0.5000 \text{ L})$$

$$P_2 = \frac{(1.0 \text{ atm})(0.2000 \text{ L})}{0.5000 \text{ L}} = 0.40 \text{ atm}$$

Mathematically, this happens because conversions between units of volume and pressure involve multiplying the given value by a conversion factor. If you multiply the numerator and denominator of a ratio by the same number, that number essentially cancels out.

$$\frac{a \cdot x}{b \cdot x} = \frac{a}{b}$$

The same thing happens in a Boyle's law calculation. To convert each volume from liters to milliliters, you multiply by the same term ($1 \text{ mL}/10^{-3} \text{ L}$), which gets factored out of the equation.

$$P_2 = \frac{(1.0 \text{ atm})(0.2000 \, \cancel{\text{L}} \times \cancel{1 \text{ mL}/10^{-3} \text{ L}})}{0.5000 \, \cancel{\text{L}} \times \cancel{1 \text{ mL}/10^{-3} \text{ L}}} = 0.40 \text{ atm}$$

However, conversions between our two main units of temperature—Celsius and Kelvin—are done by *addition*, not multiplication. When you add the same number to the numerator and denominator of a ratio, it doesn't cancel out like it does with multiplication.

$$\frac{a + x}{b + x} \neq \frac{a}{b}$$

If you're having trouble understanding this distinction, just know this: solving a Charles' law problem with the temperature in Celsius gives you a *completely different* answer than when the units are in Kelvin.

$$\frac{3.5 \text{ L}}{80 \, ^\circ\text{C}} = \frac{V_2}{130 \, ^\circ\text{C}}$$

$$V_2 = \frac{(3.5 \text{ L})(130 \, ^\circ\cancel{\text{C}})}{80 \, ^\circ\cancel{\text{C}}} = 5.7 \text{ L}$$

or

$$\frac{3.5 \text{ L}}{353 \text{ K}} = \frac{V_2}{403 \text{ K}}$$

$$V_2 = \frac{(3.5 \text{ L})(403 \cancel{\text{K}})}{353 \cancel{\text{K}}} = 4.0 \text{ L}$$

Obviously only one volume can be the correct answer, but which? If one disobeyed Charles's law that would make the decision a little easier, but in both cases the volume increases with temperature, as expected.

Remember, though, that Kelvin is an absolute scale whereas Celsius is a relative one that some guy based on the freezing and boiling points of water (see Chapter 1). Imagine if the initial temperature in this problem was *minus* 80°C. That would give us a volume of -5.7 L, which is impossible. With the Kelvin scale being an absolute scale, there are no negative temperatures, which means impossible answers like that won't normally occur. Therefore, when performing a Charles's law calculation, all temperatures must be in units of Kelvin, which means our answer for the above problem is actually the second one, 4.0 L.

Avogadro's Law: Volume vs. Amount

One of the reasons that Avogadro's number (6.022502 x 10^{23}) is named after Amedeo Avogadro is his studies of how the amount of a gas affects its volume. **Avogadro's law** states that at a constant temperature and pressure, the amount of gas is directly proportional to its volume. In Chapter 4, we learned that a modern chemist usually thinks of amount on the mole scale, which is often represented mathematically by the letter n. Avogadro's law can be written mathematically as

$$V \alpha n$$

or, using the same bit of algebraic magic that was done with Boyle's and Charles' laws, we can write it as

$$\frac{V_1}{n_1} = \frac{V_2}{n_2}$$

Example: If 2.33 mol of gas has a volume of 40.0 L at a given temperature and pressure, what would the volume be if the amount was increased to 4.00 mol?

This problem is essentially the same "plug-n-chug" type of calculation we saw with the previous two laws. First, we sort out our data,

$$V_1 = 40.0 \text{ L} \qquad V_2 = ?$$
$$n_1 = 2.33 \text{ mol} \qquad n_2 = 4.00 \text{ mol}$$

and then plug these into our equation for Avogadro's law.

$$\frac{40.0 \text{ L}}{2.33 \text{ mol}} = \frac{V_2}{4.00 \text{ mol}}$$

$$V_2 = \frac{(40.0 \text{ L})(4.00 \text{ mol})}{2.33 \text{ mol}} = 68.7 \text{ L}$$

The Ideal Gas Law

Notice that the three gas laws mentioned so far all have a term in common: volume.

$$V \alpha \ 1/P \qquad\qquad V \alpha \ T \qquad\qquad V \alpha \ n$$

These three can be combined into a single equation

$$V \alpha \ \frac{nT}{P}$$

As before, factoring in a constant can turn this proportionality into an equality, but unlike our previous constants, this one is actually used quite a bit and is known as the *ideal gas constant* (*R*).

$$V = R \cdot \frac{nT}{P}$$

or, as it's more commonly written

$$PV = nRT$$

The value of R can be expressed in different units, depending on the equation, which in turn affects its numeric value. For this equation, $R = 0.08206$ atm·L/mol·K.

This equation is known as the **ideal gas law**. An *ideal gas* is basically one whose behavior can be predicted by the above equation. In other words, if you know three of the four variables (V, n, T, P) you can use the ideal gas law to find the fourth. Practically all gases behave ideally under normal temperatures and pressures. We'll discuss what causes non-ideal behavior later in the chapter.

Example: Find the pressure of 1.00 g of helium in a 750.0mL container at 25°C.

Notice that, unlike our previous gas laws, this equation still includes a constant, and that constant has units associated with it. Therefore, any of the other values that we plug into this equation must match those found in the gas constant. Here, we need to convert grams to moles,

$$1.00 \ \cancel{g \ He} \times \frac{1 \ mol \ He}{4.00 \ \cancel{g \ He}} = 0.250 \ mol \ He$$

milliliters to liters,

$$750.0 \text{ mL} \times \frac{10^{-3} \text{ L}}{1 \text{ mL}} = 0.7500 \text{ L}$$

and Celsius to Kelvin.

$$25 \text{ °C} + 273 = 298 \text{ K}$$

From there, it's a simple matter of plugging the values into the ideal gas law.

$$P(0.7500 \text{ L}) = (0.250 \text{ mol})(0.08206 \frac{\text{atm} \cdot \text{L}}{\text{mol} \cdot \text{K}})(298 \text{ K})$$

$$P = \frac{(0.250 \text{ mol})(0.08206 \frac{\text{atm} \cdot \text{L}}{\text{mol} \cdot \text{K}})(298 \text{ K})}{0.7500 \text{ L}} = 8.15 \text{ atm}$$

Notice how the unwanted units cancel out? Regardless of what type of calculation you're performing, be it a unit conversion or an equation-based calculation, it's *always* important to pay attention to units.

Try It Yourself

P2. At 23 °C, a sample of gas has a volume of 5.00 L and exerts a pressure of 3.85 atm.
a) Calculate the amount of gas present (in mol).
b) If the volume is compressed to 1.77 L while holding the temperature constant, what will be the new pressure (in atm)?
c) If the temperature is increased to 50 °C while keeping the pressure at 3.85 atm, what will be the new volume (in L)?

P3. At 315.2 K, a 0.250 mol sample of gas occupies a volume of 855.1 mL.
a) Calculate the pressure (in atm) exerted by the gas.

b) What temperature is required to expand the volume to 1.30 L while keeping the pressure constant?
c) What would be the volume (in L) of this gas at 315.2 K if the amount was increased to 0.6011 mol, assuming the pressure remained the same?

Part 3: Using the Ideal Gas Law

In Part 2, we saw how the ideal gas law can be used for straightforward, "plug-n-chug" types of calculations (given all but one variable, solve for the unknown), but it has other useful applications as well. In this section, we'll discuss a few of its more common uses.

Deriving Other Gas Laws

Many students will try to learn the historical gas laws discussed in Part 2 (Boyle, Charles, and Avogadro's) by rote memorization, but all three of the relationships—plus others that weren't mentioned—can be derived using the ideal gas law and the same bit of algebra we've used before.

Picture a gas under two sets of conditions (P, V, n and T), each following the ideal gas law

$$P_1V_1 = n_1RT_1$$
$$P_2V_2 = n_2RT_2$$

Remember that R's a constant, so there's no need to write R_1 and R_2. Like our previous gas laws, we can rewrite these two equations so the constant is by itself

$$R = \frac{P_1V_1}{n_1T_1}$$

$$R = \frac{P_2V_2}{n_2T_2}$$

As before, if the two sets of values are both equal to the R, they're equal to each other, giving an equation that's often called the **combined gas law**.

$$\frac{P_1 V_1}{n_1 T_1} = \frac{P_2 V_2}{n_2 T_2}$$

Recall that in each of the first three gas laws discussed, something was held constant. In Boyle's Law, for example, temperature is held constant, which means T_1 and T_2 are the same temperature. If that's the case then there's no need for the 1's and 2's and we can simply use a T in the combined gas law.

$$T_1 = T_2 = T$$

$$\frac{P_1 V_1}{n_1 T} = \frac{P_2 V_2}{n_2 T}$$

Additionally, unless you're specifically told that the amount of gas is changing, one usually assumes that n is also being held constant.

$$n_1 = n_2 = n$$

$$\frac{P_1 V_1}{nT} = \frac{P_2 V_2}{nT}$$

If T and n are the same value on each side of the equation, they cancel out, leaving us with the same expression of Boyle's law we derived previously.

$$\frac{P_1 V_1}{\cancel{nT}} = \frac{P_2 V_2}{\cancel{nT}}$$

$$P_1 V_1 = P_2 V_2$$

Example: A container of gas exerts a pressure of 3.2 atm at 25°C. What would the pressure be if the temperature increased to 85°C while holding the volume constant?

If the volume is being held constant, then V_1 and V_2 are the same value.

$$V_1 = V_2 = V$$

and since the problem didn't mention changing the amount of gas, we can assume that the same is true for n_1 and n_2
$n_1 = n_2 = n$.

Applying these to the combined gas law gives us

$$\frac{P_1 V}{n T_1} = \frac{P_2 V}{n T_2}$$

which can be simplified to

$$\frac{P_1}{T_1} = \frac{P_2}{T_2}$$

Now that we have the right equation (which, by the way, is known as the *Gay-Lussac law*), we can begin our calculation. First, we set up our known values.

$$P_1 = 3.2 \text{ atm} \qquad P_2 = ?$$
$$T_1 = 25\ °C \qquad T_2 = 85\ °C$$

And don't forget that temperature will need to be in units of Kelvin.

$$25\ °C + 273 = 298 \text{ K}$$
$$85\ °C + 273 = 358 \text{ K}$$

Finally, we can plug our known values into our equation and solve for P_2

$$\frac{3.2 \text{ atm}}{298 \text{ K}} = \frac{P_2}{358 \text{ K}}$$

$$P_2 = \frac{(3.2 \text{ atm})(358 \text{ \cancel{K}})}{298 \text{ \cancel{K}}} = 3.8 \text{ atm}$$

Determination of Molar Mass

Example: A 9.21g sample of a gas occupies a volume of 1.30 L at 24 °C and 765 torr. Calculate its molar mass.

Recall from Chapter 4 that the units of molar mass are typically grams per mole (g/mol). We know the mass of our sample, so if we can determine the number of moles present we can divide the two to find its molar mass. Since the volume, temperature and pressure of the gas are given, and R is a known constant, we can use the ideal gas law to find moles.

$$
\begin{array}{ccccc}
\checkmark & \checkmark & ? & \checkmark & \checkmark \\
P & V & = \ n & R & T
\end{array}
$$

First, however, we must make sure that all of the given values are in the correct units, matching those found in the gas constant, R (0.08206 atm·L/mol·K). The volume is already in liters, but pressure and temperature have to be converted to atmospheres and Kelvin, respectively.

$$24 \text{ °C} + 273 = 297 \text{ K}$$

$$765 \text{ \cancel{torr}} \times \frac{1 \text{ atm}}{760 \text{ \cancel{torr}}} = 1.01 \text{ atm}$$

Next, we can use the ideal gas law to find the number of moles present.

$$PV = nRT$$

$$n = \frac{(1.01 \text{ atm})(1.30 \text{ L})}{(0.08206 \frac{\text{atm} \cdot \text{L}}{\text{mol} \cdot \text{K}})(297 \text{ K})} = 0.0538 \text{ mol}$$

Finally, we use this amount with the given mass to calculate molar mass.

$$\frac{9.21 \text{ g}}{0.0538 \text{ mol}} = 171 \text{ g/mol}$$

Determining the Density of a Known Gas

Example: Calculate the density of helium (in g/L) at 1.00 atm pressure and 100 °C.

Comparing what's given to what's in the ideal gas law, only two of the four variables in that equation—pressure and temperature— are given.

$$
\begin{array}{cccccc}
\checkmark & ? & & ? & \checkmark & \checkmark \\
P & V & = & n & R & T
\end{array}
$$

With two unknown variables, at first glance it looks like there isn't enough information given to use this equation , but there is one other thing we're told: the identity of the gas. Helium has a molar mass of 4.00 g/mol, so we know the mass of 1 mole of helium. If we use the ideal gas law to find the *volume* of 1 mole of helium...

$$PV = nRT$$

$$V = \frac{(1 \ \cancel{mol})(0.08206 \ \frac{atm \cdot L}{\cancel{mol} \cdot \cancel{K}})(373 \ \cancel{K})}{1.00 \ \cancel{atm}} = 30.6 \ L$$

we can calculate its density.

$$\frac{4.00 \ g}{30.6 \ L} = 0.131 \ g/L$$

Stoichiometry

Example: How many liters of hydrogen are produced when 20.0g of Zn reacts with an excess of sulfuric acid at 1.00 atm and 298K?

The first thing we need to do is come up with the equation for this reaction. In Chapter 5, we learned that reactions between a metal and an acid usually produce hydrogen gas and a salt.

$$Zn(s) + H_2SO_4(aq) \rightarrow ZnSO_4(aq) + H_2(g)$$

Next, we'll find the number of moles of hydrogen gas produced from 20.0 g Zn.

$$20.0 \ \cancel{g \ Zn} \times \frac{1 \ \cancel{mol \ Zn}}{65.39 \ \cancel{g \ Zn}} \times \frac{1 \ mol \ H_2}{1 \ \cancel{mol \ Zn}} = 0.306 \ mol \ H_2$$

which can be plugged into the ideal gas law to find its volume at the given pressure and temperature.

$$V = \frac{(0.306 \ \cancel{mol})(0.08206 \ \frac{atm \cdot L}{\cancel{mol} \cdot \cancel{K}})(298 \ \cancel{K})}{1.00 \ \cancel{atm}} = 7.48 \ L$$

Try It Yourself

P4. Show how the ideal gas law can be used to derive a) Charles' law, b) Avogadro's law.

P5. A 2.44 g sample of gas exerts a pressure of 1.22 atm in a 500.0 mL container at 20 °C. Calculate the molar mass of this gas.

P6. Calculate the density of nitrogen gas, in g/L, at 45.2 °C and 748 mmHg (remember that nitrogen is a diatomic element, N_2).

P7. Copper and nitric acid react as follows:

$$Cu(s) + 4HNO_3(aq) \rightarrow Cu(NO_3)_2(aq) + 2NO_2(g) + 2H_2O(l)$$

a) How many moles of nitrogen dioxide can be produced from the reaction of 5.00 grams of copper? If the gas was collected in a 250.0 mL container, what pressure (in atm) would the gas exert at 22 °C?
b) If the NO_2 produced from 250.0 mL of 3.51 M nitric acid exerted a pressure of 788 torr at 26 °C, what is the volume of the gas (in L)?

P8. For the reaction between hydrochloric acid and calcium sulfate

$$2HCl(aq) + CaSO_3(s) \rightarrow H_2O(l) + SO_2(g) + CaCl_2(aq)$$

a) If 10.0 g $CaSO_3$ reacts with excess HCl in a closed 1.00 L container at 26 °C, what will be the pressure exerted by the SO_2 produced?
b) How many milliliters of 1.5 M hydrochloric acid would be needed to be produce 2.00 L of sulfur dioxide at 3.10 atm and 295 K?

Part 4: Gas Mixtures

So far, this chapter has only focused on pure substances, but the ideal gas law also works with mixtures of gases. One reason is that under normal conditions the actual identity of the gas isn't important. Look back at some of the earlier examples in this chapter. Sometimes, the question only refers to "a gas."

Avogadro was one of the first to notice this in what's known today as **Avogadro's hypothesis**, which states that under normal conditions, two gases of equal volume will contain equal amounts. The reason it's not considered a scientific law is because this observation fails at very small volumes (more on that later). There were, however, other observations that did eventually lead to laws, two of which we'll discuss here.

Dalton's Law

In addition to the law of multiple proportions and his atomic theory, John Dalton also studied the behavior of gas mixtures. He discovered that the total pressure of a mixture of gases is equal to the sum of the partial pressures of each gas in that mixture, an observation known today as **Dalton's law**. The *partial pressure* of a gas is the pressure it would exert if that same amount were by itself under the same volume and temperature.

Example: A 3.0L flask contains 0.30 mol H_2 and 0.40 mol He at 298 K. Calculate the pressure inside the flask.

We can use the ideal gas law to calculate the partial pressure of each gas.

$$P_{H2} = \frac{(0.30 \ \cancel{mol})(0.08206 \ \frac{atm \cdot \cancel{L}}{\cancel{mol} \cdot \cancel{K}})(298 \ \cancel{K})}{3.0 \ \cancel{L}} = 2.4 \ atm$$

$$P_{He} = \frac{(0.40 \ \cancel{mol})(0.08206 \ \frac{atm \cdot \cancel{L}}{\cancel{mol} \cdot \cancel{K}})(298 \ \cancel{K})}{3.0 \ \cancel{L}} = 3.3 \text{ atm}$$

According to Dalton's Law, the total pressure would equal the sum of the partial pressures.

$$P_T = P_{H2} + P_{He}$$
$$P_T = 2.4 + 3.3 \text{ atm} = 5.7 \text{ atm}$$

Notice that we would get this same pressure if there were 0.70 mol of a single gas.

$$P = \frac{(0.70 \ \cancel{mol})(0.08206 \ \frac{atm \cdot \cancel{L}}{\cancel{mol} \cdot \cancel{K}})(298 \ \cancel{K})}{3.0 \ \cancel{L}} = 5.7 \text{ atm}$$

Again, under normal ("ideal") conditions, it's not identity that's important, but rather the amount of gas present.

Graham's Law

Scottish chemist Thomas Graham (1805–1869) studied the rates (speeds) of gases as they traveled through a hole or tube, a process known as *effusion* (you're probably more familiar with a similar process, *diffusion*, which refers to the mixing of gases). Graham discovered that the effusion rate of a gas was inversely proportional to the square root of its mass, M (molar mass, in our case).

$$\text{Rate } \alpha \ \sqrt{\frac{1}{M}}$$

In other words, larger molecules will effuse (or diffuse) more slowly.

When comparing the rates of two gases, we can use the same algebra we did in Part 1 of this chapter to derive the following equation.

$$\frac{\text{Rate A}}{\text{Rate B}} = \sqrt{\frac{\mathcal{M}_B}{\mathcal{M}_A}}$$

For example, comparing the diffusion rates of He and SF_6, we see that helium is predicted to be about six times faster than sulfur hexafluoride.

$$\frac{\text{Rate He}}{\text{Rate SF}_6} = \sqrt{\frac{146.07 \text{ g/mol}}{4.00 \text{ g/mol}}}$$

$$\frac{\text{Rate He}}{\text{Rate SF}_6} = 6.04$$

Example: An unknown gas (Gas X) diffuses at a rate of 206 cm/min. Under the same conditions, helium's rate of diffusion is 785 cm/min. Calculate the molar mass of Gas X.

Using Graham's Law, we can plug in the three known variables and solve for the unknown. Like our previous "1-2" types of equations, it doesn't matter which gas is assigned as A and which is B. You'll get the same answer either way.

$$\frac{\text{Rate He}}{\text{Rate X}} = \sqrt{\frac{\mathcal{M}_X}{\mathcal{M}_{He}}}$$

$$\frac{785 \text{ cm/min}}{206 \text{ cm/min}} = \sqrt{\frac{\mathcal{M}_X}{4.00 \text{ g/mol}}}$$

$$\mathcal{M}_X = 58.1 \text{ g/mol}$$

Try It Yourself

P9. Calculate the partial pressures and total pressure of each the following mixtures in a 4.00 L vessel at 296 K.
a) 0.444 mol oxygen and 0.801 mol carbon dioxide.
b) 0.82 mol H_2, 0.11 mol Kr, and 0.31 mol NO_2
c) 10.0 g Ne and 14.5 g N_2

P10. Comparing the effusion rates of neon and carbon dioxide...
a) Which is predicted to effuse faster?
b) Relatively speaking, how much faster will the quicker gas diffuse?
c) If neon diffuses at a rate of 2.16 x 10^{-3} m/s, what would be carbon dioxide's rate of diffusion under the same conditions?

Part 5: Kinetic Molecular Theory

In Chapter 1, we discussed how scientific laws don't explain *why* things happen, only that they will (or should) happen, based on previous observations. The gas laws in this chapter are no different. Boyle's law, for instance only says the pressure exerted by a gas should increase if you decrease its volume, but not why. To figure out the "why" part requires experimentation and collecting enough data to formulate a theory. The most common theory used to explain gas behavior is the **kinetic molecular theory of gases**. The principle ideas of the theory can be broken down into five main points:

1. Gas particles are in constant, random motion.
2. When gas particles collide—with each other or the container walls—there is no significant attractive or repulsive forces involved (the collisions are elastic, if you're familiar with that term).
3. When gas particles collide there is no net loss or gain of kinetic energy.
4. The average kinetic energy of a particle is proportional to its temperature.
5. Gas particles are much smaller than the distances between them, effectively making their volumes negligible.

Particle energy and speed

To understand the first four parts of the theory, we have to examine the relationship between kinetic energy, temperature and molecular speed. The average kinetic energy (KE) of a gas particle can be determined by the following equation

$$\overline{KE} = \frac{1}{2}m\bar{u}^2$$

where m is the particle's mass (in kg) and u is its *molecular speed* (in m/s). The bar over KE and u is the mathematical symbol for a mean average. If you look at the units on the right side of this equation, multiplying the mass times squared speed gives us kinetic energy in kg·m²/s² or Joules (J), which we briefly mentioned in Chapter 1 as the SI unit for energy (and a unit we'll use quite a bit in the next chapter).

$$1 \text{ J} = 1 \, \frac{\text{kg·m}^2}{\text{s}^2}$$

The average squared speed of a gas particle can be calculated using the equation

$$\bar{u}^2 = \frac{3RT}{\mathcal{M}}$$

although it's more common to show it after taking the square root of both sides. Technically speaking, though, this doesn't simply give us the speed, u, but rather the *root mean squared* speed, u_{rms} (but don't let that throw you; we're still just talking about how fast the particles are traveling).

$$u_{rms} = \sqrt{\frac{3RT}{\mathcal{M}}}$$

We've used all the terms on the right-hand side of this equation previously, but here the gas constant is written as 8.314 J/mol·K. It's the same constant, though, just in different units.

$$R = 0.08206 \text{ atm·L/mol·K} = 8.314 \text{ J/mol·K}$$

In addition, molar mass is in units of *kilograms* per mole (kg/mol). The reason we use these different versions of R and $\mathcal{M}$ is so everything on right side of the equation will work out to give the proper units for u_{rms} (m/s). The temperature and mole unit cancels out as we saw in previous problems

$$\sqrt{\frac{\left(\frac{J}{\cancel{mol \cdot K}}\right)(\cancel{K})}{kg/\cancel{mol}}} = \sqrt{\frac{J}{kg}}$$

and if we show Joules as $kg \cdot m^2/s^2$, we can see how the mass unit drops out as well.

$$\sqrt{\frac{J}{kg}} = \sqrt{\frac{\frac{\cancel{kg} \cdot m^2}{s^2}}{\cancel{kg}}} = \sqrt{\frac{m^2}{s^2}} = \frac{m}{s}$$

Example: Calculate the root-mean-squared speed of oxygen (O_2) at 25 °C.

The molar mass of O_2 is 32.00 g/mol or 0.03200 kg/mol. Plugging this mass into the equation for u_{rms}, we get

$$u_{rms} = \sqrt{\frac{3(8.314 \frac{J}{mol \cdot K})(298 \ K)}{0.03200 \ kg/mol}} = 481 \text{ m/s}$$

This speed (which, for you non-metric folks, is equal to 1,080 mi/hr) is typical for most gases under normal temperatures and pressures, which explains the first four parts of kinetic molecular theory. At these speeds, gas particles simply won't be in contact with each other long enough to feel any attractive or repulsive forces (point #2 of kinetic molecular theory) or to transfer energy between them (point #3). They'll simply bounce around randomly (point #1). And as the temperature increases, so does the speed of the gas particles, which in turn increases their kinetic energy (point #4).

Particle volumes

Finally, to understand the final point of kinetic molecular theory, imagine an empty 2.0 L bottle of soda at room temperature (25°C or 298 K) and standard atmospheric pressure (1.0 atm). The amount of air in that bottle would be

$$n = \frac{PV}{RT} = \frac{(1.0 \text{ atm})(2.0 \text{ L})}{(0.08206 \frac{\text{atm} \cdot \text{L}}{\text{mol} \cdot \text{K}})(298 \text{ K})} = 0.082 \text{ mol}$$

Using Avogadro's number, 0.082 mol of gas is about 4.9×10^{22} particles

$$0.082 \text{ mol} \times \frac{6.02 \times 10^{23} \text{ particles}}{1 \text{ mol}} = 4.9 \times 10^{22} \text{ particles}$$

A typical molecule has a volume that's around 10^{-27} L, which means that the total volume of gas particles in that bottle is

$$4.9 \times 10^{22} \text{ particles} \times \frac{10^{-27} \text{ L}}{1 \text{ particle}} = 4.9 \times 10^{-5} \text{ L}$$

So approximately 49 μL (0.0025%) of what's inside that 2.0 L bottle is actually air. The other 99.9975% is empty space. That's pretty negligible in most cases. This also explains why gases are so compressible and why Avogadro's hypothesis is true under normal conditions.

Gas Laws Revisited

To see how kinetic molecular theory can be used to explain gas behavior, let's look back at the first three gas laws we discussed:

Boyle's Law: When a gas is compressed at a constant temperature, the number of gas particles in a given area increase. This means that the number of collisions against the container walls will increase, which in turn causes an increase in pressure. Likewise, if the volume is expanded, then there will be fewer collisions per area and the pressure will drop.

Charles' Law: Looking at the equation for root mean square speed (u_{rms}), increasing the temperature will cause the speed of the molecules to increase. This should result in more collisions between particles, but if pressure's held constant the number of collisions per area must remain the same. For this to happen, the surface area of the container walls must increase, meaning the volume of the container has to expand.

Avogadro's Law: Increasing the number of gas particles in a container will result in more collisions. As with Charles' law, if the pressure is to remain constant the container volume must also increase to keep the collisions per area constant.

Try It Yourself

P11. Calculate the molecular speeds of the following gases at 22 °C. a) neon, b) nitrogen dioxide, c) oxygen, d) sulfur dioxide?

P12. How do your answers for P11 compare with what you'd predict according to Graham's law?

Part 6: Non-ideal Behavior

Basically, an ideal gas is one that follows kinetic molecular theory and obeys the ideal gas law. In other words, if you know three of the four variables in the ideal gas law (P, V, n, and T), you can find the fourth with a high degree of accuracy. Under normal conditions, most gases exhibit ideal behavior. However, there are circumstances where non-ideal behavior can occur, causing any calculations done with the ideal gas law to have significant errors.

There are two primary places where you find non-ideal behavior:

1) High pressures. Remember that pressure is a result of gas particles colliding against the container walls. At a high enough pressure, there are so many particles present that their volumes will no longer be negligible, as assumed in point 5 of kinetic molecular theory (and Avogadro's hypothesis).

2) Low Temperatures. As discussed in Part 5, under normal temperatures the gas particles are moving too quickly to significantly interact with colliding particles or the container surface (points 2 and 3 of kinetic molecular theory). At a low enough temperature, however, the particles will move so slowly that such interactions can actually occur. If, for example, a gas particle is interacting significantly with other nearby particles, it will affect the force of its collision against the container wall (i.e., pressure).

As such, gases tend to behave most ideally at low pressures and high temperatures. Of course, "low" and "high" are relative terms. Where you actually see non-ideal behavior can vary from gas to gas.

When working with gases under non-ideal conditions, the ideal gas law has to be modified to account for the haforementioned deviations from kinetic molecular theory. Dutch physicist Johannes van der Waals (1837-1923) successfully did this using what is now known as the **van der Waals equation**

$$\left(P + \frac{an^2}{V^2} \right) (V - bn) = nRT$$

If you look closely at this equation, you'll see it's essentially a modified form of the ideal gas law with two correction factors, an^2/V^2 and nb, that are included to correct the measured pressure and volume, respectively, under non-ideal conditions. Each gas has its own set of constants a and b that are used in this equation. In general, the term an^2/V^2 is added to the measured pressure to account for the number of gas particles interacting with each other in a given space. In other words, it's "adding back" the pressure that should have been measured if the particles hadn't been interacting with each other. Likewise, the term nb is subtracted from the measure volume to effectively "remove" particle volume from the equation.

Learning Beyond

- We mentioned several important scientists in this chapter. Why not learn more about them?
- Learn how carbon dioxide and other "greenhouse gases" play a part in the planet's climate.
- Learn why the properties of chlorofluorocarbons (CFCs) that revolutionized the refrigeration industry also made it an environmental hazard.
- You've undoubtedly seen the effect helium has on the human voice. Check out a similar demonstration using sulfur hexafluoride (SF_6)

Test Your Skills

★ Wine Coolers

1. A 2.00 L sample of gas exerts a pressure of 849 mmHg. What would be the pressure (in mmHg) if the volume was changed to 4.75 L at a constant temperature?

XP: +3

2. A balloon has a volume of 4.88×10^5 L at 22 °C. What temperature (in °C) would the air need to be heated to increase the volume to 1.82×10^6 L?

XP: +3

3. If 0.328 mol of gas has a volume of 10.0 L, what would be new volume (in L) if the amount was increased to 0.705 mol?

XP: +3

4. What is the pressure (in atm) of 0.250 mol of oxygen in a 3.00 L container at 21 °C?

XP: +3

5. What volume (in mL) would an 8.00 g sample of SF_6 exert a pressure of 4.25 atm at 23 °C?

XP: +4

6. A 2.58 mol sample of gas has a pressure of 3.84 atm. What would the pressure be (in atm) if the amount was increased to 4.71 mol at the same volume and temperature?

XP: +3

7. A 1.00 g sample of a gas occupies a volume of 122 mL 21 °C, with a pressure of 912 mmHg. Calculate its molar mass.

XP: +4

8. Calculate the density (in g/L) of each of the following gases at 22 °C and 1.10 atm: a) NO_2, b) Ne, c) SF_6.

XP: +4 each

9. Potassium superoxide (KO_2) produces oxygen when combined with water, and is used to generate oxygen in rebreathers, spacecraft, and submarines.

$$KO_2(s) + H_2O(l) \rightarrow 4KOH(s) + 3O_2(g)$$

a) How many liters of oxygen can be produced from 40.0 g KO_2 at 20.0 °C and 1.10 atm?
b) Suppose 12 L of oxygen was generated by this reaction at 26 °C, exerting a pressure of 3.1 atm. How many grams of potassium hydroxide was produced?

XP: +4 each

10. As we discussed in Chapter 5, when sulfuric acid and sodium bicarbonate react, carbon dioxide is produced.

$$H_2SO_4(aq) + 2NaHCO_3(aq) \rightarrow Na_2SO_4(aq) + 2H_2O(l) + 2CO_2(g)$$

If a 250.0 mL solution of 1.50 M sodium carbonate reacts with an excess amount of acid, how many liters of carbon dioxide can be produced at 25 °C and 750 mmHg?

XP: +4

11. Calculate the partial pressures and the total pressure of a mixture containing 0.82 mol O_2 and 0.15 mol N_2 in a 10.0 L flask at 30 °C.

XP: +4

226

12. Comparing the diffusion rates of chlorine and bromine:
a) Which is predicted to diffuse the slowest?
b) Relatively speaking, how much slower will the slower gas diffuse?
c) If bromine diffuses at a rate of 4.2 x 10^3 mm/min, how fast would chlorine diffuse under these same conditions?

XP: +4 each

★XP: _____   Total XP: _____

If your XP is 47 or higher, you're ready to move up to…

★★Mixed Drinks

13. A container with 15.00 g of argon has a pressure of 2.51 atm. Calculate the pressure when the amount is reduced to 9.44 g at the same temperature and volume.

XP: +4

14. A sample of gas was originally 2.00 L and 1.72 atm at 22 °C. If the temperature was increased to 48 °C as the volume was expanded to 5.00 L, what would be the new pressure, assuming the amount remains constant?

XP: +5

15. A 5.00 L flask contains 22.0 grams of nitrogen dioxide at 32 °C. Calculate the pressure exerted by the gas.

XP: +5

16. "Molar volume" is defined as the volume occupied by one mole of gas at a given temperature and pressure. "Standard temperature and pressure" (STP) is currently defined as 0 °C and 1.00 atm. What would be the molar volume of a gas at STP?

XP: +5

17. An unknown gas is found to be 2.2 times faster than iodine gas. Calculate its molar mass.

XP: +5

18. A mixture of 8.30 g carbon dioxide and an unknown amount of sulfur dioxide exerts a pressure of 3.70 atm in a 2.48 L container at 25°C.
a) What is the partial pressure of carbon dioxide (in atm)?
b) How many grams of sulfur dioxide are in the container?

XP: +4 each

19. An apparatus similar to the one below contains two gases. The left side is a 2.00 L flask containing argon at 1.88 atm and the right is a 5.00 L flask containing neon at 3.01 atm.

If the central valve is opened and the two gases are mixed, what will be the new pressure inside the apparatus?

XP: +5

20. Calcium carbonate will decompose into calcium oxide and carbon dioxide when heated.

$$CaCO_3(s) \rightarrow CaO(s) + CO_2(g)$$

Suppose 5.00 g $CaCO_3$ is placed in a 3.00 L flask at 22 °C, sealed closed, and heated to 855 °C.
a) If the air inside the flask was originally 1.00 atm, what would be the partial pressure of the air after heating (assuming the volume of the solid in the container is negligible)?
b) Calculate the partial pressure of carbon dioxide after heating.
c) What would be the total pressure inside the flask after heating?

XP: +5 each

21. You probably already know that hot air rises; as seen in hot air balloons, for instance. Explain, qualitatively (that is, without using any calculations) why this is true.

XP: +5

22. The Gay-Lussac law (briefly mentioned in Part 3) states that the pressure and temperature of a gas are directly proportional when the volume is held constant. How could you explain this using kinetic molecular theory?

XP: +5

★★XP: _____   Total XP: _____

If your total XP is 87 or higher, let's see if you can handle...

★★★Straight, No Chaser

23. A container of pure oxygen has a pressure of 2.83 atm at 25 °C. Calculate its concentration in units of molarity.

XP: +10

24. Stoichiometric amounts of two gases (just enough of one to react with the other), A and B, were combined in a flask at room temperature. The total pressure inside the flask was 2.84 atm. The flask was heated and the two gases reacted according to the following equation:

$$A(g) + 3B(g) \rightarrow 2C(g)$$

When the flask was returned to its original room temperature, what is the pressure exerted by gas C?

XP: +10

25. A 1.00 L flask at 22 °C contains a 5.00 g mixture of oxygen and an unknown gas. The oxygen was removed chemically,

causing the pressure to drop from 3.48 to 1.21 atm. Calculate the molar mass of the unknown gas.

XP: +10

26. A 5.00 g piece of magnesium was placed in a 1.00 L flask containing 500.0 mL of hydrochloric acid and the flask was immediately closed. If the air pressure inside the flask was 750 torr at the temperature was 22 °C, what would be the total pressure (in atm) after all of the magnesium reacted? Assume the volume of the solution didn't change significantly.

XP +10

27. In an apparatus similar to the one from question 19, the left flask contains a gas mixture of 5.00 moles of neon and 5.00 moles of argon. The valve was opened for a brief period and the two gases were allowed to effuse into the flask on the right. If the right side contained 1.80 moles of neon, how many moles of argon were present?

XP: +10

28. Ammonium sulfate, a common component of fertilizers, can be prepared by the reaction of ammonia with sulfuric acid:

$$2NH_3(g) + H_2SO_4(aq) \rightarrow (NH_4)_2SO_4(aq)$$

If 500.0mL of NH_3 at a pressure of 1.50 atm at 25.0°C was reacted with a 150.0 mL of 1.3M sulfuric acid, what would be the theoretical yield of $(NH_4)_2SO_4$ (in grams)?

XP: +10

29. Calculate the kinetic energy (in J) of one molecule of CO_2 at 24 °C

XP: +10 each

30. Water was once thought to have the formula HO, but eventually Avogadro—with the help of his hypothesis—showed

that it was actually H_2O (thus sparing the world from countless water-themed prostitution jokes). Suppose you react a liter of oxygen with a liter of hydrogen.

a) According to Avogadro's hypothesis, how many liters of hydrogen would be required if the formula was HO? How many would be required if it was H_2O?

b) Using this same reaction, and knowing that water's formula is H_2O, how could we verify that hydrogen and oxygen are both diatomic elements and not monatomic?

XP: +10 each

★★★XP: _____   Total XP: _____

If your total XP is 155 or higher: Level up!

Achievement Unlocked: Silent, but Deadly!
Completed Chapter 6

You're now ready to learn about thermochemistry.

Chapter 7
Thermochemistry
(Part I)

Part 1: Thermochemistry

Thermodynamics is the study of energy: how it behaves, its different forms, etc. Like other areas of modern science, it's a very broad and diverse field that branches out into other areas, including chemistry. **Thermochemistry** is the branch of thermodynamics that studies the relationship between energy and chemical reactions. In this chapter we'll introduce many of the basic principles of thermodynamics and thermochemistry. Later, in Chapter 19, we'll dive into the subject a little more deeply.

When discussing thermodynamics, there are several common terms that you should familiarize yourself with. To begin with, the thing that you're studying—usually a chemical reaction, in this book—is referred to as the **system**. Everything else (the solvent, the beaker, the lab bench, the lab, etc) collectively makes up the **surroundings**. In nearly every process, chemical or otherwise, there is usually some transfer of energy between the system and its surroundings. An **exothermic** process is one where the system is releasing heat into the surroundings, while in an **endothermic** process the system is absorbing heat (remember: exo- = heat *ex*its the system; endo- = heat *en*ters the system).

Systems can be studied in one of two ways. In a **closed system**, only energy is transferred between the system and surroundings. **Open systems**, on the other hand, allow for the transfer of both energy and matter, which inherently makes them more complicated. As such, in this chapter we'll focus exclusively with closed systems.

One of the fundamental laws of chemistry discussed in Chapter 2 was the law of conservation of mass, which says matter cannot be created or destroyed during a reaction. In thermodynamics, there's the **law of conservation of energy** (sometimes called the *first law of thermodynamics*), which states that *energy* is neither created nor destroyed during a chemical reaction. For this reason, you'll sometimes see these two laws combined into the *law of conservation of mass and energy* (which

Einstein would probably agree with, since he considers them to be two different forms of the same thing, but that's a discussion for another textbook).

Energy primarily exists in two forms: potential energy and kinetic energy. Generally speaking, **potential energy** is stored energy while **kinetic energy**—which was briefly discussed in the previous chapter—is energy that's being used. For example, when throwing a ball you usually cock your arm back first, which allows your body to build up potential energy. As you bring your arm forward, your body converts this potential energy into kinetic energy. You're probably already familiar with, at least in name, the two main types of kinetic energy: heat and work. **Heat** is energy that results in a temperature change, while **work** is the application of a force over some distance. In this chapter we'll focus primarily on heat and save our discussion of work for Chapter 19.

Calorimetry

A subset of thermodynamics is **calorimetry**, the measuring of heat as it's transferred between a system and its surroundings. This heat transfer (q) can be determined using the following equation.

$$q = mc\Delta T$$

Here, *m* is the mass of the system (in grams), while ΔT is the change in temperature. In mathematics, a capital Greek letter delta (Δ) is often used to represent change and is determined by subtracting the initial value from the final ("final − initial"). When performing calorimetry measurements, it's important to measure ΔT in this specific manner because this will affect the sign of q. Exothermic processes will have a negative value of q, since a loss in heat will cause the system's temperature to decrease ($-\Delta T$). Conversely, an endothermic process will have a positive value of q, since absorbing heat will cause an increase in the system's temperature (+ΔT).

Finally, c represents the **specific heat capacity** of the system. Specific heat capacity (or *specific heat*, for short) is defined as the amount of heat required to raise the temperature of 1 gram of a substance by 1 degree. The units of specific heat are either J/g·°C or J/g·K, but since we're only looking at the *difference* in temperature, and the Celsius and Kelvin scales are in the same increments (one's just 273 units higher), the value is the same regardless of which one you use. For example, 100 °C to 25°C and 373 K to 298 K are both ranges of 75 degrees. The following table lists the specific heat capacities of a few common substances.

Substance	Specific Heat (J/g·°C)
Aluminum	0.900
Copper	0.385
Carbon (graphite)	0.720
Carbon (diamond)	0.502
Ethanol	0.385
Gold	0.129
Iron	0.444
Water (solid)	2.092
Water (liquid)	4.184
Water (gas)	2.008

You might have noticed that liquid water has a significantly higher specific heat compared to other substances in this table, even other liquids. It's actually one of several unique things about a substance that we usually think of as "ordinary." Chemically speaking, though, water is quite the freak of nature. Not only can it hold twice as much heat as most other liquids of similar size (see ethanol's specific heat, by comparison), but it also has a unusually large liquid range of 100 degrees, it's one of the few substances whose solid is less dense than its liquid form (ice floats), and it can dissolve a larger variety of solutes than other, similar liquids (more on that in a later chapter). All of these play a significant role in making Earth a livable planet. For example, because of its relatively large specific heat capacity, our sweat can absorb a large amount of heat before evaporating. On a larger scale, the oceans absorb the heat from the sun, which helps prevent large fluctuations in the planet's temperature during the night.

Calorimetry studies are often performed in a well-insulated container known as a **calorimeter**. While high-tech, electronic versions of these instruments can be found in a research laboratory, most general chemistry labs use the simple—yet still effective—model consisting of a coffee cup and a thermometer (or two cups, one inside the other, if you wish to make it a bit more insulated).

Example: How much heat (in Joules) is required to raise the temperature of a 13.0g piece of aluminum from 20.0°C to 50.0°C?

From our table of specific heats, we see that aluminum's specific heat capacity is 0.900 J/g·°C. Plugging this and the other given information into our calorimetry equation gives us

$$q = (13.0 \text{ g})(0.900 \text{ J/g·°C})(50.0 - 20.0 \text{ °C})$$
$$q = 351 \text{ J}$$

Going back to the sign convention for q, notice that our answer is a positive value. This makes sense, as the metal is absorbing heat, making it an endothermic process.

Example: 500.0 g of an unknown metal is heated to 100.0 °C then placed in a calorimeter containing 50.0 g of water at 25.0 °C. The temperature of the water increased to 63.0 °C. Determine the specific heat of the metal.

Comparing the information given about the metal with the equation $q = mc\Delta T$, we know the mass, and the problem specifically states that the metal was initially 100.0°C. As for its final temperature, we can assume that it will be the same as the water it's submerged in, 63.0 °C, which means we know the metal's ΔT. One thing we're not told, however, is the amount of heat released from the metal as it's cooled.

$$\begin{array}{cccc} ? & \checkmark & ? & \checkmark \\ q = & m & c & \Delta T \end{array}$$

Think about it, though: what happened to the heat released by the metal? Assuming our calorimeter was well insulated, it should have been absorbed by the water surrounding it.

$$-q_{metal} = q_{water}$$

We're given the mass of the water, its initial and final temperature, and its specific heat is given in the table on the previous page,

$$\begin{array}{cccc} ? & \checkmark & \checkmark & \checkmark \\ q = & m & c & \Delta T \end{array}$$

so we have everything required to calculate the amount of heat absorbed by the water.

$$q_{water} = (50.0 \text{ g})(4.184 \text{ J/g·°C})(63.0\text{-}25.0 \text{ °C}) = 7{,}950 \text{ J}$$

Again, if our calorimeter was properly insulated to prevent significant heat loss, this is the amount of heat released by the metal, only with a negative value to reflect an exothermic process.

$$q_{water} = -q_{metal} = -7950 \text{ J}$$

Now we can calculate the specific heat of the metal.

$$-7950 \text{ J} = (500.0\text{g})(c)(63.0 - 100.0°\text{C})$$

$$c = \frac{-7950 \text{ J}}{(500.0\text{g})(-37.0°\text{C})} = 0.430 \text{ J/g·°C}$$

This method of indirectly measuring heat transfer is a very common one in calorimetry.

Try It Yourself

P1. Calculate q (in Joules) for each of the following:
a) heating a 25.0 g piece of iron from 80.0 °C to 220.0 °C.
b) heating 2.0 kg of water from 18 °C to 77 °C.
c) cooling a 560 g piece of graphite from 325 °C to 32 °C.

P2. For each of the following, if the mass was 100.0 g and the initial temperature was 22 °C, what would be the temperature after adding 5,525 J of heat?
a) aluminum, b) ethanol, c) water.

P3. A 200.0 g sample of an unknown substance was heated to 142 °C then placed in a calorimeter containing 100.0 g of water at 23 °C. The temperature of the water increased to 72 °C.
a) Calculate the amount of heat was absorbed by the water.
b) Calculate the specific heat of the substance.

Part 2: Enthalpy Change

Enthalpy Change (ΔH) is a measure of heat transfer (q) at constant pressure. Under normal lab conditions, unless you're deliberately changing the pressure as part of your experiments, it's usually assumed to stay constant, so for all intents and purposes ΔH and q can be thought of as meaning the same thing, much in the same way that mass and weight are often used interchangeably. As such, the sign convention we use for ΔH is the same as q's: a negative value of ΔH represents an exothermic process while a positive ΔH denotes an endothermic one.

Thermochemical Equations

In thermochemistry it's often useful to show reactions as **thermochemical equations**, which basically means the reaction's relative enthalpy change is included as part of the balanced chemical equation. For example, when one mole of methane (CH_4) undergoes combustion it releases 890 kJ of heat. The thermochemical equation would look like this

$$CH_4(g) + 2O_2(g) \rightarrow CO_2(g) + 2H_2O(l) \qquad \Delta H = -890 \text{ kJ}$$

It's important to remember that the enthalpy change shown is per mole of the substances in the reaction, relative to the equation's stoichiometry. In other words, one mole of methane reacts with two moles of oxygen, producing a mole of carbon dioxide, two moles of water, *plus* 890 kJ of heat.

$$CH_4(g) + 2O_2(g) \rightarrow CO_2(g) + 2H_2O(l) + 890 \text{ kJ}$$

An example of an endothermic reaction can be found in most of the commercially available "cold packs" used in first aid.

Most simply work by dissolving ammonium nitrate in water, as shown in the following thermochemical equation

$$NH_4NO_3(s) \rightarrow NH_4^+(aq) + NO_3^-(aq) \qquad \Delta H = 28 \text{ kJ}$$

From this equation, we see that one mole of ammonium nitrate absorbs 28 kJ of heat in order to dissociate into ions.

$$NH_4NO_3(s) + 28 \text{ kJ} \rightarrow NH_4^+(aq) + NO_3^-(aq)$$

It absorbs this heat from the water (its immediate surroundings), which lowers the water's temperature.

Enthalpy Change and Stoichiometry

The thermochemical equation for the combustion of ethane gas (C_2H_6) is

$$2C_2H_6(g) + 7O_2(g) \rightarrow 4CO_2(g) + 6H_2O(l) \qquad \Delta H = -3120 \text{ kJ}$$

We see that 2 moles of C_2H_6 will undergo combustion to produce 3,120 kJ of heat. But what if you have 8.0 g of C_2H_6? How much heat will be produced then?

This is just another example of a stoichiometry problem, the only difference being that instead of converting from one substance to another, we're converting from one substance to heat. Like every stoichiometry problem from the past three chapters, the first step will be to take the amount given and convert it to units of moles

$$8.0 \text{ g } C_2H_6 \times \frac{1 \text{ mol } C_2H_6}{30.07 \text{ g } C_2H_6}$$

Previously, we used a given chemical equation to convert between moles of one chemical to moles of another. We can also use a thermochemical equation to convert between moles of one chemical to heat released (or absorbed). In this example, according to the given equation, 2 moles of C_2H_6 should produce 3,120 kJ of heat.

$$8.0 \ \cancel{g \ C_2H_6} \times \frac{1 \ mol \ C_2H_6}{30.07 \ \cancel{g \ C_2H_6}} \times \frac{-3120 \ kJ}{2 \ \cancel{mol \ C_2H_6}} = -420 \ kJ$$

Enthalpy Change and Phase Changes

If you added a constant supply of heat to a block of ice and tracked its temperature over time, you would get a graph that looked something like this:

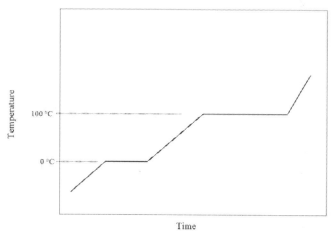

Notice the points where the temperature levels off: 0 °C and 100 °C, which you might recognize as the melting and boiling points of water, respectively. At these two temperatures, the heat being added isn't used to increase the temperature, but rather to break the attractive forces that are holding the molecules together as either a solid or a liquid (more on that in Chapter 13).

The heat required to melt a substance is known as the **enthalpy of fusion** (ΔH_{fus}) while the heat needed to boil is called the **enthalpy of vaporization** (ΔH_{vap}). The amount required varies with substance. In the case of water, its enthalpy of fusion is 6.01 kJ/mol and its enthalpy of vaporization is 40.8 kJ/mol. Each process can be represented as a thermochemical equation.

$$H_2O(s) \rightarrow H_2O(l) \quad \Delta H_{fus} = 6.01 \text{ kJ}$$
$$H_2O(l) \rightarrow H_2O(g) \quad \Delta H_{vap} = 40.8 \text{ kJ}$$

Whenever you're performing calorimetry calculations, it's very important to factor in the heat required to cause a phase change if one is occurring.

Example: How much heat is required to increase the temperature of 10.0 g of water from -10.0 to 50.0 °C.

At first glance, this problem seems identical to one we did in Part 1 of this chapter, only with water instead of aluminum, so you might initially try to solve it with a single calorimetry calculation.

$$q = m \quad c \quad \Delta T$$

$$q = (10.0 \text{ g})(4.184 \text{ J/g·°C})[50 - (-10 \text{ °C})]$$
$$q = 2510 \text{ J or } 2.51 \text{ kJ}$$

This answer, however, ends up being off by quite a bit.

There are a couple of problems with this calculation, both of which are due to the fact that we have a phase change occurring at 0 °C. Not only does solid water have a different specific heat than liquid water (see the specific heat table), but the above calculation doesn't factor in the the heat required to convert solid water to liquid (the enthalpy of fusion).

A problem such as this has to be examined in three stages. First, we use the calorimetry equation to calculate the heat required to take us to the phase change, which in this case would be from -10 to 0 °C.

$$q = (10.0 \text{ g})(2.09 \text{ J/g·°C})[0 - (-10 \text{ °C})]$$
$$q = 209 \text{ J}$$

Next, we calculate the heat required to take us *through* the phase change, which is a stoichiometry problem, using water's enthalpy of fusion.

$$10.0 \text{ g } H_2O \times \frac{1 \text{ mol } H_2O}{18.02 \text{ g } H_2O} \times \frac{6.01 \text{ kJ}}{1 \text{ mol } H_2O} = 3.34 \text{ kJ}$$

Finally, we use the calorimetry equation to determine how much heat would be needed to heat the liquid water from 0 °C to 50.

$$q = (10.0 \text{ g})(4.184 \text{ J/g·°C})(50 - 0 \text{ °C})$$
$$q = 2,090 \text{ J}$$

Therefore, the total heat required for this process is

-10 to 0 °C:	209 J
melting:	3,340 J
0 to 50 °C:	2,090 J
Total:	5,640 J or 5.64 kJ

Try It Yourself

P4. In Chapter 4, we discussed how ammonia can be prepared from elemental nitrogen and hydrogen (using what's known as the Haber process). The thermochemical equation for this reaction is

$$N_2(g) + 3H_2(g) \rightarrow 2NH_3(g) \quad \Delta H = -91.8 \text{ kJ}$$

a) Calculate the heat released (in kJ) when 50.0 g of nitrogen is converted to ammonia.
b) How many grams of ammonia would need to be produced to release 2.43×10^5 kJ of heat?

P5. In Chapter 5, we discussed the precipitation reaction that occurs between sodium chloride and silver nitrate. The thermochemical equation for this reaction is

$$NaCl(aq) + AgNO_3(aq) \rightarrow NaNO_3(aq) + AgCl(s) \quad \Delta H = -65.7 \text{ kJ}$$

a) How much heat (in kJ) would be released from the reaction of 85.0 mL of 2.00 M sodium chloride?
b) How many liters of 1.2 M silver nitrate would be required to produce 3,340 kJ of heat?

P6. How much heat (in kJ) would be required to heat a 100.0 g sample of water from 44.0 °C to 138 °C?

Part 3: Hess's Law

Recall from algebra class that two equations can be added together.

$$\begin{array}{rl} x + y &= 3 \\ 2x &= 2 + y \\ \hline 3x &= 5 \end{array}$$

Chemical equations can be added in a similar manner. What's more, in 1840 Russian chemist Germain Hess discovered what is now known as **Hess's law**, which states that the enthalpy change of an equation obtained by adding two or more thermochemical equations together is equal to the sum of the enthalpy changes of the added equations. For example, the combustion of elemental carbon is known to release 393.5 kJ of heat per mole of carbon.

$$C(s) + O_2(g) \rightarrow CO_2(g) \qquad \Delta H = \text{-}393.5 \text{ kJ}$$

Meanwhile, the incomplete combustion of carbon can lead to the formation of carbon monoxide.

$$C(s) + \tfrac{1}{2}O_2(g) \rightarrow CO(g) \qquad \Delta H = \text{-}110.5 \text{ kJ}$$

and the conversion of CO to CO_2 can occur by the following reaction

$$CO(g) + \tfrac{1}{2}O_2(g) \rightarrow CO_2(g) \quad \Delta H = \text{-}283.0 \text{ kJ}$$

Notice that not only will these last two equations add together to give the combustion of carbon,

$$\begin{array}{ll} C(s) + \tfrac{1}{2}O_2(g) & \rightarrow \cancel{CO(g)} \\ \cancel{CO(g)} + \tfrac{1}{2}O_2(g) & \rightarrow CO_2(g) \\ \hline C(s) + O_2(g) & \rightarrow CO_2(g) \end{array}$$

246

but their values of ΔH also add together to give the enthalpy of change of the first equation.

$$C(s) + \tfrac{1}{2}O_2(g) \rightarrow \cancel{CO(g)} \quad\quad \Delta H = -110.5\ kJ$$
$$\cancel{CO(g)} + \tfrac{1}{2}O_2(g) \rightarrow CO_2(g) \quad \Delta H = -283.0\ kJ$$
$$\overline{C(s) + O_2(g) \quad\quad \rightarrow CO_2(g) \quad \Delta H = -393.5\ kJ}$$

The reason Hess's law works is because enthalpy change is a **state function**, which only depends on the initial and final states, not the path in-between. In other words, it doesn't matter *how* you get from point A to point B. It only matters what the actual values of A and B are. A more familiar example of a state function would be altitude. If you go to the 20th floor of a skyscraper, it doesn't matter if you take the elevator directly to that floor or take the stairs and zigzag your way from floor-to-floor. In the end you'll still be twenty stories up. It's more or less the same for chemical reactions. It doesn't matter if carbon is converted to carbon dioxide in a single step or if it's a two-step process (more on that in Chapter 14). Either way, the net enthalpy change will be -393.5 kJ.

Example: Calculate the enthalpy change of

$$C_2H_2(g) + 2Cl_2(g) \rightarrow C_2H_2Cl_4(l)$$

using the following thermochemical equations:

1) $2C(s) + H_2(g) \rightarrow C_2H_2(g)$ $\Delta H = 227\ kJ$
2) $2C(s) + H_2(g) + 2Cl_2(g) \rightarrow C_2H_2Cl_4(l)$ $\Delta H = 130\ kJ$

Before you say the answer's 357 kJ, take another look at the two equations given. Adding them together as written doesn't give the reaction we're interested in. You'll often encounter this when trying to solve a problem using Hess's law, where you first need to modify one or both equations in a way that allows them to add together properly. To see which equations require modifying and which, if any, are O.K. as given, look at each of the given equations one at a time and pick a substance you can use as a point of reference. When possible, your reference should a) be in the equation you're trying to obtain and b) in only one of the given equations.

In equation 1, for instance, the only substance present that's also in our desired equation is C_2H_2. What's more, of the two given equations, this is the only one with C_2H_2, which means that however we modify equation 1, C_2H_2 must be placed on the proper side with the proper coefficient. In a case like this, there's no need to bother looking at the other reactants or products in this equation. As we'll see in a second, if you pick a good reference, the other chemicals in that equation will work themselves out in the end.

Comparing equation 1 to the reaction in question, equation 1 has one mole of C_2H_2 on the product side, and the reaction in question has one mole of C_2H_2 on the *reactant* side, so it looks like we'll need to flip equation 1 around.

$$\text{Desired eqn:} \quad \mathbf{C_2H_2(g) + 2Cl_2(g) \rightarrow C_2H_2Cl_4(l)}$$
$$\text{Eqn 1):} \quad 2C(s) + H_2(g) \rightarrow \mathbf{C_2H_2(g)}$$
$$\text{Needs to be:} \quad \mathbf{C_2H_2(g)} \rightarrow 2C(s) + H_2(g)$$

When we modify a chemical equation, its ΔH needs to be adjusted accordingly. Here, flipping an equation around causes the sign of ΔH to "flip" as well.

$$C_2H_2(g) \rightarrow 2C(s) + H_2(g) \qquad \Delta H = -227 \text{ kJ}$$

If you're having trouble understanding why the sign changes, remember that when a reaction is endothermic, heat is essentially a reactant in the overall process.

$$2C(s) + H_2(g) + 227 \text{ kJ} \rightarrow C_2H_2(g)$$

When the equation is flipped around, what was originally a reactant becomes a product, including heat.

$$C_2H_2(g) \rightarrow 2C(s) + H_2(g) + 227 \text{ kJ}$$

Moving on to equation 2, we can use either Cl_2 or $C_2H_2Cl_4$ as a reference, since both appear in the equation we're trying to obtain, plus neither one is present in equation 1. As before, whatever we do to this equation, these two chemicals must end up on the proper side with the proper coefficient in front of it. No matter which one you pick as your reference, though, they already seem to be on the proper side with the proper coefficient, so we can use this equation as it's given.

Desired eqn: $C_2H_2(g) + 2Cl_2(g) \rightarrow C_2H_2Cl_4(l)$

Eqn 2): $2C(s) + H_2(g) + 2Cl_2(g) \rightarrow C_2H_2Cl_4(l)$

Our two given equations now look like this:

$$C_2H_2(g) \rightarrow 2C(s) + H_2(g) \qquad \Delta H = -227 \text{ kJ}$$
$$2C(s) + H_2(g) + 2Cl_2(g) \rightarrow C_2H_2Cl_4(l) \qquad \Delta H = +130.0 \text{ kJ}$$

To double-check our work up to this point, we add the two chemical equations together to confirm that they do indeed give us the desired reaction.

$$C_2H_2(g) \rightarrow \cancel{2C(s)} + \cancel{H_2(g)} \qquad \Delta H = -227 \text{ kJ}$$
$$\cancel{2C(s)} + \cancel{H_2(g)} + 2Cl_2(g) \rightarrow C_2H_2Cl_4(l) \qquad \Delta H = +130.0 \text{ kJ}$$
$$\overline{C_2H_2(g) + 2Cl_2(g) \rightarrow C_2H_2Cl_4(l)}$$

According to Hess's law, the enthalpy change of this equation should be sum of the ΔH's of the added equations.

$$C_2H_2(g) \rightarrow \cancel{2C(s)} + \cancel{H_2(g)} \qquad \Delta H = -227 \text{ kJ}$$
$$\underline{\cancel{2C(s)} + \cancel{H_2(g)} + 2Cl_2(g) \rightarrow C_2H_2Cl_4(l) \qquad \Delta H = +130.0 \text{ kJ}}$$
$$C_2H_2(g) + 2Cl_2(g) \rightarrow C_2H_2Cl_4(l) \qquad \Delta H = -97 \text{ kJ}$$

Example: Calculate the enthalpy change of

$$Cu(s) + Cl_2(g) \nrightarrow CuCl_2(s)$$

given the following:

1) $2Cu(s) + Cl_2(g) \rightarrow 2CuCl(s)$ $\qquad \Delta H = -274.4 \text{ kJ}$
2) $2CuCl(s) + Cl_2(g) \rightarrow 2CuCl_2(s)$ $\qquad \Delta H = -165.8 \text{ kJ}$

As before, we'll look at each equation one at a time using one substance as a reference. Looking at the two given equations, though, notice that while Cl_2 is in our desired equation, it's in *both* of the given equations, so we should avoid making this our reference (if we can help it).

Starting with equation 1, $Cu(s)$ looks to make the best reference, as it's in the equation we're trying to derive and equation 1 is the only one of the two that has this particular chemical. Comparing equation 1 to our desired equation, copper seems to be on the correct side, but it has the wrong coefficient in front of it. To fix this, we can simply divide the coefficients by two.

Desired eqn: **$Cu(s) + Cl_2(g) \rightarrow CuCl_2(s)$**
Eqn 1): **$2Cu(s) + Cl_2(g) \rightarrow 2CuCl(s)$**
Needs to be: **$Cu(s) + \frac{1}{2}Cl_2(g) \rightarrow CuCl(s)$**

Remember, there's a stoichiometric relationship between the chemical equation and its ΔH. If the amount of each substance is cut in half, so is the amount of heat released.

$$Cu(s) + \frac{1}{2}Cl_2(g) \rightarrow CuCl(s) \qquad \Delta H = -137.2 \text{ kJ}$$

Whenever you multiply or divide the coefficients of an equation, you must also modify the value of ΔH in the same way.

Looking at equation 2, CuCl isn't in the equation we want and we've already said that Cl_2 wouldn't make an ideal reference in this problem. That leaves copper (II) chloride, which thankfully does fit our two criteria for a good reference. Just like equation 1, it seems the reference is on the correct side, but the coefficients need to be divided by two,

$$\begin{array}{ll} \text{Desired eqn:} & Cu(s) + Cl_2(g) \rightarrow \mathbf{CuCl_2(s)} \\ \text{Eqn 2):} & 2CuCl(s) + Cl_2(g) \rightarrow \mathbf{2CuCl_2(s)} \\ \text{Needs to be:} & CuCl(s) + \tfrac{1}{2}Cl_2(g) \rightarrow CuCl_2(s) \end{array}$$

and so the ΔH is halved as well.

$$CuCl(s) + \tfrac{1}{2}Cl_2(g) \rightarrow CuCl_2(s) \qquad \Delta H = -82.9 \text{ kJ}$$

Checking our work so far, adding these two modified equations does give the equation we want,

$$\begin{array}{ll} Cu(s) + \tfrac{1}{2}Cl_2 \rightarrow \cancel{CuCl(s)} & \Delta H = -137.2 \text{ kJ} \\ \underline{\cancel{CuCl(s)} + \tfrac{1}{2}Cl_2(g) \rightarrow CuCl_2(s)} & \underline{\Delta H = -82.9 \text{ kJ}} \\ Cu(s) + Cl_2(g) \rightarrow CuCl_2(s) & \end{array}$$

so adding the two ΔH's together should give us the enthalpy change of our new equation.

$$\begin{array}{ll} Cu(s) + \tfrac{1}{2}Cl_2 \rightarrow \cancel{CuCl(s)} & \Delta H = -137.2 \text{ kJ} \\ \underline{\cancel{CuCl(s)} + \tfrac{1}{2}Cl_2(g) \rightarrow CuCl_2(s)} & \underline{\Delta H = -82.9 \text{ kJ}} \\ Cu(s) + Cl_2(g) \rightarrow CuCl_2(s) & \Delta H = -220.1 \text{ kJ} \end{array}$$

Try It Yourself

P7. Given the following thermochemical equation

$$H_2(g) + Cl_2(g) \rightarrow 2HCl(g) \qquad \Delta H = -184.6 \text{ kJ}$$

determine the enthalpy changes of
a) $2HCl(g) \rightarrow H_2(g) + Cl_2(g)$
b) $3H_2(g) + 3Cl_2(g) \rightarrow 6HCl(g)$
c) $\frac{1}{2}H_2(g) + \frac{1}{2}Cl_2(g) \rightarrow HCl(g)$
d) $\frac{1}{2}HCl(g) \rightarrow \frac{1}{4}H_2(g) + \frac{1}{4}Cl_2(g)$

P8. Calculate the enthalpy change for

$$2A + B \rightarrow D + 2E$$

given the following equations:
    1) $A + \frac{1}{2}B \rightarrow C$ $\Delta H = 150 \text{ kJ}$
    2) $D + 2E \rightarrow 2C$ $\Delta H = 200 \text{ kJ}$

P9. Thionyl chloride ($SOCl_2$) is an important reagent in organic chemistry. It's often prepared by reacting sulfur trioxide and sulfur dichloride.

$$SO_3(g) + SCl_2(g) \rightarrow SOCl_2(l) + SO_2(g)$$

Calculate the enthalpy change for this reaction using the following equations:
    1) $2SO_2(g) + O_2(g) \rightarrow 2SO_3(g)$ $\Delta H = -198.2 \text{ kJ}$
    2) $2SCl_2(g) + O_2(g) \rightarrow 2SOCl_2(l)$ $\Delta H = -456.1 \text{ kJ}$

Part 4: Enthalpies of Formation

The **enthalpy of formation** (ΔH_f) of a substance is the enthalpy change required to form one mole of that substance from each of its elements in their standard states. The **standard state** of an element is its state in pure form at 1 atm. The following is a list of common standard states, many of which you're probably already familiar with by this point.

1. Metals are monatomic solids (except mercury, which is a liquid)
2. Five of the seven diatomic elements are gases in their standard states: hydrogen, nitrogen, oxygen, fluorine, and chlorine. Bromine is a liquid while iodine is a solid.
3. The standard state of carbon is graphite, written as either C(graphite) or C(gr).
4. The standard state of phosphorus is white phosphorus, P(white).
5. The standard state of sulfur is rhombic sulfur, S(rhombic).

For example, to find the enthalpy of formation of carbon dioxide, you'd need to first find a way to form it by the reaction of graphite and oxygen.

$$C(gr) + O_2(g) \rightarrow CO_2(g)$$

The experimentally derived enthalpy change for this reaction would be –393.5 kJ per mole of CO_2

$$C(gr) + O_2(g) \rightarrow CO_2(g) \qquad \Delta H = -393.5 \text{ kJ}$$

From this, the enthalpy of formation of $CO_2(g)$ is said to be –393.5 kJ/mol.

In another example, the equation showing the formation of one mole of N_2O from each element in their standard states is

$$N_2(g) + \tfrac{1}{2}O_2(g) \rightarrow N_2O(g)$$

The enthalpy change for this reaction has been measured as 81.6 kJ

$$N_2(g) + \tfrac{1}{2}O_2(g) \rightarrow N_2O(g) \quad \Delta H = 81.6 \text{ kJ}$$

Therefore, N_2O is said to have $\Delta H_f = 81.6$ kJ/mol.

    Over the years, chemists have determined the enthalpies of formation for just about every chemical you can imagine. A few are given in the following table. The superscript circle next to the enthalpy of formation symbol (ΔH_f°) means these are standard values measured at 25 °C (298 K) and 1 atm.

Substance	ΔH_f° (kJ/mol)	Substance	ΔH_f° (kJ/mol)
Ag(s)	0	H_2(g)	0
AgCl(s)	-127.0	H_2O(g)	-241.8
Al(s)	0	H_2O(l)	-285.8
Al_2O_3(s)	-1669.8	H_2O_2(l)	-187.6
Br_2(l)	0	I_2(s)	0
HBr(g)	-36.2	HI(g)	259
C(graphite)	0	Mg(s)	0
C(diamond)	1.90	$MgCl_2$(s)	-641.8
CO(g)	-110.5	$MgCO_3$(s)	-1112.9
CO_2(g)	-393.5	N_2(g)	0
CH_4(g)	-74.85	NH_3(g)	-46.3
$C_6H_{12}O_6$(s)	-1274.5	NO(g)	90.4
Ca(s)	0	NO_2(g)	33.85
$CaCO_3$(s)	-1206.9	N_2O_4(g)	9.66
CaO(s)	-635.6	O_2(g)	0
Cl_2(g)	0	O_3(g)	142.2
HCl(g)	-92.3	P(white)	0
Cu(s)	0	P(red)	-18.4
$CuSO_4$(s)	-769.86	P_4O_{10}(s)	-3012.48
F_2(g)	0	S(rhombic)	0
HF(g)	-271.6	S(monoclinic)	0.30
Fe(s)	0	SO_2(g)	-296.1
FeO(s)	-272.0	SO_3(g)	-395.2
Fe_2O_3(s)	-822.2	H_2S(g)	-20.15

254

Something that tends to stand out in this list is the many entries with an enthalpy of formation equal to zero. Look closer and you'll see that they're all for elements in their standard states. As we discussed previously, measurements are based on either an absolute scale (such Kelvin) or a relative one (like Celsius). In the case of enthalpies of formation, it's the latter. By assigning standard states a relative value of zero, any heat absorbed or released in a formation reaction, like the ones for CO_2 and N_2O, will be assigned to the compound being produced.

Using ΔH_f to Determine ΔH_{rxn}

Enthalpies of formation give us a fairly direct method of determining the enthalpy change for any reaction (ΔH_{rxn}). Because enthalpy change is a state function (see Part 3), the ΔH for any reaction will be the sum of the enthalpies of formation of its products minus the sum of the enthalpies of formation of its reactants. We can write this mathematically by the following equation (in math, a Greek letter sigma, Σ, means "sum").

$$\Delta H_{rxn} = \Sigma \Delta H_f(products) - \Sigma \Delta H_f(reactants)$$

Example: Determine the enthalpy change from the combustion of glucose, $C_6H_{12}O_6$.

$$C_6H_{12}O_6(s) + 6O_2(g) \rightarrow 6CO_2(g) + 6 H_2O(g)$$

In our table of ΔH_f's, we find the following values

	ΔH_f (kJ/mol)
$C_6H_{12}O_6(s)$	-1274.5
$O_2(g)$	0
$CO_2(g)$	-393.5
$H_2O(g)$	-241.8

Be mindful of the fact that these values are given in kJ *per mole*. For each substance in an equation, you have to multiply its enthalpy of formation by the coefficient in front of it.

$$\Delta H_{rxn} = [6 \text{ mol}(-393.5 \text{ kJ/mol}) + 6(-241.8)] - [(-1274.5) + 6(0)]$$
$$\Delta H_{rxn} = -2537.3 \text{ kJ}$$

Multiplying each substance's coefficient (moles) by its ΔH_f (kJ/mol) causes the mole unit to cancel out, as seen with CO_2 above (I didn't show it for every substance to conserve space), giving an answer in units of kJ.

Try It Yourself

P10. Calculate the enthalpy changes (in kJ) for the following reactions using enthalpies of formation.
a) $CaCO_3(s) \rightarrow CaO(s) + CO_2(g)$
b) $2H_2S(g) + 3O_2(g) \rightarrow 2SO_3(g) + 2H_2O(g)$
c) $2Al(s) + Fe_2O_3(s) \rightarrow 2Fe(s) + Al_2O_3(s)$

Learning Beyond

- Learn what a bomb calorimeter is (though you may not find it to be as cool as the name suggests).
- One of the more popular classroom demos of an exothermic reaction is that between sucrose (usually in the form of a gummy bear) and potassium chlorate. There are several videos of this reaction on the internet.

256

Test Your Skills

★ Smoke on the Water

1. A 35.0 g piece of metal was heated from 25°C to 105 °C. Calculate the heat required (in J) to do this when the metal is a) iron, b) gold, c) aluminum.

XP: +3 each

2. Suppose 3.36 kJ of heat was added to 150.0 g of a liquid. By how much would the temperature change if the liquid was a) ethanol, b) water

XP: +3 each

3. A 55.3 g sample of a liquid was heated to 59.1 °C then mixed in a calorimeter with 49.8 g of benzene (specific heat = 1.73 J/g·°C) that was initially at 22.7 °C. The final temperature of the mixture was 35.9 °C. Find the specific heat of the other liquid.

XP: +4

4. When heated, copper (II) nitrate will decompose by the following reaction:

$$2Cu(NO_3)_2(s) \rightarrow 2CuO(s) + 4NO_2(g) + O_2(g) \quad \Delta H = 430.8 \text{ kJ}$$

a) How much heat (in kJ) is required to decompose 200.0 g of copper (II) nitrate?
b) If 4.50 x 10^5 kJ of heat are added to a sample of copper (II) nitrate, how many grams of copper (II) oxide can be produced (assuming enough $Cu(NO_3)_2$ is present)?

XP: +4 each

5. Sodium and water will react to form sodium hydroxide and hydrogen gas, according to the following equation:

$$2Na(s) +2 H_2O(l) \rightarrow 2NaOH(aq) + H_2(g) \quad \Delta H = -367.6 \text{ kJ}$$

a) How much heat is released by the reaction of 10.0 g Na?
b) How many grams of water are needed to produce 9.42×10^4 kJ of heat?

XP: +4 each

6. Cyclohexane (C_6H_{12}) has the following properties:

melting pt.:   7 °C ΔH_{vap}:   32 kJ/mol

boiling pt.:   80.7 °C   specific heats: 1.85 J/g·°C (liq.),
                                                 1.25 J/g·°C (gas)

a) Using this information, calculate the heat required to increase the temperature of 74.0 g cyclohexane from 45 °C to 150 °C.
b) How much heat would be required to increase the temperature of 74.0 g water from 45 °C to 150 °C?

XP: +4 each

7. Calculate the enthalpy change of the reaction

$$SO_2(g) + O_3(g) \rightarrow SO_3(g) + O_2(g)$$

using the following equations:
    1) $2O_3(g) \rightarrow 3O_2(g)$ $\Delta H = -284.4$ kJ
    2) $2SO_3(g) \rightarrow 2SO_2(g) + O_2(g)$ $\Delta H = 198.2$ kJ

XP: +4

8. Hydrogen peroxide is prepared commercially using an elaborate process involving an organic catalyst. The overall reaction, however, is fairly simple:

$$H_2(g) + O_2(g) \rightarrow H_2O_2(l)$$

Calculate the enthalpy change for this reaction using the following:

1) $H_2O_2(l) \rightarrow H_2O(l) + \frac{1}{2}O_2(g)$ $\Delta H = -98.0$ kJ
2) $2H_2(g) + O_2(g) \rightarrow 2H_2O(l)$ $\Delta H = -571.6$ kJ

XP: +4

9. Using the table of enthalpies of formation found in Part 4 to verify your answers to questions 7 and 8.

XP: +4 each

10. Using the table of enthalpies of formation found in Part 4, calculate the enthalpy changes (in kJ) for the following reactions:
a) $4NO_2(g) + 6H_2O(g) \rightarrow 4NH_3(g) + 7O_2(g)$
b) $2H_2S(g) + SO_2(g) \rightarrow 3S(rhombic) + 2H_2O(g)$
c) $CaO(s) + 2HF(g) \rightarrow CaF_2(s) + H_2O(l)$
  (the ΔH_f of $CaF_2(s)$ is -1215 kJ/mol)

XP: +4 each

★XP: _____

If your XP is 46 or higher, maybe you can handle...

★★Back in Black

11. Calculate the mass of liquid water that can absorb 3,910 J without undergoing a temperature change greater than 10 degrees. If the same mass of copper absorbed this much heat, by how much would the temperature increase?

XP: +5 each

12. A piece of iron weighing 30.0 g was heated to 125 °C then placed in a calorimeter with 200.0 g of water that was initially at 22 °C. What was the final temperature of the water?

XP: +5

13. In Part 2, the thermochemical equation for the dissociation of ammonium nitrate was given as

$$NH_4NO_3(s) \rightarrow NH_4^+(aq) + NO_3^-(aq) \qquad \Delta H = 28 \text{ kJ}$$

a) How much heat is required to dissolve 5.00 g of ammonium nitrate?
b) If this mass of ammonium nitrate was dissolved in 40.0 g of water that was initially at 22 °C, what would be the final temperature?

XP: +5 each

14. Sublimation is a phase change where a solid is converted to a gas. Using Hess' law and the water's enthalpies of fusion and vaporization, calculate water's enthalpy of sublimation.

XP: +5

15. Hydrazine can be prepared by the reaction between ammonia and hydrogen peroxide

$$2NH_3(g) + H_2O_2(l) \rightarrow N_2H_4(l) + 2H_2O(l)$$

Calculate the enthalpy change for this reaction using the following equations

1) $3N_2H_4(l) \rightarrow 4NH_3(g) + N_2(g)$ $\qquad \Delta H = -334.8 \text{ kJ}$
2) $2H_2(g) + O_2(g) \rightarrow 2H_2O(l)$ $\qquad \Delta H = -571.6 \text{ kJ}$
3) $2H_2O_2(l) \rightarrow 2H_2O(l) + O_2(g)$ $\qquad \Delta H = -196.0 \text{ kJ}$
4) $N_2(g) + 3H_2(g) \rightarrow 2NH_3(g)$ $\qquad \Delta H = -92.6 \text{ kJ}$

XP: +5

16. Write thermochemical equations showing the formation of one mole of each of the following from their standard state elements: a) $HBr(g)$, b) $MgCO_3(s)$, c) $C_6H_{12}O_6(s)$

XP: +5 each

17. If you rewrote an equation as a net ionic, would its enthalpy change be different? Why or why not?

XP: +5

18. Calcium sulfate can be prepared by the following reaction:

$2CaO(s) + 2SO_2(g) + O_2(g) \rightarrow 2CaSO_4(s)$

If the enthalpy change of this reaction is -1002 kJ, what is enthalpy of formation of calcium sulfate?

XP: +5

★★XP: _____   Total XP: _____

If your total XP is 91 or higher, crack your knuckles and thrash on...

★★★Hot for Teacher

19. The Atlantic Ocean contains 3.547×10^8 km^3 of water. The specific heat of sea water is approximately 3.93 J/g·°C with a density of 1.025 g/mL. How much heat (in J) would be required to increase the temperature of the entire Atlantic by two degrees?

XP: +10

20. A solution of 0.20 mol of acid HA in 50.0g water was prepared, then another solution was prepared containing 0.20 mol of an alkali metal hydroxide, MOH in 50.0g water. Both solutions were initially 22.0°C, but after combining the two the temperature increased to 38.0°C. Use this information to determine the enthalpy change of this reaction.

XP: +10

21. Copper and nitric acid react by the following equation:

$Cu(s) + 4HNO_3(aq) \rightarrow Cu(NO_3)_2(aq) + 2NO_2(g) + 2H_2O(l)$ $\Delta H = -26.4$ kJ

a) How much heat would be released if a 5.00 g piece of copper is placed in 100.0 mL solution of 1.80 M nitric acid?
b) If 114 kJ of heat was released during this reaction, how many liters of NO_2 was released at 1.00 atm and 24 °C?

XP: +10 each

22. Explosions are usually characterized as exothermic reactions that coincide with a large increase in volume. ANFO explosives (ammonium nitrate/fuel oil) are commonly used by the mining industry and—unfortunately—terrorists. Using the molecular formula $C_{17}H_{36}$ as an average formula for the components in fuel oil, the equation for the reaction between ammonium nitrate and fuel oil can be written as

$52NH_4NO_3(s) + C_{17}H_{36}(l) \rightarrow 52N_2(g) + 17CO_2(g) + 122H_2O(g)$

a) The ΔH_f of $NH_4NO_3(s)$ is -365.6 kJ/mol and an approximate value for compounds with the formula $C_{17}H_{36}$ is -479.9 kJ/mol. Use this and the ΔH_f table in Part 4 to estimate the energy released by the above reaction.
b) Fertilizers are commonly sold in 50.0 pound bags. If 50.0 lbs of ammonium nitrate underwent the above reaction, how much heat would be released?
c) How many moles of gas would be produced by 50.0 lbs of ammonium nitrate? What volume would this amount of gas occupy at 25 °C and 1.00 atm?

XP: +10 each

23. The ΔH_f of benzene (C_6H_6) is 49.04 kJ/mol. Calculate the energy released from the combustion of 100.0 g of benzene.

XP: +10

★★★XP: _____   Total XP: _____

If your total XP is 151 or higher: Level up!

Achievement Unlocked: Don't sweat it
Completed Chapter 7

You're now ready to learn about electron arrangement.

Chapter 8
Electron Arrangement
(Part I)

Part 1: The Dual Nature of Light

During our introduction to the atom in Chapter 2, we only noted that electrons exist in a "cloud" around the nucleus. It's important to have a greater understanding of how electrons are arranged in atoms, as it'll lead to a better understanding of how most chemical reactions occur, not to mention why they occur in the first place.

Before jumping into electron arrangement, however, it'll be helpful to start with a bit of "back story," involving electromagnetic (EM) radiation. In many ways, you're already familiar with the different parts of the EM spectrum, at the very least by name:

Spectrum	Wavelength	Frequency (Hz)	Examples
Gamma	1 – 10 pm	$> 10^{19}$	PET scans, Comic book superpowers
X-rays	10 pm – 10 nm	$10^{16} – 10^{19}$	X-rays, Determination of chemical structures
Ultraviolet (UV)	10 nm – 400 nm	$10^{15} – 10^{16}$	black lights, tanning beds
Visible	400 – 700 nm	10^{14}	anything you can see
Infrared (IR)	700 nm – 1 mm	$10^{12} – 10^{14}$	TV remotes, several types of imaging, satellites
Microwave	1 mm – 1 m	$10^8 – 10^{11}$	microwave ovens, cell phones, Wi-Fi
Radio	1 m – 1 km	$1000 – 10^8$	radios, TV

While the majority of examples in this chapter will use the visible part of the spectrum, the concepts discussed can apply to any of the others as well.

The Wave Behavior of Light

Chances are, when you think of EM radiation you think of it as waves of radiation (one region is even called micro*wave*). Waves are defined by three parts. The **wavelength (λ)**, as the name implies, describes how long a wave is. Visible light, for example, occurs in a range of 400-700 nm. The **frequency (ν)** describes the number of times a wave cycles through in a second. The units of frequency are inverse seconds (1/s or s^{-1}; it's usually not written as "cycles/s"), which is also known as a Hertz (Hz), after the German physicist Heinrich Hertz (1857 – 1894).

$$1 \ s^{-1} = 1 \ Hz.$$

Finally, there's the **amplitude**, which describes the height of the wave.

Looking at the two waves below,

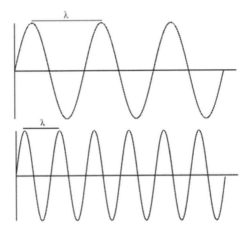

if both are occurring over the same period of time, we can see an inverse relationship between frequency and wavelength. Waves with longer wavelengths have shorter frequencies (fewer cycles per second).

$$\lambda \propto \frac{1}{\nu}$$

As we saw several times in Chapter 6, a constant is required to convert a proportionality into an equality. In the case of wavelength and frequency, the constant happens to be the speed of light (c): 3.00×10^8 m/s.

$$\lambda = c \cdot \frac{1}{\nu}$$

or

$$c = \lambda\nu = 3.00 \times 10^8 \text{ m/s}$$

Example: If a wave has a wavelength of 345 nm, what is its frequency, in Hertz?

As mentioned previously, with most calculations it's very important to be mindful of units. To get an answer in Hz (s^{-1}), the units of length must cancel out in our calculation. It doesn't matter what unit of length you pick, as long as it's the same for both c and λ. In problems like this, I typically convert nanometers to meters.

$$345 \text{ nm} \times \frac{10^{-9} \text{ m}}{1 \text{ nm}} = 3.45 \times 10^{-7} \text{ m}$$

Now we can use the speed of light equation to find frequency.

$$c = \lambda\nu$$
$$3.00 \times 10^8 \text{ m/s} = (3.45 \times 10^{-7} \text{ m})\nu$$

$$\nu = \frac{3.00 \times 10^8 \text{ m/s}}{3.45 \times 10^{-7} \text{ m}}$$

$$\nu = 8.70 \times 10^{14} \text{ s}^{-1} \text{ or } 8.70 \times 10^{14} \text{ Hz}$$

The Particle Behavior of Light

In 1900, physicist Max Planck (with a little help five years later from Albert Einstein) discovered that EM radiation could behave as *particles* in addition to behaving as waves. Planck discovered that radiation was **quantized**, meaning it was absorbed or released by a system in fixed amounts. We call these tiny particles of light **photons**. While the term "quantization," might be a new word for you, it isn't an entirely foreign concept. When you climb a ladder, for example, your height from the ground is quantized since each rung is a fixed distance from the ground (sure, if you've got the arm strength you can pull up your feet and dangle between the rungs, but that's cheating).

The energy of a photon can be calculated using the equation

$$E_{photon} = h\nu$$

Here, ν is still frequency and h is a constant, usually referred to as Planck's constant, 6.63×10^{-34} J·s. For example, in our previous example, we calculated the frequency of a 345 nm wave to be 8.70×10^{14} Hz. A photon emitting at this frequency would be

$$E_{photon} = (6.63 \times 10^{-34} \text{ J} \cdot \text{s})(8.70 \times 10^{14} \text{ s}^{-1})$$
$$E_{photon} = 5.77 \times 10^{-19} \text{ J}$$

That's a pretty small number, so it's common to express the energy of photons on the mole scale.

$$\frac{5.77 \times 10^{-19}}{1 \text{ photon}} \times \frac{6.022 \times 10^{23}}{1 \text{ mol}} = 3.47 \times 10^5 \text{ J/mol} \ (347 \text{ kJ/mol})$$

Try It Yourself

P1. Convert the following wavelengths to frequencies (in Hz):
a) 81.0 pm, b) 442 nm, c) 7.52 mm

P2. Convert the following frequencies, given in Hz, to wavelengths (in m):
a) 749.21, b) 4.043×10^5, c) 1.349×10^{10}, d) 9.23×10^{14}

P3. Calculate the energy of a photon with each of the frequencies from P2.

P4. Calculate the energy of a mole of photons (in J) with each of the frequencies from P2.

Part 2: The Bohr Model

Emission Spectra of Elements

Humans have known for a long, long time that different elements give off different colors of light when heated, going back to at least the invention of fireworks by Chinese alchemists. For example, when copper compounds are placed in a flame, they give off a green light, sodium compounds are yellow, while lithium compounds are purple. Neon gives off an orange glow when you run a current through it (any other colors from neon signs come from the color of the glass) and when hydrogen burns it gives off a purple color. These colors that you see aren't just a single wavelength from the visible spectrum, but rather a mixture of several different wavelengths.

As you may already know, visible light can be separated into individual wavelengths by passing it through a prism. Raindrops act as prisms to give rainbows, separating white light into the entire visible spectrum. And of course there's the famous cover to Pink Floyd's *Dark Side of the Moon*. The light emitted by heated elements can be separated in a similar manner. If, for example, you take the purple light we see from hydrogen and pass it through a prism, you can see the different wavelengths that give you that purple color. We call this set of wavelengths an **emission spectrum** or line spectrum. Every element has its own unique emission spectrum.

The Rydberg Equation

In 1888, physicist Johannes Rydberg studied the emission spectrum of hydrogen and discovered that each line in that spectrum fit the following equation.

$$\frac{1}{\lambda} = R_H \left(\frac{1}{n_A^2} - \frac{1}{n_B^2} \right)$$

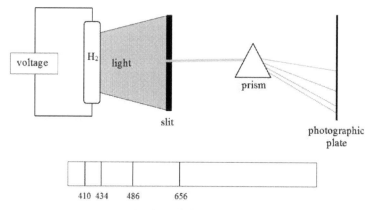

Emission spectrum of hydrogen (visible region), nm

410 434   486   656

As before, λ is the wavelength, while R$_H$ is a constant, 1.097 x 10^7 m^{-1}. The two *n*'s are simply any two whole-number integers (1, 2, 3, etc.) where n$_B$> n$_A$. You get the visible part of the spectrum when n_A = 2. For example, when the two values of *n* are 2 and 4, we get the green line of hydrogen's emission spectrum.

$$\frac{1}{\lambda} = (1.097 \times 10^7 \text{ m}^{-1})\left(\frac{1}{2^2} - \frac{1}{4^2}\right)$$

$$\frac{1}{\lambda} = 2.057 \times 10^6 \text{ m}^{-1}$$

$$\lambda = 4.862 \times 10^{-7} \text{ m} = 486.2 \text{ nm}$$

Keep in mind, this equation is based on *data*, not theory. In other words, Rydberg took hydrogen's emission spectrum, examined the numbers, and discovered an equation that matched the observed wavelengths, relating them to these mystery integers, *n*.

So, going back to our discussion of the scientific method (Chapter 1), we have a series of observations. The next step would be to ask, "What the heck is going on here?" What is it about atoms that cause each to have its own unique emission spectra? And what exactly is behind those n's in Rydberg's equation? Scientists of the late 19th and early 20th centuries wondered this as well, and in 1913 a guy named Niels Bohr figured out a big piece of the puzzle.

The Bohr Model of the Atom

Physicist Niels Bohr (1885-1962) is famous for a couple of reasons. One was his series of arguments with Einstein that most historians like to describe as friendly (many know Einstein's famous quote, "God doesn't play dice with the universe;" as legend tells it, Bohr's response was "Don't tell God what to do with his dice."). His other place in history was his theory connecting Rydberg's equation with the electronic structure of the atom.

Bohr believed that the energy of an electron was quantized, just like light, meaning electrons could only possess fixed amounts of energy, which we call **energy levels**. You can also think of energy levels as being the equivalent of fixed distances from the nucleus. Electrons can only occupy these fixed energy levels, "orbiting" the nucleus similar to the way the planets orbit the sun. However, unlike the orbits of our solar system, these energy levels can hold more than a single electron.

The lowest allowed energy level (the closest to the nucleus) would be n = 1, the second lowest n = 2, and so on. The energy an electron would possess (E) at a given level (n) can be calculated as

$$E_n = -\frac{B}{n^2}$$

where B is a constant, 2.18 x 10[-18] J. The allowed energy for level 2 (n = 2), for example, would be

$$E_n = -\frac{2.18 \times 10^{-18} \text{ J}}{2^2} = -5.45 \times 10^{-19} \text{ J}$$

The negative value of E_n is due to the idea that an electron in an atom has a lower energy than a "free" electron (one not interacting with a nucleus). In other words, the negative sign is a relative term and doesn't imply that an electron possesses a "negative" amount of energy.

To explain the lines of hydrogen's emission spectrum, Bohr said that electrons are usually in the lowest possible energy level, known as the **ground state**. This ground state doesn't have to be n = 1. If that level's already full it would be n = 2, and so on. If an electron absorbs a photon of energy (like being exposed to a flame or current), it "jumps" to a higher energy level, which we call the **excited state**.

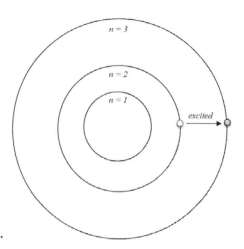

When the electron "cools off" and returns to its ground state, it'll release that energy, and if it's within the visible part of the EM spectrum, you'll see it as some color of light.

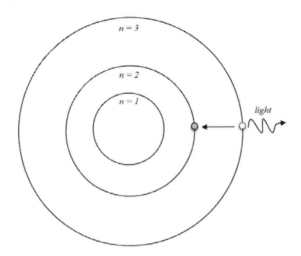

The energy of the photon absorbed (and later released) by the electron is just the difference between the two levels. If we let n_A be the ground state and n_B be the excited state, similar to what was done in Rydberg's equation, we end up with

$$\Delta E = E_{n_B} - E_{n_A}$$

$$\Delta E = \frac{-B}{n_B^2} - \frac{-B}{n_A^2}$$

or

$$\Delta E = B \left(\frac{1}{n_A^2} - \frac{1}{n_B^2} \right)$$

So let's say a hydrogen electron is excited from the second to the fourth energy level. The amount of energy absorbed (and later released) would be

$$\Delta E = 2.18 \times 10^{-18} \left(\frac{1}{2^2} - \frac{1}{4^2} \right) = 4.09 \times 10^{-19} \, J$$

We can use Planck's equation to find the frequency of this photon

$$E = h\nu$$
$$4.09 \times 10^{-19} \text{ J} = (6.63 \times 10^{-34} \text{ J} \cdot \text{s})\nu$$
$$\nu = 6.17 \times 10^{14} \text{ s}^{-1}$$

If we go on to find its wavelength, we get the same one obtained by Rydberg's equation for these two values of n.

$$c = \lambda\nu$$
$$3.00 \times 10^8 \text{ m/s} = \lambda(6.17 \times 10^{14} \text{ s}^{-1})$$
$$\lambda = 4.86 \times 10^{-7} \text{ m} = 486 \text{ nm}$$

So imagine hydrogen's electron, resting in a ground state of $n = 1$. You run a current through it and it absorbs energy to jump to an excited state, and then releases that heat to return to its ground state. But if that energy source is still present, it might actually absorb more energy *before* returning to the first energy level. Maybe it only makes it to the second. You can picture that electron (along with the electrons of the other hydrogen atoms in your sample), absorbing and releasing energy, zigzagging up and down the different energy levels to give you all the possible lines in its spectrum.

Problem solved, right? Well, not quite. While Bohr did get a Nobel Prize for his work, his theory could only successfully explain the lines of hydrogen's emission spectrum (and remember, that's all Rydberg's equation was good for, as well). It couldn't account for all of the observed lines in the spectra of any other element. The fact that it worked for hydrogen, though, meant that he was close, and over the decades that followed Bohr and other scientists were able to fill in the missing pieces of his theory. They just had to look at electrons a little differently.

Try It Yourself

P5. Using the Rydberg equation, calculate the wavelengths (in m) from hydrogen's emission spectrum that have the following values of n: a) 1 and 5, b) 2 and 4, c) 3 and 6

P6. Using Bohr's equation, calculate the energy (in J) required for a hydrogen electron to jump between the following energy levels: a) 1 to 5, b) 2 to 4, c) 3 to 6

P7. Using Planck's equation and your answers from P6, calculate the wavelength (in m) of a photon released during these transitions.

Part 3: The Dual Nature
of Electrons

Electrons as Waves

In 1924, Louis de Broglie proposed a pretty radical idea: electrons, like light, had a dual nature. Before then, scientists essentially thought of electrons as these tiny particles that "orbit" a nucleus (just as you probably do) and thought of them as only having particle-like behavior. But de Broglie realized that electrons also exhibited *wave behavior*. Specifically, he realized that electrons behaved as **standing waves** – waves that close at the same point it begins.

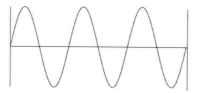

A nonstanding wave would be one that ended anywhere else, like this one…

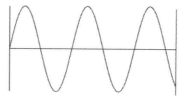

If you think of electrons as orbiting the nucleus in a circular path, the allowed energy levels that Bohr discovered are the only distances from the nucleus that result in a standing wave, which can be pictured as a single, continuous path.

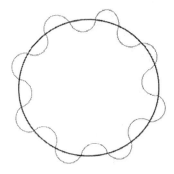

At any other distance, the wave will behave as a nonstanding wave. If this happens, every successive "orbit" would overlap with the previous one to some degree, which in turn causes part of the wave to cancel out.

Overlap

As a result, this circular wave will grow smaller and smaller until the orbits finally reaches zero amplitude. Essentially this means the electron would eventually spiral into the nucleus and no longer exist. With this discovery, scientists were soon able to understand how electrons arranged themselves around a nucleus and explain what was missing in Bohr's model.

The Schrödinger Wave Equation

In 1926, Erwin Schrödinger developed an equation that allowed one to determine the most probable location of an electron as it "orbits" a nucleus. You'll notice that I keep putting the word *orbit* in quotation marks. That's because electrons aren't thought to really orbit a nucleus like planets orbit a sun, although we still use that term. This model is purely mathematical in nature, even though we often use illustrations to emphasize some of its important points.

You might also notice that I said Schrödinger's equation found the most *probable* location of an electron. This is because of a discovery by Werner Heisenberg today known as the **Heisenberg uncertainty principle**, which states that one cannot determine the exact location and momentum of a particle simultaneously. There will always be some degree of uncertainty. Even something like a baseball being thrown has *some* degree of uncertainty, albeit one that's very small and essentially insignificant. However, as an object gets smaller that uncertainty will increase, so that when you get to something the size of an electron, which is only 9 x 10^{-28} grams, that uncertainty becomes very significant.

Schrödinger's theory involves equations that most would see as complicated, to say the least. Here's a sample

$$p^2 \Psi = \left(p_x^2 + p_y^2 + p_z^2\right) \Psi = -\hbar^2 \left(\frac{\delta^2}{\delta x^2} + \frac{\delta^2}{\delta y^2} + \frac{\delta^2}{\delta z^2}\right) \Psi = -\hbar^2 \nabla^2 \Psi$$

If this makes complete sense to you, you're probably either a) already the owner of a graduate degree in math or physics, b) not worried about a General Chemistry course adversely affecting your 4.0 grade point average, or c) the janitor that inspired Matt Damon's character in *Good Will Hunting*. Fortunately, for the rest of us, we don't have to use the Schrödinger equation directly to get a general understanding of how electrons arrange themselves in an atom. Some will find it odd that we're looking at an equation (and the mathematical model that comes from it) in a purely qualitative fashion, but this isn't really the first time you've done this. Recall from Chapter 1 that many scientific laws and theories (such as Newton's law of gravity) are mathematical in nature, but can be understood or explained without performing any actual calculations.

Part 4: The Quantum Model

Quantum Numbers

Quantum numbers are used to describe an electron and its probable location around a nucleus. We'll discuss four of them, three of which come from the Schrödinger equation. How they're used mathematically isn't really a concern for us. In this chapter, we're going to use them strictly in a qualitative sense.

One way to think of quantum numbers is they give you an electron's "address." For example, the address of the U.S. president is

1600 Pennsylvania Avenue
Washington, DC 20500

The bottom part of the address tells you the city and state, while the top line is a little more specific, telling you the street in that city, as well as the building on that street. As we'll see, quantum numbers can—more or less—tell us the same thing about an electron's location.

The Principle Quantum Number

The first quantum number we'll discuss was actually introduced in Part 2. The **principle quantum number (n)** is essentially the same n used by Rydberg, then later used by Bohr to describe the allowed energy levels of an electron, though today we often use the term **shell** instead of "level" as a way to emphasize the fact that they're actually three-dimensional in nature and not flat, 2-D orbits.

As before, n can be any positive whole number integer

$$n = 1, 2, 3...$$

The principle quantum number essentially describes the *size* of the shell. Larger values n have larger shells (in other words, their electrons get further away from the nucleus). This isn't an entirely foreign concept. The further away a planet is from the sun, the larger its orbit will be.

The Angular Momentum Quantum Number

Bohr's theory accounted for the presence of shells (levels), but what he didn't realize at the time was that these shells can contain various types of *subshells*. Going back to our address analogy, it's similar to how different building on a street can have a different number of rooms.

The **angular momentum quantum number (l)** is used to describe the number and type of subshells in a given shell. For any shell, n, the allowed values of l can be zero to n-1

$$l = 0, 1, \ldots n\text{-}1$$

As before, these numbers are used mathematically in some equation, but that's not important here. We're looking at this model in a much more qualitative sense. In this case, the number of allowed values of l tells us how many subshells are present in a given shell. For instance, in the first shell ($n = 1$), l can only equal 0. Because we only have one allowed value of l, there can only be one type of subshell in the first shell.

n	allowed l's	translation
1	0	One subshell in 1st shell

In the second shell, $n = 2$, there are two allowed values of l: 0 and 1. Therefore the second shell has two types of subshells. And so on…

n	allowed l's	translation
1	0	One subshell in 1st shell
2	0,1	Two subshells in 2nd shell
3	0,1,2	Three subshells in 3rd shell
		etc.

Notice a trend, here? The nth shell has n number of subshells. We'll soon see that there are several convenient trends to help us understand this model.

To make it easier for one to describe a given subshell, letters are often assigned to each possible value of l. The first four values (0-3) are assigned the following letters

$$l: \quad 0 \quad 1 \quad 2 \quad 3$$
$$\text{symbol:} \quad s \quad p \quad d \quad f$$

These letters actually stand for something (or used to), but it's not really worth going into at the moment. After $l=3$, it was decided to just go alphabetical after f

$$l: \quad 0 \quad 1 \quad 2 \quad 3 \quad 4 \quad 5$$
$$\text{symbol:} \quad s \quad p \quad d \quad f \quad g \quad h \quad \text{etc...}$$

So instead of saying "the $l = 1$ subshell in the 3rd shell," we can simply say "subshell 3p." The number tells you the shell while the letter represents the subshell (notice that, conveniently enough, n represents the *number* and l represent the *letter*).

n	allowed l's	symbol
1	0	1s
2	0	2s
	1	2p
3	0	3s
	1	3p
	2	3d
	etc.	

The Magnetic Quantum Number

Just as different shells can have a different number of subshells, different subshells have a different number of **orbitals**. The term *orbital* is sort of a throwback to Bohr's theory, but don't forget that physical orbits don't really exist. Here, an orbital is defined as the region around a nucleus where a given electron spends most of its time (its most probable locations). The **magnetic quantum number (m_l)** tells us how many orbitals are in a given subshell, similar to how l tells us the number of subshells in a shell.

For any given subshell (l), the allowed values of m_l are $-l$ to $+l$, including zero.

$$m_l = -l...0...+l$$

The number of allowed values equals the number of orbitals in that subshell. For example, an *s* subshell has $l = 0$. The only allowed value of m_l is 0. This means that an *s* subshell is just a single orbital. A *p* subshell ($l = 1$), however, has three values of m_l: -1, 0, and +1, which tells us that a *p* subshell contains three orbitals.

subshell	allowed m_l	translation
s ($l = 0$)	0	one s orbital
p ($l = 1$)	-1, 0, 1	three p orbitals
d ($l = 2$)	-2, -1, 0, 1, 2	five d orbitals
	etc.	

Notice another handy trend: the number of orbitals in any subshell (l) equals $2(l) + 1$

Different types of orbitals have different "shapes," or areas where a given electron will spend most of its time. For example, as you plot out all the probable locations for an *s* electron, you get an overall spherical pattern.

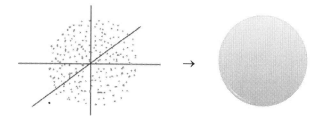

It should be noted (or admitted) that the above plot is an extreme simplification of an actual plot for a 1s electron, which would contain many, many more points.

For a *p* electron, you get a "dumbbell" or 3D figure-eight shape for each of the three orbitals.

All three orbitals are perpendicular to one another, so you can picture each one lying on one of the three axes in 3D space.

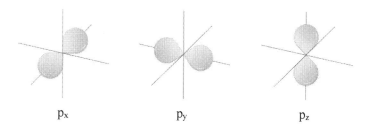

p_x p_y p_z

The Electron Spin Quantum Number

The fourth quantum number that we'll discuss actually doesn't come from the Schrödinger equation and is independent of the other three. The **electron spin quantum number** (m_s) describes the two possible "spins" of an electron that give rise to two possible types of magnetic fields.

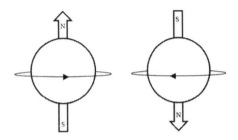

These two possible spins are assigned m_s values of $+\frac{1}{2}$ and $-\frac{1}{2}$. Like the other quantum numbers we discuss, these two numbers have some mathematical meaning that's beyond the scope of this textbook. What's important to us is that this quantum number only has two values. More on that later.

Bohr's Model Revisited

The discovery of subshells and orbitals eventually led to a better understanding of why Bohr's theory could only successfully predict the emission spectrum of hydrogen. Bohr's original model only consisted of single energy levels for each value of n. Earlier in this chapter, this was illustrated using circular orbits, but here we'll use a ladder-like diagram.

It was later discovered that these levels (shells) actually contained sublevels (subshells) and sub-sublevels (orbitals). For a one-electron system like hydrogen (or any hypothetical ion, such as He^+, Li^{2+}, etc), the subshells of each shell are **degenerate**, meaning they all have the same energy, as shown below.

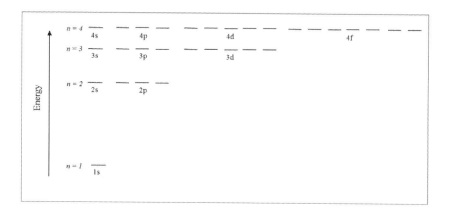

So when a hydrogen electron jumps from shell 2 to 3, it doesn't matter if it's actually happening between 2s and 3s, or 2s and 3p, and so on. It's the same difference in energy (ΔE), so you'll see the same wavelength of light emitted regardless of what the actual subshells are.

For systems with two or more electrons around that nucleus, however, the subshells are no longer degenerate, due to things like repulsive effects between the like-charged electrons, and the different shapes of orbitals that can affect the attraction between an electron and the protons in the nucleus (an effect known as *electron shielding*). In such cases, the subshells within each shell are no longer degenerate, with the energy of each subshell increasing as l increases (s < p < d < f ...etc.).

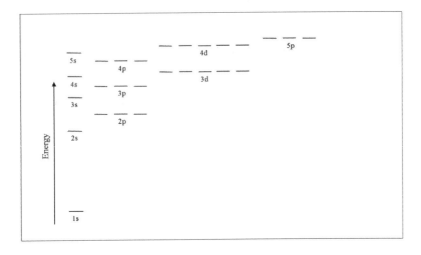

Now when an electron jumps between shells 1 and 2, the actual subshell it's in *will* matter. A jump between 2s and 3s, for instance, will have a different ΔE than one between 2s and 3p, which can potentially give rise to two lines in that element's emission spectrum. And as the electron jumps further out to higher shells that contain more subshells, the number of possible transitions increase, which in turn increases the number of possible emission lines.

Try It Yourself

P8. What are the allowed values of l when n is a) 4, b) 8, c) 12

P9. What letters are assigned to each of the subshells from question P8.

P10. What are the allowed values of m_l when l is a) 3, b) 6, c) 8

P11. What are the values of n and l for the following subshells: a) 3p, b) 5f, c) 7g, d) 9j

P12. How many orbitals are present in the following subshells:
a) *f*, b) *h*, c) *m*

Learning Beyond

- Many parts of the EM spectrum are used by scientists for chemical analysis, such as X-ray crystallography, IR spectroscopy, and UV spectroscopy. Find out how.
- We talked about the shapes of *s* and *p* orbitals. Look up the shapes of *d* and *f* orbitals.
- Learn more about Max Planck, Johannes Rydberg, Niels Bohr, Louis de Broglie, Erwin Schrödinger (especially his cat), and Werner Heisenberg.

Test Your Skills

★ Slow-pitch

1. Convert the following frequencies, given in Hz, to wavelengths (in m): a) 5.02×10^6, b) 7.44×10^{10}, c) 2.91×10^{14}

XP: +3 each

2. Calculate the energy of a photon (in Joules) with each of the frequencies from question 1.

XP: +3 each

3. Convert the following wavelengths to frequencies (in Hz):
a) 874 pm, b) 661 nm, c) 803 μm

XP: +3 each

4. A photon has a frequency of 1.08×10^8 Hz. Calculate the energy (in J) of a) 1 photon, b) 1 mole of photons, c) 5 mole of photons.

XP: + 3 each

5. Which line in hydrogen's emission spectrum (in nm) have the following sets of n: a) 1 and 3, b) 3 and 7, c) 2 and 5

XP: +3 each

6. Calculate the energy (in J) absorbed by a hydrogen electron that jumps between each of the following energy levels from question 5.

XP: +3 each

7. Identify—by letter—the subshells that are present in a) the 4th shell, b) the 7th shell, c) the 9th shell.

XP: +3

8. How many orbitals are present in each of the following subshells: a) g, b) k, c) l

XP +4

9. Complete the following table:

	Subshell	n	l	m_l
a)	4d	___	___	_____
b)	___	3	1	_____
c)	___	5	___	-3, -2, -1, 0, 1, 2, 3

XP: +3 each blank

★XP: _____

If your XP is 109 or higher, maybe you can handle...

★★Fastballs

10. Planck's equation can also be written with respect to wavelength instead of frequency. Derive that equation.

XP: +4

11. Calculate the energy (in J) of a photon with the following wavelengths: a) 671 nm, b) 39.3 cm, c) 9.8×10^4 pm

XP: +4 each

12. At what frequency (in Hz) will 3.8 mol of photons emit 5.2 kJ of energy?

XP: +4

13. A hydrogen electron is excited to the 9th energy level then releases light with a wavelength of 1.818 μm. Calculate its new ground state.

XP: +4

14. If a hydrogen electron residing in the first energy level absorbs 2.04×10^{-18} J of energy, what will be its excited state?

XP: +4

15. Calculate the frequency of light (in Hz) emitted by a hydrogen electron that's moving between the following energy levels: a) 1 and 2, b) 3 and 5.

XP +4 each

16. Which of the following set of quantum numbers are allowed? For those that aren't explain why.
a) $n = 4$, $l = 3$, $m_l = -2$, b) $n = 2$, $l = 2$, $m_l = 1$, c) $n = 3$, $l = 2$, $m_l = 3$, d) $n = 5$, $l = 1$, $m_l = 0$

XP: +4 each

17. Which of the following subshells cannot theoretically exist? For those that don't, explain why.
a) 8f, b) 6j, c) 9k, d) 7m

XP: +4 each

★★XP: _____   Total XP: _____

If your total XP is 160 or higher, let's see if you can handle...

★★★Sliders

18. Calculate the total number of orbitals in each of the first 5 shells. What trend do you see?

XP: +10

19. When an electron is excited from the 3rd shell to the 4th, how many emission lines would you predict for a one-electron system? For a multi-electron system?

XP: +10

20. A hydrogen electron, originally in the first energy level, absorbs 2.093 x 10^{-18} J of heat, and then releases light with a wavelength of 1,280 nm. What is its new ground state?

XP: +10

21. Most cellular phones transmit at a frequency of around 1800 GHz (G = Giga = 10^9). As of 2011, approximately 5.6 billion are being used globally. Using this data, estimate the total energy being released by these devises a) per photon, b) per mole of photons.

XP: +10

★ ★ ★ XP: _____   Total XP: _____

If your total XP is 190 or higher: Level up!

Achievement Unlocked: I'm So Excited.
Completed Chapter 8

You're ready to learn about electron configurations.

Chapter 9
Electron Arrangement
(Part II)

Part 1: Electron Configurations

Electrons are believed to fill the orbitals around a nucleus in their order of increasing energy, an idea commonly known as the **Aufbau principle** (*aufbau* is German for "building up"). In a perfect world (for students, anyway), that would mean electrons simply fill up the first shell, then the second, and so on. However, looking back at our discussion on multi-electron systems at the end of Chapter 8, notice that as *n* increases the shells get closer together. With multi-electron systems, this will cause a sort of overlap to occur between shells. For example, subshell 3d ends up being slightly higher in energy than 4s.

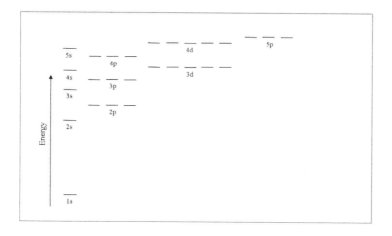

As a result, the actual order of subshells, up to 7p, is

1s 2s 2p 3s 3p 4s 3d 4p 5s 4d 5p 6s 4f 5d 6p 7s 5f 6d 7p

In 1925, Austrian physicist Wolfgang Pauli discovered a fundamental rule for electron arrangement, now known as the **Pauli exclusion principle**, which says that no two electrons can have the exact same set of quantum numbers. This means that any three electrons can occupy the same shell,

Electron A $n = 3$
Electron B $n = 3$
Electron C $n = 3$

and can be in the same subshell,

Electron A $n = 3$ $l = 2$
Electron B $n = 3$ $l = 2$
Electron C $n = 3$ $l = 2$

but if you try to put them in the same orbital

Electron A $n = 3$ $l = 2$ $m_l = 0$
Electron B $n = 3$ $l = 2$ $m_l = 0$
Electron C $n = 3$ $l = 2$ $m_l = 0$

you run into a problem because there are only two values of m_s

Electron A $n = 3$ $l = 2$ $m_l = 0$ $m_s = +\frac{1}{2}$
Electron B $n = 3$ $l = 2$ $m_l = 0$ $m_s = -\frac{1}{2}$
Electron C $n = 3$ $l = 2$ $m_l = 0$ $m_s = ??$

Therefore, *no orbital can hold more than 2 electrons.* Any additional electrons will violate the Pauli exclusion principle. This means the maximum electrons allowed in each subshell are

subshell	number of orbitals	max. electrons
s	1	2
p	3	6
d	5	10
f	7	14
	etc.	

From the Aufbau and Pauli exclusion principles, the predicted filling order (or **electron configuration**) for the first

118 electrons is shown below. The superscript notes the number of electrons present in a given subshell.

$$1s^2\, 2s^2\, 2p^6\, 3s^2\, 3p^6\, 4s^2\, 3d^{10}\, 4p^6\, 5s^2\, 4d^{10}\, 5p^6$$
$$6s^2\, 4f^{14}\, 5d^{10}\, 6p^6\, 7s^2\, 5f^{14}\, 6d^{10}\, 7p^6$$

For any of the previous 117 elements, you simply start with the lowest energy subshell (1s) and work your way up the order until you run out of electrons.

Example: Write the predicted electron configuration for each of the following atoms: a) H, b) Li, c) S, d) Fe, e) Se

a) A hydrogen atom only has one electron (see Chapter 2), and according to the Aufbau principle it should go in the lowest energy orbital, 1s. Therefore, hydrogen's electron configuration is

$$1s^1$$

b) Lithium has a total of three electrons. The first two should go in 1s

$$1s^2$$

That leaves one more electron, which will go into the next subshell, 2s

$$1s^2 2s^1$$

c) Sulfur has 16 electrons. Again, the first two will go into subshell 1s

$$1s^2$$

and the next two into 2s

$$1s^2 \mathbf{2s^2}$$

Four down, twelve to go. Next up is subshell 2p, which you'll recall can hold up to *six* electrons since it has a total of three orbitals.

$$1s^22s^2\mathbf{2p^6}$$

The next two go into 3s

$$1s^22s^22p^6\mathbf{3s^2}$$

and finally the last four will go into 3p.

$$1s^22s^22p^63s^23p^4$$

d) Iron has 26 electrons. The first twelve go into the first 4 subshells, just as it did with sulfur.

$$1s^22s^22p^63s^2$$

The next six go into 3p

$$1s^22s^22p^63s^2\mathbf{3p^6}$$

We have eight left, but they *don't* all go into subshell 3d. Remember, this is where the overlap starts to occur. Subshell 4s actually comes next and, like any s subshell, it can hold 2 electrons in its one orbital

$$1s^22s^22p^63s^23p^6\mathbf{4s^2}$$

That leaves six electrons that are predicted to go into 3d.

$$1s^22s^22p^63s^23p^64s^23d^6$$

e) Selenium has 34 electrons. The first twenty go into the same subshells as before

$$1s^2 2s^2 2p^6 3s^2 3p^6 4s^2$$

Next up is the 3d subshell, which has 5 orbitals that can hold a total of 10 electrons.

$$1s^2 2s^2 2p^6 3s^2 3p^6 4s^2 \mathbf{3d^{10}}$$

There are four electrons left, which will go into 4p

$$1s^2 2s^2 2p^6 3s^2 3p^6 4s^2 3d^{10} 4p^4$$

In this chapter, we'll refer to configurations written this way as **standard notation**. Later, we'll discuss a couple of other ways to write electron configurations.

Valence Electrons

Valence electrons are the electrons used by an atom for chemical bonding (more on that in Chapter 10). For atoms of main group elements, this number is the *total* number of electrons in the highest shell (n) of its electron configuration (it's not as simple with transition elements, but in this book we generally assume that those form ionic compounds, so they won't be discussed here). Looking at our previous examples, hydrogen's highest occupied shell is $n = 1$, which has one electron. Lithium's highest is $n = 2$, which also has one electron.

Atom	Valence Electrons
H	1
Li	1

Sulfur's highest shell is $n = 3$, which has a *total* of 6 electrons – two in 3s and four in 3p.

Atom	Valence Electrons
H	1
Li	1
S	6

Similarly, selenium's highest shell is $n = 4$, and it also has a total of 6 electrons – two in 4s and 4 in 4p.

Atom	Valence Electrons
H	1
Li	1
S	6
Se	6

Now, look at these examples and compare their valence electrons to their location in the periodic table. Do you notice anything?

Part 2: Electron Configurations & the Periodic Table

Looking back at our examples at the end of Part 1, notice that lithium and hydrogen both end in ns^1 and, therefore, both have one valence electron. In the periodic table, these elements are found in group 1A. In fact, if you predict the electron configurations for any other group 1A element, you'll see they too have one valence electron in subshell ns^1, such as sodium:

$$Na: 1s^2 2s^2 2p^6 3s^1$$

Similarly, sulfur and selenium both end in np^4 and both have six valence electrons. Both elements are found in group 6A of the periodic table. In fact, if you predict the electron configuration of any other 6A element, guess how many valence electrons it will have? Nitrogen is in group 5A. How many electrons would you guess it has?

$$N: 1s^2 2s^2 2p^3$$

In the case of transition metals, you'll notice there isn't a similar correlation between valence electrons and group number.

$$Fe: 1s^2 2s^2 2p^6 3s^2 3p^6 4s^2 3d^6$$

Actually, if you predict the electron configurations of any other transition metal, you'll see that they're all predicted to have two valence electrons, since a higher s subshell fills before any remaining electrons go in a d. Take molybdenum, for instance,

$$Mo: 1s^2 2s^2 2p^6 3s^2 3p^6 4s^2 3d^{10} 4p^6 5s^2 4d^4$$

There is another trend, however. Iron ends with six electrons in a d subshell ($3d^6$) and it's in the sixth group of transition metals.

Similarly, molybdenum is in the fourth group of transition metals and ends in d^4. While we're counting groups, how many groups of transition metals are there? And how many electrons did we say a d subshell could hold?

Now look at the main group elements (the A groups). See how it's split across the transition metals, with two groups on the left side of the B groups and six on the right, which happens to be the maximum number of electrons that the s and p subshells can hold, respectively. Looking at sulfur and selenium again, notice that group 6A is the fourth main group right of the transition metals. Finally, look down at the inner transition elements (the lanthanide and actinide series). There are fourteen groups, the same number that the f subshell can hold.

Back in Chapter 2, we discussed how Mendeleev devised his periodic table based on common physical and chemical properties. We went on to say that our modern table is essentially Mendeleev's with some minor tweaking. Those tweaks occurred due to our understanding of electron arrangements. The reason, for example, that the alkali metals have similar properties is because they have similar electron configurations.

The Periodic Table Revisited

Since the modern periodic table is based on electron configurations, it can be used to help us remember the order that subshells fill. First, we divide the periodic table into four "blocks." The first two main groups are dubbed the "s block," the six on the other end are the "p block," the transition metals are the "d block," and the inner transition group is the "f block" (I know it sounds like a prison; hopefully you don't find any irony or symbolism in that).

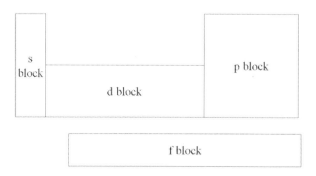

In general, you can get the filling order by starting at the top of the table and working your way down, row by row. When you pass through the *s* or *p* block, the *n* will be the same as the period. When you pass through the *d* block, the *n* will be equal to the period minus one and for the *f* block it will be period minus two.

s and p blocks	n = period
d block	n = period−1
f block	n = period−2

There are, however, two exceptions to keep in mind. The first is with helium. If the table was based *solely* on predicted configurations, helium would be placed in group 2A since, like the alkaline earth metals, its configuration ends in ns^2. Chemically, however, it makes more sense to place it with the other inert gases in group 8A. The other exception occurs around the *f* block elements. Based on what we've discussed thus far, the Aufbau principle would predict that lanthanum's last electron would go into a 4f orbital and actinium's would be in a 5f orbital, but they're actually in 5d and 6d, respectively. That's because an atom's actual electron configuration isn't always what you'd predict it to be (more on that later). If this wasn't the case, the *f* block would actually begin immediately after the *s* block with lanthanum and actinium. Instead, it ends up following the first group of *d* block elements, with cerium and thorium.

Example: Predict the electron configuration of Germanium (Ge).

When using the periodic table as a guide, it helps to start at the end of the configuration. Germanium is in the fourth period and in the second group of the p block. From this we can predict that its configuration will end with $4p^2$

$$...4p^2$$

Even though there's an exception with the first period, hopefully you've seen enough examples by this point to know that every configuration begins with $1s^2$ (except hydrogen, of course).

$$\mathbf{1s^2}...4p^2$$

To get everything in between, we continue on to period 2, which passes through the s and p blocks, where n is equal to the period. What's more, since there are two columns in the s block and six in the p block, we have a way to remember how many electrons each subshell can hold.

$$1s^2\mathbf{2s^22p^6}...4p^2$$

Now we move to period 3, where we again only pass through the s and p blocks.

$$1s^22s^22p^6\mathbf{3s^23p^6}...4p^2$$

Next is period 4. First, we pass through the s block ($4s^2$)

$$1s^22s^22p^63s^23p^6\mathbf{4s^2}...4p^2$$

followed by the d block, but remember that in the d block n is equal to the period-1 ($3d^{10}$). Also, there are ten groups in the d

block, which reminds us that this subshell can hold up to ten electrons.

$$1s^22s^22p^63s^23p^64s^2\mathbf{3d^{10}}...4p^2$$

Finally, we've reached the fourth row of the p block, which is where we predicted the configuration would end.

$$1s^22s^22p^63s^23p^64s^23d^{10}4p^2$$

Try It Yourself

P1. Using the periodic table as a guide, determine the subshell that each of the following atom's electron configuration should end with: a) phosphorus, b) calcium, c) iodine, d) mercury

P2. For each of the elements in question P1, use the periodic table to determine how many electrons should be in the last subshell of their electron configurations.

P3. Write the predicted electron configurations for each of the elements in P1 (in standard notation).

P4. Determine the number of valence electrons for each of the elements in P1.

Part 3: Other Ways to Write Electron Configurations

Rare Gas Notation

Comparing the electron configurations of neon, magnesium, and aluminum, we see that they're identical up to the first three subshells.

$$
\begin{array}{ll}
\text{Ne} & 1s^2 2s^2 2p^6 \\
\text{Mg} & 1s^2 2s^2 2p^6 3s^2 \\
\text{Al} & 1s^2 2s^2 2p^6 3s^2 3p^1
\end{array}
$$

An alternate method of writing an element's electron configuration, known as a **rare gas notation**, is to put the rare gas that immediately precedes it in brackets, and then write the remainder of the configuration as usual. Magnesium and aluminum's rare gas configurations would be

$$
\begin{array}{ll}
\text{Mg} & [\text{Ne}]3s^2 \\
\text{Al} & [\text{Ne}]3s^2 3p^1
\end{array}
$$

There's a reason why rare gases were picked as the one that's put in brackets, but we'll save that for a little later.

Example: What is the predicted rare gas configuration for platinum?

Platinum (Pt) is found in period 6, in the 8th group of the d block. From this, we predict its configuration will end with $5d^8$.

$$\ldots 5d^8$$

The rare gas that immediately precedes platinum is xenon.

$$[\text{Xe}]...5\text{d}^8$$

Working our way from xenon to platinum, we first go through period 6 of the s block.

$$[\text{Xe}]\mathbf{6s^2}...5\text{d}^8$$

Don't forget that in the last two periods, you're also going through the f block (where n = period-2).

$$[\text{Xe}]6\text{s}^2 4\text{f}^{14} 5\text{d}^8$$

As you can see, rare gas configurations can be a convenient shorthand for writing electron configurations, particularly those at the bottom of the periodic table. It's only really a shorthand, though, if you understand the relationship between the table and electron configurations we discussed in Part 2.

Orbital Diagrams

Another common way to write electron configurations are as **orbital diagrams** (also known as *box notation*). Here, boxes are used to represent the orbitals of each subshell

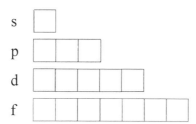

Electrons are shown as arrows. The orbital diagrams of the first five elements are shown below.

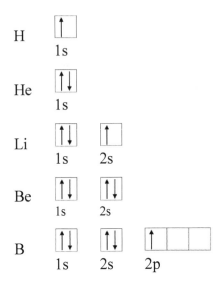

Notice that when there are two electrons in an orbital, they point in *opposite* directions. This is to emphasize the fact that their spins are opposite (one has an m_s of $+\frac{1}{2}$ and the other is $-\frac{1}{2}$). When there's only one electron in an orbital it doesn't matter which way the arrow points. In cases like boron, where there's only one electron in a subshell, it doesn't matter which box it's in, either (though we still show the entire subshell).

In carbon's electron configuration ($1s^2 2s^2 2p^2$), we have two electrons in 2p. **Hund's rule** states that the most stable electron arrangement is the one with the most parallel spins (the same value of m_s). Essentially, what this means is a) you don't pair up electrons in a given subshell until every orbital has one and b) any unpaired electrons must point in the same direction—up or down, doesn't matter which. This gives carbon the following orbital diagram.

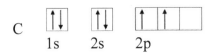

The arrows in 2p can be in any two of the three boxes and can point in either direction. As a final example, iron's orbital diagram would be

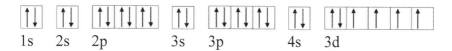

1s   2s   2p   3s   3p   4s   3d

Again, notice that in the last subshell, electrons aren't paired up until necessary. Since iron has six electrons and only five orbitals, two electrons must pair up.

Para- and Diamagnetism

The presence of unpaired electrons can affect a substance's magnetic properties. **Paramagnetic** substances are those with one or more unpaired electrons, which makes them strongly attracted to a magnetic field. On the other hand, in a **diamagnetic** substance all electrons are paired, so that every magnetic moment created by an electron spinning in one direction is canceled by one spinning in the opposite direction. As a result, such substances are either weakly attracted or repelled by a magnetic field. In the previous examples, helium and beryllium atoms are predicted to be diamagnetic while hydrogen, boron, carbon, lithium and iron atoms are predicted to be paramagnetic.

Anomalous Electron Configurations

As mentioned earlier, sometimes the actual configuration of an atom doesn't match what's predicted. For example, we predict that the *f* block should begin with lanthanum, not cerium, since lanthanum's electron configuration is predicted to be $[Xe]6s^24f^1$. However, experimental evidence shows it's configuration to actually be $[Xe]6s^25d^1$.

La: predicted configuration: $[Xe]6s^24f^1$
     actual configuration $[Xe]6s^25d^1$

There are several anomalous configurations in the inner transition group (the f block) where the energies of the outer subshells lie closer to one another. Sometimes an f block element will follow the Aufbau principle,

$$Nd: [Xe]6s^24f^4$$

while others actually have an anomalous configuration similar to lanthanum's

$$U: [Rn]7s^25f^36d^1$$

You also see anomalous configurations in a few transition metals. Copper, for example, is predicted to be $[Ar]4s^23d^9$, but experimentally we see that it prefers to have the 4d subshell filled instead of 4s.

Cu: predicted configuration: $[Ar]4s^23d^9$
     actual configuration $[Ar]4s^13d^{10}$

Try It Yourself

P5. Write the predicted electron configurations for each of the following elements in rare gas notation: a) phosphorus, b) calcium, c) iodine, d) mercury

P6. Write the predicted electron configurations for each of the elements from P5 as orbital diagrams.

P7. Which of the elements from P5 are diamagnetic? Paramagnetic?

Want more practice? Simply pick any element on the periodic table and try to predict its electron configuration. You can easily check your answer online using a site such as Wolfram|Alpha or Wikipedia. Just remember that these will be the actual configurations, so you will occasionally run into an anomalous configuration that doesn't match what you'd normally predict.

Part 4: Ion Configurations

When a neutral atom is converted to an ion, electrons are added or removed from the *valence shell* (highest n) first. In Part 1, we predicted that the electron configuration of sodium would be

$$1s^2 2s^2 2p^6 3s^1 \text{ or } [Ne]3s^1$$

Before that, back in Chapter 3, we learned that sodium usually forms a +1 ion. The electron is removed from the valence shell ($n = 3$), giving this configuration:

$$1s^2 2s^2 2p^6 \text{ or } [Ne]$$

Likewise, the configuration of oxygen is

$$1s^2 2s^2 2p^4$$

As a group 6A element, oxygen typically forms an -2 ion. These two additional electrons will go in subshell 2p, since it can hold up to 6.

$$1s^2 2s^2 2p^6 \text{ or } [Ne]$$

Notice that in both instances, the ions of sodium and oxygen have the same electron configuration as neon. The term often used here is **isoelectronic**, which means they have the same number of electrons. In this case, Na^+, O^{2-} and Ne all have 10 electrons. Also, recall that group 8A is often referred to as the *inert* gas group since elements of this group don't typically react or form ions. It turns out that there's something special about the electron configurations of group 8A elements ($ns^2 np^6$) that makes them particularly stable (or "happy" if you want to be anthropomorphic). In fact, when most main group elements form compounds, be it ionic or—as we'll see in the next chapter—covalent, they're often doing so in order to obtain this "magic" configuration of eight valence electrons. Chemists often refer to this phenomenon as the **octet rule**.

Pseudo-rare gas configurations

There are a few metals, found in the lower left corner of the p block, that are unable to obtain a rare gas configuration. Gallium, for example has the following configuration:

$$[Ar]4s^23d^{10}4p^1$$

Like other metals in group 3A, gallium's most common ion is Ga^{3+}. Here, the valence shell is $n = 4$ and, despite the fact that it's split by the 3d subshell, those are still the electrons that are removed first, giving us

$$[Ar]3d^{10}$$

In order to obtain a rare gas configuration, it would have to lose all ten electrons in subshell 3d, which would result in a Ga^{+13} ion! Energy requirements aside (which we'll discuss momentarily), removing that many electrons seems a bit excessive. Therefore, the closest gallium can reasonably come to a rare gas configuration,[Rg], is what's often known as a **pseudo-rare gas configuration**, which is a rare gas configuration plus a filled d subshell

$$[Rg]xd^{10}$$

or a rare gas configuration plus filled d and f subshells

$$[Rg]xf^{14}yd^{10}$$

Try It Yourself

P8. Write the predicted electron configurations of each of the following ions in standard notation: a) phosphide, b) calcium ion, c) iodide, d) mercury (II)

P9. Write the electron configurations of the ions from P8 in rare gas notation.

P10. Write the electron configurations of the ions from P8 as orbital diagrams.

P11. Which of the ions from P8 have a pseudo-rare gas configuration?

Part 5: Atomic Radius

Throughout the history of modern chemistry, the most common way to visualize atoms has been as spheres. In geometry, a common way to measure the size of a sphere is its *radius*. As such, atomic radius is often used to describe the size of atoms.

When comparing the atomic radii of main group elements, we see an increase in size when going down a group and across a period, right to left.

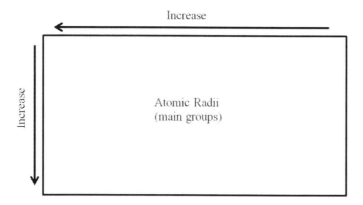

Going down a group, it makes sense that the trend should be an increase, since the valence shell increases from period to period. The trend across a period stems from the fact that the atomic number (i.e., number of protons) is increasing. This increase in positive charge will pull electrons closer to the nucleus.

When the actual values of atomic radii are available, one can usually do a relative comparison by using the lower left and upper right corners as reference points. In most cases, the closer an element is to francium on the table, the larger it is. Likewise, the closer it is to helium, the smaller it's predicted to be. A general method for gauging how close a given element is to our two reference points is to count by "blocks," vertically and horizontally (but *not* diagonally).

Example: Predict the order of increasing atomic radii for the following elements: Al, O, and Se.

Since we're on the right side of the table, we'll use He as our reference. Oxygen is the closest, being 3 blocks away from helium, while selenium is 5 blocks away and aluminum 7.

5	6	7	8	3	2
					He
B	C	N	O	F	Ne
10.81	12.01	14.01	16.00	19.00	20.18
13	14	15	16	17	7 18
Al	Si	P	S	Cl	Ar
26.98	28.09	30.97	32.07	35.45	39.95
31	32	33	34	35	5
Ga	Ge	As	Se	Br	Kr
69.72	72.64	74.92	78.96	79.90	83.80

Therefore, we predict oxygen to be the smallest, followed by selenium, then finally aluminum.

$$O < Se < Al$$

Ionic Radii

When an atom is converted to a cation, the atomic radii will usually decrease. One reason for this is there are fewer repulsive forces around the nucleus (due to a decrease in the number of electrons), which allows the protons in the nucleus to pull the remaining electrons in more closely. For example, comparing the radii of sodium and magnesium with their respective ions

Na: 186 pm   Na$^+$: 98 pm
Mg: 160 pm   Mg^{2+}: 78 pm

Notice that even though the resulting ions are isoelectronic, with both having 10 electrons, the magnesium ion is smaller. That's because magnesium has an additional proton, giving it a larger positive charge that can pull those 10 electrons closer to the nucleus.

When an atom is converted to an anion, the radii will increase, since an increase in negatively charged electrons would result in an increase in repulsive forces, pushing the electrons further out. For example,

O: 73 pm   O^{2-}: 140 pm
F: 72 pm   F$^-$: 133 pm

Similar to our cation example, we see that even though the resulting ions are isoelectronic (10 electrons each), fluorine's atomic radius is smaller due to the greater positive charge in its nucleus.

Try It Yourself

P12. Using the periodic table, predict the order of increasing atomic radius for the following elements: antimony, lead, and nitrogen.

Part 6: Ionization Energy

Ionization Energy (IE) is the energy required to remove an electron from an atom in its gaseous state.

$$X(g) \rightarrow X^+(g) + e^- \qquad \Delta H = 1^{st} \text{ IE}$$
$$X^+(g) \rightarrow X^{2+}(g) + e^- \qquad \Delta H = 2^{nd} \text{ IE}$$

etc.

Let's take a look at the ionization energies for periods 2 and 3 (given in kJ/mol):

Element	1st	2nd	3rd	4th	5th	6th
Li	520	7,300	11,815			
Be	899	1,757	14,850	21,005		
B	801	2,430	3,660	25,000	32,820	
C	1,086	2,350	4,620	6,220	38,000	47,261
N	1,400	2,860	4,580	7,500	9,400	53,000
O	1,314	3,390	5,300	7,470	11,000	13,000
F	1,680	3,370	6,050	8,400	11,000	15,200
Ne	2,080	3,950	6,120	9,370	12,200	15,000
Na	496	4560	6,900	9,540	13,400	16,600
Mg	738	1,450	7,730	10,500	13,600	18,000
Al	578	1,820	2,750	11,600	14,800	18,400
Si	786	1,580	3,230	4,360	16,000	20,000
P	1,012	1,904	2,910	4,960	6,240	21,000
S	1,000	2,250	3,360	4,660	6,990	8,500
Cl	1,251	2,297	3,820	5,160	6,540	9,300
Ar	1,521	2,666	3,900	5,770	7,240	8,800
K	419	3,052	4,410	5,900	6,500	8,100
Ca	590	1,145	4,900	6,500	8,100	11,000

Notice that with both alkali metals (lithium and sodium), there's a significant difference between the first and second IE. With the alkaline earth metals (Be and Mg), however, the first and second IE's are closer in value, and we don't see a similar large jump until the third IE. And with the group 3A elements the big increase occurs with the *fourth* IE. In each of these cases, the sharp increase in ionization energy occurs during the removal of an electron from a rare gas configuration (Li^+, Be^{2+}, B^{3+}, and so on). Observations such as this are what lead to the discovery of the aforementioned octet rule.

From this table we can also see a general trend for the first ionization energy. Overall it seems to be the opposite of the size trend, increasing going up a group and left to right across a period.

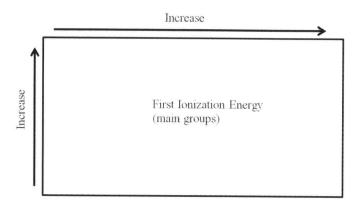

If you think about it, it makes sense that this trend is the opposite of atomic radii. As the size increases, the valence shell gets further away from the positive charge in the nucleus. Furthermore, the like-charged electrons between the valence shell and the nucleus will reduce the effective charge of the nucleus. Both of these factors should make it easier to remove an electron from the valence shell.

You can also explain the trend in general terms using the octet rule. Looking at the second period, for example, in order for lithium to get a rare gas configuration, it only has to lose one valence electron, so it would only make sense that its first ionization energy is the lowest of that period. Likewise, it seems natural that it would take more energy to remove an electron from atoms as they get closer to having a rare gas configuration, and since a rare gas already has that octet, it would be the highest in that period.

However, there are two significant deviations from this trend, which are easier to see in a graph.

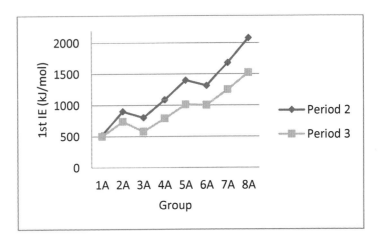

We see a set of "dips" in the graph that always seem to occur with elements of groups 3A and 6A, and this trend continues with the fourth and fifth periods (which I've omitted to keep the plot from getting too messy). If these deviations occur within specific groups, it probably has something to do with their electron configurations.

While eight valence electrons is the most stable configuration for most elements, electron configurations with filled or half-filled subshells are more stable than other partially filled configurations. With group 3A, removing an electron causes the electron configuration to go from an ns^2np^1 to just ns^2.

For atoms in group 6A, the configuration goes from np^4 to a half-filled np^3.

ns np   → ns np   + e⁻

In both cases, the result is a more stable configuration, so it will take less energy than one would otherwise predict from the other six elements in the same period. Think of energy as money. The closer an atom is to getting that octet, the more they want to hold on to the electrons they currently have, so you'll need to "pay" more energy to get one. But it just so happens that the atoms in groups 3A and 6A have a p electron that they could do without, so you don't have to pay as much to take it as the other six groups would lead you to believe.

Try It Yourself

P13. Using the periodic table, predict the order of increasing first ionization energy for the following elements: carbon, chlorine, sodium.

Part 7: Electron Affinity

Electron Affinity (EA) is defined as the enthalpy change that occurs when an electron is added to an atom (again, in the gaseous state).

$$X(g) + e^- \rightarrow X^-(g)$$

The greater the EA, the more energy an atom is willing to "spend" to obtain it. However, since this process is usually exothermic ($-\Delta H$), it's customary to flip the sign around to make most of the values positive, which usually makes comparisons a little easier. For example, a fluorine atom will release -328 kJ/mol to get an additional electron

$$F(g) + e^- \rightarrow F^-(g) \quad \Delta H = -328 \text{ kJ}$$

Its electron affinity, therefore, is given as 328 kJ/mol.

The electron affinities of the main group elements are given below (in kJ/mol).

H							He
73							< 0
Li	**Be**	**B**	**C**	**N**	**O**	**F**	**Ne**
60	≤ 0	27	122	0	141	328	< 0
Na	**Mg**	**Al**	**Si**	**P**	**S**	**Cl**	**Ar**
53	≤ 0	44	134	72	200	349	< 0
K	**Ca**	**Ga**	**Ge**	**As**	**Se**	**Br**	**Kr**
48	2.4	29	118	77	195	325	< 0
Rb	**Sr**	**In**	**Sn**	**Sb**	**Te**	**I**	**Xe**
47	4.7	29	121	101	190	295	< 0

From this data we see that the general trend for groups 1A-7A is similar to that of the 1st IE trend, where there is an overall increase as one goes up a group or across a period, left to right.

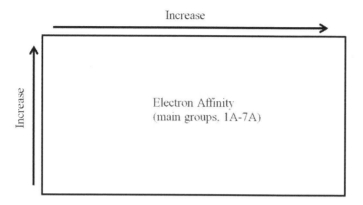

It seems logical that the two trends would be identical. Lithium, for example, has a relatively low first ionization energy because giving up an electron gives it a rare gas configuration. Spending energy to obtain an *additional* electron seems counter-productive, doesn't it?

Like the 1st IE trend, exceptions to this trend can be found in two groups, in this case 2A and 5A. The reason for this exception again has to do with filled and half-filled subshells being more stable than other partially filled shells. Atoms from these two groups already have these configurations, so adding an electron results in one that's *less* favorable.

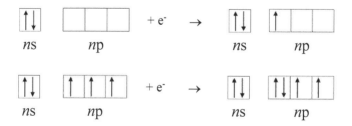

As a result, elements of groups 2A and 5A wouldn't spend as much energy to get an electron as you'd predict by looking at the other elements in that period. This is why electron affinities of the first two alkaline earth metals are believed to be negative or close to zero, because adding an electron is actually an endothermic process (remember, we've flipped the sign). Keeping with the whole energy/money analogy, this means you actually have to "pay" Be and Mg to take those electrons. This is also why the group 8A elements also have negative electron affinities, since they already have an octet.

Try It Yourself

P14. Using the periodic table, predict the order of increasing electron affinity for the following elements: carbon, chlorine, sodium.

Test Yer Skills

★Landlubber

1. Write the predicted electron configurations for the following atoms in standard notation: a) argon, b) rubidium, c) seaborgium

XP: +3 each

2. Write the predicted electron configurations for the following atoms in rare gas notation: a) arsenic, b) potassium, c) bismuth

XP: +3 each

3. Write the predicted electron configurations for following atom as orbital diagrams: a) magnesium, b) cobalt, c) osmium

XP: +3 each

4. Which of the atoms from question 3 are predicted to be diamagnetic?

XP: +3

5. Write the predicted electron configurations for the following ions in standard notation: a) P^{3-}, b) Fe^{2+}, Sn^{4+}

XP: +3 each

6. Arrange the following atoms in the predicted order of increasing atomic radius: aluminum, calcium, sodium, barium.

XP: +3

7. Arrange the following atoms in the predicted order of decreasing atomic radius: arsenic, lead, nitrogen, gallium.

XP: +3

8. Arrange the following atoms in the predicted order of increasing first ionization energy: beryllium, bismuth, fluorine, phosphorus

XP: +3

9. Arrange the following atoms in the predicted order of decreasing electron affinity: lithium, oxygen, potassium, silicon.

XP: +3

★XP: _____

If yer XP be 36 or higher, stop swingin' the lead and go for...

★★Sea Dog

10. Identify the following elements from their electron configuration:
a)$1s^2 2s^2 2p^6 3s^2 3p^2$
b)$1s^2 2s^2 2p^6 3s^2 3p^6 4s^2 3d^3$
c)$[Kr]5s^2 4d^{10} 5p^5$

XP: +4 each

11. Write the electron configuration of the following ions in rare gas notation: a) Ti^{2+}, b) Ru^{3+}, c) W^{4+}

XP: +4 each

12. Predict the two common charges of bismuth. Which of these two is probably the most common?

XP: +4

13. The electron configuration for a Ag^+ ion is actually an anomalous configuration. What is it?

XP: +4

14. Arrange the following in order of predicted increasing atomic radius: Ar, Ca^{2+}, Cl^-, K^+

XP: +4

15. Write orbital diagrams for each of the following:
a) a *g* subshell with 13 electrons
b) an *h* subshell with 18 electrons
c) a *k* subshell with 25 electrons

XP: +4 each

★★XP: _____   Total XP: _____

If yer XP be 72 or more, maybe it's time to parley about becoming a...

★★★Pirate King

16. Given our discussion of ionization energy, where would you expect an exception to occur within the transition metal groups?
XP: +4

17. Based on your experience with electron configurations thus far, predict the order of subshells from 7p to 9p.
XP: +5

18. The following f block elements follow the Aufbau principle. Predict their electron configurations in standard notation: a) americium (Am), b) dysprosium (Dy), c) fermium (Fm).
XP: +5 each

18. Write the orbital diagrams of the elements from question 17.
XP: +5 each

20. The following electron configurations contain an excited electron. Identify the element.
a) $1s^2 2s^2 2p^6 3s^2 3p^3 4p^1$
b) $1s^2 2s^2 2p^6 3s^2 3p^6 4s^1 3d^{10} 6s^1$

XP: +5 each

330

★★★XP: _____   Total XP: _____

If you be earnin' 104 XP or more: Avast!

Achievement Unlocked: Trendy
Completed Chapter 9

You're now ready to learn about chemical structures.

Chapter 10
Chemical Structures
(Part I)

Part 1: Covalent Compounds Revisited

Covalent compounds were introduced way back in Chapter 3, but we only went as far as defining them as compounds that share electrons instead of forming ions. In this chapter, and the two that follow, we're going to discuss covalent compounds in a little more detail.

For starters, the electrons that are shared are often thought to be *valence* electrons, which we defined in Chapter 9 as the electrons in the highest occupied shell (n). In that chapter, we also saw that one of the benefits of the A/B grouping system that we've been using is that we don't have to write an electron configuration to figure out the number of valence electrons for a main group atom. The number is equal to whatever group it's in (group 1A elements have one valence electrons, 2A elements have two, etc).

The sharing of electrons between two atoms is known as a **covalent bond**. There are actually a couple of prevalent theories that explain covalent bonding, which we'll discuss in Chapter 12, but the underlying principle in both is that bonds are formed through an overlap or combining of orbitals. The **bond length** of a covalent bond is defined as the distance between the two nuclei of the atoms sharing electrons (usually measured in picometers). The ideal bond length is one where the two atoms are close enough to overlap orbitals, but still far enough apart to minimize repulsive forces between the protons in their nuclei.

Ionic, Covalent, and the Octet Rule

From the periodic trends discussed in Chapter 9, we can begin to have a better understanding of why metals and nonmetals usually combine to form ionic compounds, while those with two or more nonmetals are usually covalent. For a compound like NaCl, sodium's ionization energy is significantly lower than chlorine's, as is its electron affinity. This is to be expected when one considers the octet rule of main group elements. Sodium only needs to rid itself of a single electron to obtain eight valence electrons while chlorine needs to *obtain* one to get its octet. When the two elements are combined (under the proper conditions, of course), sodium has no problem giving up its electron to form Na^+ and chlorine will readily spend the energy required to accept that electron and form Cl^-.

On the other hand, in a compound with two nonmetals, such as PCl_3, both elements are in the top right corner of the table, meaning they both have relatively high ionization energies and electron affinities. *Both* elements would prefer to get their octet by obtaining electrons, so neither will readily form a cation. Therefore, they must share their valence electrons in a way that gives each atom a total of eight.

Lewis Structures

Until now, we've only looked at covalent compounds as *molecular compounds*, where only the type and number of each element are given. A **structural formula**—as the name would indicate—also provides information about the molecule's structure, allowing one to see which atoms are sharing electrons and how many are being shared (and sometimes, as we'll see in Chapter 11, what the molecule looks like in 3D space).

The most common type of structural formula used is a **Lewis structure**, named after its creator, Gilbert Lewis (1875 – 1946), who was one of the first to understand the concept of covalent bonding. In a Lewis structure, an atom's valence electrons are shown as dots around its element symbol. The Lewis symbols of period 2 are given below.

Li·   ·Be·   ·B·   ·C·   ·N·   :O·   :F·   :Ne:

There are a couple of things to keep in mind when writing the Lewis symbol of an atom. First, you can place the dots/electrons on any of the four sides around the element that you wish (left, right, top, bottom), so long as you're showing the correct number. With group 1A atoms, for example, that one dot representing an alkali metal's one valence electron can be on any of the four sides. However, notice that you don't pair up your dots until you have to (when you have 5 or more valence electrons). When two electrons are paired up in a Lewis structure, they are known as a **lone pair**. Oxygen's Lewis symbol, for example (along with the other group 6A elements), has two lone pairs and two unpaired electrons.

Lewis Structures of Diatomic Compounds

Fluorine

To show how Lewis structures are drawn, let's start with a few simple diatomic molecules, starting with fluorine, F_2. The Lewis symbol of fluorine has three lone pairs and one unpaired electron. We can picture the two fluorine atoms sharing their unpaired electrons so that each has a total of eight (to borrow a term from the legal system, the shared electrons would be considered "joint property" of the two atoms).

$$:\!\ddot{F}\cdot \quad \cdot\ddot{F}\!: \quad \rightarrow \quad :\!\ddot{F}\!:\!\ddot{F}\!:$$

Usually, instead of showing all the electrons as dots, a shared pair is symbolized with a single line (you'll appreciate this more when we start looking at bigger molecules).

$$:\!\ddot{F}\!-\!\ddot{F}\!:$$

A shared pair of electrons (one line) is known as a **single bond**.

Oxygen

Next, we'll look at oxygen, O_2. As a Lewis symbol, oxygen's six valence electrons are shown as two lone pairs and two unpaired electrons. Sharing just two electrons between them will only give each atom seven electrons,

$$:\ddot{O}\cdot \quad \cdot\ddot{O}: \quad \rightarrow \quad :\ddot{O}-\ddot{O}:$$

but there's an additional set of unpaired electrons that can be shared in order to obey the octet rule (and we'll move the lone pairs on the side to the bottom to make it look a little nicer, or at least more symmetrical).

$$:\ddot{O}-\ddot{O}: \quad \rightarrow \quad \ddot{O}=\ddot{O}$$

The sharing of four electrons (two shared pairs) is called a **double bond**.

Nitrogen

Finally, let's look at nitrogen, N_2. The two nitrogen atoms initially have five valence electrons apiece: one lone pair and three unpaired electrons. For each to get an octet, a total of six electrons must be shared between the two atoms.

$$:\dot{\ddot{N}}\cdot \quad \cdot\dot{\ddot{N}}: \quad \rightarrow \quad :N\equiv N:$$

Sharing six electrons (as you may have guessed) is a **triple bond**.

Though we won't encounter any in this book, it should be noted that it's possible that more than six electrons can be shared. We've been assuming that transition metal compounds are ionic, but it was noted in Chapter 4 that this is a broad generalization that we use for the sake of simplicity. In actuality, there are several known transition metal compounds that contain quadruple bonds (eight shared electrons) and even quintuple bonds (ten).

Bond Order

Bond order is simply a way to describe the bonding between two atoms. In most cases it's fairly simple: the bond order is equal to the number of bonds.

Bond Type	Bond Order
Single	1
Double	2
Triple	3

Fractional bond orders are also possible, but those won't be discussed here.

A common trend that's observed in chemical structures is bonds will become shorter and stronger as bond order increases. For example, for compounds with a nitrogen-nitrogen bond, the following bond lengths are observed

Bond type:	N-N	N=N	N≡N
Bond length:	147 pm	125 pm	110 pm

We can compare their relative strengths by comparing the energy required to break each type of bond.

Bond type:	N-N	N=N	N≡N
Energy required to break bond (kJ/mol):	193	418	941

The more energy needed, the stronger the bond is.

338

Try It Yourself

P1. Write the Lewis symbols of each of the following atoms:
a) Al, b) Cs, c) Se, d) Cl

P2. Draw Lewis structures for the following diatomic molecules, starting with their Lewis symbols: a) HBr, b) CO_2, c) NF_3

Part 2: Inorganic Structures

In our earlier examples, giving each atom an octet was essentially a matter of pairing up unpaired electrons in a way that allowed all atoms to obey the octet rule. While this same approach can be taken with larger inorganic molecules (as you hopefully saw after trying a couple in problem P2), this "puzzle piece" approach can sometimes be a bit more involved and time-consuming, particularly when you're just starting to learn how to draw Lewis structures.

Back in Chapter 3, it was mentioned that most covalent inorganic compounds are binary, consisting of just two types of atoms. Many of these compounds—especially those discussed in this book—have the general formula AX_n, where there is only one of the first atom and n number of the second (CO_2, NH_3, SO_4^{2-}, etc). In these cases, we can employ a more stepwise, systematic approach to predict its Lewis structure.

For an inorganic compound of type AX_n:

1. A is a central atom bonded to n number of outer atoms (X).
2. Add up the total number of valence electrons.
3. Bond all outer atoms to the central atom using single bonds.
4. Add the remaining electrons as lone pairs, starting with the outer atoms. If you've counted correctly, you should have enough to give the outer atoms an octet.
5. If any electrons remain after all outer atoms have an octet, add those to the central atom as lone pairs.
6. If the central atom still needs 8 electrons, remove a lone pair from one of the outer atoms and replace its single bond with a double bond. If the central atom still doesn't have 8 electrons, either form another double bond with a different outer atom or convert the double bond you made into a triple. Remember to remove a lone pair for each shared pair you create.

This method works particularly well for polyatomic ions and molecules where the central atom has an expanded valence (which we'll discuss in Part 4). If a compound doesn't fit this general formula, you can usually get a correct structure by starting with their Lewis symbols or drawing it as you would an organic compound (which we'll discuss in the next chapter).

Example: Draw the Lewis Structure of PCl_3

This compound fits our general formula, AX_n, so phosphorus is assumed to be the central atom and the chlorines are outer atoms. The first step in determining its structure will be to tally up the number of valence electrons. Remember, for main group elements, the number of valence electrons is equal to its group number.

P	5 valence electrons
Cl	3 x 7 valence electrons
Total	26 valence electrons

Therefore, our Lewis structure must show twenty-six electrons as either shared pairs (bonds) or lone pairs.

Unless we're told otherwise, we assume that each of the outer atoms (X) is bonded to the central atom (A). And since most covalent bonds are sharing at least two electrons, we'll begin with single bonds.

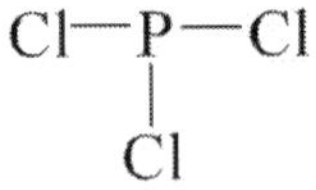

$$Cl-P-Cl$$
$$|$$
$$Cl$$

That takes care of six of our twenty-six electrons (remember, each line represents two electrons). The remaining electrons are then added to the structure as lone pairs, beginning with the outer atoms. Looking at the structure above, each chlorine needs six more electrons for an octet, so we'll give each one three sets of lone pairs.

$$:\ddot{C}l\!\!-\!\!P\!\!-\!\!\ddot{C}l:$$
$$|$$
$$:\ddot{C}l:$$

If your valence count is correct, you should at least have enough to give all of your outer atoms an octet. Any remaining electrons will go on the central atom. Here, we've used twenty-four of our twenty-six electrons at this point, so the remaining two will be placed on phosphorus.

$$:\ddot{C}l\!\!-\!\!\ddot{P}\!\!-\!\!\ddot{C}l:$$
$$|$$
$$:\ddot{C}l:$$

Once all the valence electrons have been distributed, we check to see if all atoms are obeying the octet rule. That seems to be the case here, so it looks like we're done.

Example: Draw the Lewis structure of nitrate, NO_3^-.

As with PCl_3, this compound fits our general formula, so we assume the oxygen atoms are the outer atoms and nitrogen is the central atom. We start again by adding up our valence electrons. However, since this is a polyatomic anion with a -1 charge, we must also include the one electron that has been added to the molecule.

N	5 valence electrons
O	3 x 6 valence electrons
-1 charge	1 valence electron
Total	24 valence electrons

If the ion had been a cation, we would have removed electrons from our valence count.

Putting our structure together, we start by connecting the outer atoms to the central atom

$$O\!-\!N\!-\!O$$
$$|$$
$$O$$

then the remaining electrons are added as lone pairs, starting with the outer atoms.

$$:\!\ddot{O}\!-\!N\!-\!\ddot{O}\!:$$
$$|$$
$$:\!\ddot{O}\!:$$

Don't get too dot-happy, though, and add a lone pair to nitrogen. At this point, we've used all twenty-four electrons, so we can't put a lone pair on nitrogen. "But, wait," you might be asking, "didn't we show nitrogen having a lone pair on its Lewis symbol in the last section?" True, but unlike our diatomic examples in Part 1, this method doesn't actually begin with the Lewis symbols of each element. Nitrogen's lone pair, as we'll soon see, actually ends up getting used for bonding.

When the central atom still needs an octet, this is where multiple bonding comes into play. To give nitrogen an octet and still keep our valence count at 24 electrons, we convert one of the lone pairs into a shared pair, which in turn changes one of the single bonds into a double bond. In this example, all of our outer atoms are identical, so it doesn't matter which one we choose.

$$:\!\ddot{O}\!-\!N\!-\!\ddot{O}\!:\qquad\rightarrow\qquad:\!\ddot{O}\!-\!N\!=\!\ddot{O}$$
$$|\qquad\qquad\qquad\qquad|$$
$$:\!\ddot{O}\!:\qquad\qquad\qquad\quad:\!\ddot{O}\!:$$

Try It Yourself

P3. Draw a Lewis structure for each of the following molecules using the method described in this section: a) $SiCl_4$, b) SBr_2, c) CO_3^{2-}

344

Part 3: Resonance Structures

Despite the usefulness of Lewis structures, they do have their limitations. Take ozone (O_3), for example. When drawing its Lewis structure, you end up needing a double bond to give the central oxygen eight valence electrons. Since both outer atoms are the same element, it doesn't seem to matter which one gets the double bond. In either structure, we have one single bond and one double bond.

$$\ddot{O}{=}\ddot{O}{-}\ddot{O}{:} \quad or \quad :\ddot{O}{-}\ddot{O}{=}\ddot{O}$$

Thinking back to what was said regarding bond order in Part 1, if this is actually the structure of an ozone molecule, one bond should be shorter than the other. However, experimental evidence shows that the two bonds are *identical*, with a bond length that's somewhere between those normally found for an oxygen-oxygen single bond and an oxygen-oxygen double bond:

O-O bond	146 pm
O=O bond	121 pm
Bonds in ozone	128 pm

And if you're thinking that both bonds might be double bonds because their lengths are closer to 121 than 146, try drawing a structure for ozone where both bonds are double and you've also used all eighteen electrons. You can't do it, not without breaking the octet rule, anyway.

In other words, the two bonds are neither single bonds nor double bonds, but something in between. In *other*, other words, they have a *fractional* bond order that's somewhere between 1 and 2. This means that neither of the two structures given above are accurate representations of what an ozone molecule actually looks like. The true structure is an average or composite of the two.

Ozone's structure is an example of **resonance**, where the actual structure can't be accurately represented by a single Lewis structure. Instead, we write all the possible structures we can draw (known as **resonance structures**) and link them together with a double tipped arrow.

$$\ddot{O}{=}\ddot{O}{-}\ddot{O}: \quad \leftrightarrow \quad :\ddot{O}{-}\ddot{O}{=}\ddot{O}$$

The term "resonance" can be misleading because it can lead one to think that the two bonds are resonating or oscillating between single and double. The bonding between the atoms isn't changing. It's just that the type of bond that's forming can't be accurately shown simply using straight lines and dots.

For most compounds, one sign that the structure you're trying to draw might be a resonance structure is if it's possible to put a multiple bond in more than one place. Flipping back to Part 2, this happened when we drew the Lewis structure of nitrate.

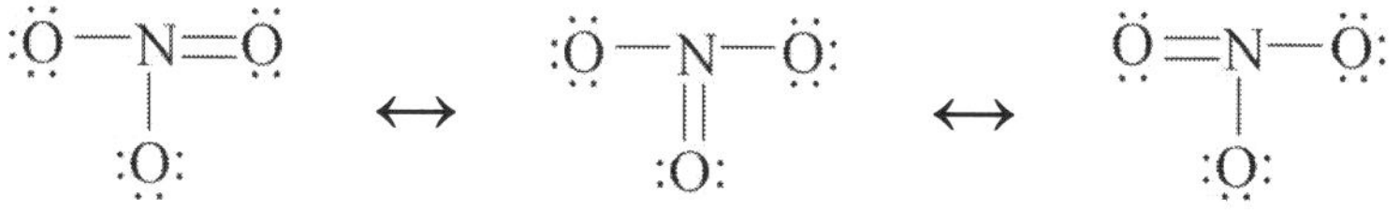

Similar to ozone, the three bonds of nitrate aren't single or double bonds, but something in between. Because of the inherent limitations of Lewis structures, the closest we can come to showing this is in the above figure.

That being said, chemists will sometimes use "cheats" for compounds with resonance structures to avoid having to draw the molecule more than once. One common trick you see for molecules that only have two resonance forms, such as ozone, is to use a dotted line in place of the resonating double bond, so you'll often see ozone written like this:

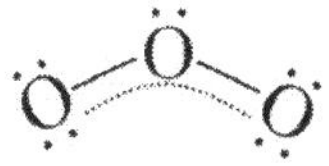

Major Structures

For both ozone and nitrate, each resonance structure essentially looks the same as the others. Each of nitrate's structures, for instance, has nitrogen singly bonded to two oxygen atoms and doubly bonded to a third. That isn't always true for every resonance structure, though. Sometimes, it's possible to come up with two or three structures that look very different. The resonance structures of thiocyanate ion (SCN⁻) are such an example.

$$:S\equiv C-\ddot{N}: \quad \leftrightarrow \quad \ddot{S}=C=\ddot{N} \quad \leftrightarrow \quad :\ddot{S}-C\equiv N:$$

In cases such as this, there's usually one structure that better represents the actual structure than the others, which we call the **major structure**. To determine which one of thiocyanate's three structures is the major one, we need to first introduce a couple of new terms.

Electronegativity

Electronegativity (EN) is a term that describes an atom's "desire" for electrons. It's similar to electron affinity (see Chapter 9), except that electronegativity isn't a direct measurement, but a relative scale that ranges from zero (lowest EN) to four (highest). The electronegativities of the main group elements are given in the following table.

H						
2.1						
Li	**Be**	**B**	**C**	**N**	**O**	**F**
1.0	1.5	2.0	2.5	3.0	3.5	4.0
Na	**Mg**	**Al**	**Si**	**P**	**S**	**Cl**
0.9	1.2	1.5	1.8	2.1	2.5	3.0
K	**Ca**	**Ga**	**Ge**	**As**	**Se**	**Br**
0.8	1.0	1.6	1.8	2.0	2.4	2.8
Rb	**Sr**	**In**	**Sn**	**Sb**	**Te**	**I**
0.7	0.9	1.7	1.8	1.9	2.1	2.5
Cs	**Ba**	**Tl**	**Pb**	**Bi**	**Po**	**At**
0.7	0.9	1.8	1.9	1.9	2.0	2.2

Like electron affinity, the electronegativity trend also increases going across a period (left to right) and up a group, only *without* any group exceptions. In general, the closer an atom is to fluorine, the more electronegative it's predicted to be (except hydrogen, which is between boron and carbon). When you don't have these values handy, you can use the same block-counting technique that was discussed with the Chapter 9 trends.

Formal Charge

Formal Charges are "fake" charges used with structural formulas, similar to how oxidation numbers are used with redox reactions (Chapter 5). To determine the formal charge of an atom in a Lewis structure, you take its original number of valence electrons and subtract the number of lone pair electrons and half the number of shared electrons.

$$FC = (\text{original \# } e^-) - (\text{\# lone pair } e^-) - (\tfrac{1}{2} \text{ \# shared } e^-)$$

For example, in the Lewis structure of PCl_3 (see Part 2), the formal charge of phosphorus would be zero

$$FC = 5 - 2 - \tfrac{1}{2}(6) = 0$$

as would each chlorine

$$FC = 7 - 6 - \tfrac{1}{2}(2) = 0$$

Formal charges can often be more "realistic" charges than oxidation numbers. Here we see that every atom in the molecule has a zero formal charge, which makes more sense for a covalent compound than the fake charges we get with oxidation numbers (+3 for P, -1 for F). That doesn't mean every neutral compound will have atoms with formal charges of zero. In carbon monoxide (:C≡O:), for example, carbon would have a formal charge of -1

$$FC = 4 - 2 - \tfrac{1}{2}(6) = -1$$

and oxygen would be +1.

$$FC = 6 - 2 - \tfrac{1}{2}(6) = +1$$

Example: Calculate the formal charges of each atom in a Lewis structure of nitrate.

Regardless of which structure we use, nitrogen is singly bonded to two oxygens and double bonded to one.

$$:\!\ddot{O}\!-\!N\!=\!\ddot{O} \qquad :\!\ddot{O}\!-\!N\!-\!\ddot{O}\!: \qquad \ddot{O}\!=\!N\!-\!\ddot{O}\!:$$
$$\quad\;\; | \qquad\qquad\qquad || \qquad\qquad\qquad |$$
$$\quad\;\; :\!\ddot{O}\!: \qquad\qquad\;\; :\!\ddot{O}\!: \qquad\qquad\;\; :\!\ddot{O}\!:$$

The formal charge of nitrogen would be +1

$$FC = 5 - 0 - \tfrac{1}{2}(8) = +1$$

the double bonded oxygen would have a formal charge of 0

$$FC = 6 - 4 - \tfrac{1}{2}(4) = 0$$

and the single bonded oxygens would each have a formal charge of -1

$$FC = 6 - 6 - \frac{1}{2}(2) = -1$$

Looking back at these three examples (PCl_3, CO, and NO_3^-), notice that the algebraic sum rule discussed with oxidation numbers and ionic compounds also applies to formal charges, as the sum of the formal charges equals the overall charge of the molecule

PCl_3	$0 + 3(0) = 0$
CO	$1 + (-1) = 0$
NO_3^-	$1 + 0 + 2(-1) = -1$

Formal charges give us an idea of how the electrons are distributed across a given a molecule. The more atoms with a formal charge of zero, the more evenly distributed the electrons are within that molecule.

Determining the Major Structure

In most cases, the major structure will meet the following two conditions:

1. It has as many atoms with a zero formal charge as possible.
2. Any negative charge will be on the atom with the highest EN (or any positive charge will be on the atom with the lowest, whichever is more applicable).

In other words, the major structure will have the electrons spread across the molecule as evenly as possible and any negative charge will be on the atom that desires it most.

Looking back at thiocyanate, the formal charges in each structure are

$$:S\equiv C-\ddot{N}: \quad \leftrightarrow \quad \ddot{S}=C=\ddot{N} \quad \leftrightarrow \quad :\ddot{S}-C\equiv N:$$
$$+1 \quad 0 \quad -2 \qquad 0 \quad 0 \quad -1 \qquad -1 \quad 0 \quad 0$$

The structure on the far left can be ruled out first, since it has the fewest atoms with a zero formal charge. The tiebreaker for the remaining two will be electronegativity. From our table of electronegativites, we see that the electronegativity of nitrogen is 3.0 while sulfur's is 2.5. Since nitrogen has the greater desire for negative charge, we predict S=C=N to be the major structure.

Formal charges and electronegativity have other uses as well, some of which we'll see later in this and future chapters.

Try It Yourself

P4. Which of the molecules from question P3 is most likely to be a resonance structure?

P5. Nitrogen monoxide (aka nitrous oxide), N_2O, has three different resonance structures.
a) Draw each resonance structure (a nitrogen is the central atom).
b) For each structure, calculate the formal charge of each atom.
c) Which resonance structure is predicted to be the major structure.

Part 4: Exceptions to the Octet Rule

While most main group atoms obtain eight valence electrons after forming covalent compounds, there are a few that are actually stable with fewer, while some elements actually have the ability to hold more than eight.

Hydrogen

In most compounds, hydrogen will only form a single bond with one other atom, giving it a total of two valence electrons. In one sense, the fact that hydrogen only needs two electrons isn't really an exception to the octet rule. Remember that most atoms are trying to get eight in order to obtain a rare gas configuration. Hydrogen's closest rare gas is helium, which only has two electrons ($1s^2$), which is actually a full shell for $n = 1$ (see Chapter 9). For example, the Lewis structure of formaldehyde, CH_2O is

$$\begin{array}{c} :O: \\ \| \\ H-C-H \end{array}$$

If you're using the method from Part 2 to draw a Lewis structure, when you get to step 4 you wouldn't place lone pairs around hydrogen. Place them around the other outer atoms, and any remaining after that would go on the central atom.

Beryllium & Boron

While most metals form ionic compounds, this is a very general rule of thumb that we used for convenience's sake back in Chapter 3. Beryllium, for instance, will often form covalent compounds because of its relatively small size and (for a main

352

group metal) high electronegativity. In the Lewis structures of these compounds, beryllium will only have four electrons, as seen in BeF_2.

$$:\ddot{F}—Be—\ddot{F}:$$

Using the method from Part 2, we'd normally convert the outer atoms' lone pairs to shared pairs to give the central atom an octet. With BeF_2, that would mean either a triple bond or two double bonds.

$$:\ddot{F}—Be\equiv F: \quad or \quad \ddot{F}=Be=\ddot{F}$$

However, while this isn't technically a resonance structure, electrons are distributed more evenly with just the two single bonds.

$$:\ddot{F}—Be—\ddot{F}: \quad :\ddot{F}—Be\equiv F: \quad \ddot{F}=Be=\ddot{F}$$
$$\;\;0\quad\;\;0\quad\quad 0\quad\;\; 0\;\; -2\;\; +2\quad +1\;\; -2\;\; +1$$

Many boron compounds, like BF_3, will also have an "incomplete octet."

$$:\ddot{F}:$$
$$:\ddot{F}—B—\ddot{F}:$$

Similar to what we saw with BeF_2, formal charges show us that the electrons are actually more evenly distributed across a molecule with this structure than one with a double bonded fluorine.

$$\quad\; 0 \quad\quad\quad\quad +1$$
$$\;\;:\ddot{F}: \quad\quad\quad\;\; :F:$$
$$:\ddot{F}—B—\ddot{F}: \quad :\ddot{F}—B—\ddot{F}:$$
$$\;\;0\quad 0\quad 0 \quad\quad 0\;\; -1\;\; 0$$

Coordinate Covalent Bonds

As single Lewis structures, beryllium and boron will often have to make due with 4 and 6 electrons, respectively. However, they are able to obtain their octets by other means. One way would be to share the lone pair of another molecule, forming a **coordinate covalent bond** (or coordinate bond, for short). For example, BF_3 is often stored as a solution in diethyl ether, $CH_3CH_2OCH_2CH_3$ (we'll talk more about organic formulas in the next chapter). The oxygen has two lone pairs, one of which will be shared with boron.

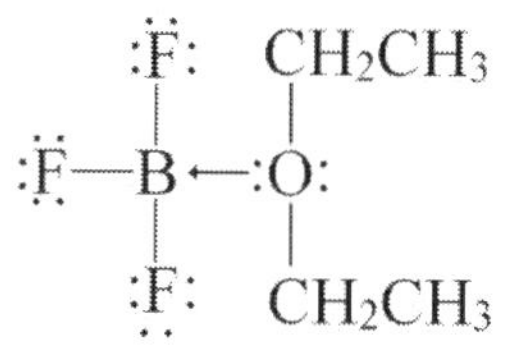

$$\begin{array}{ccc} :\ddot{F}: & CH_2CH_3 \\ | & | \\ :\ddot{F}-B\leftarrow:\ddot{O}: \\ | & | \\ :\ddot{F}: & CH_2CH_3 \end{array}$$

Compounds that form from coordinate covalent bonds are sometimes referred to as **adducts**.

A common way to differentiate coordinate bonds from a "normal" covalent bond (where each atom contributes one electron) is to show it as we did above, where the lone pair is kept on its original atom and an arrow is used to show the electrons being shared with an electron deficient atom. However, it is just as common to see them drawn like any other bond.

Molecules with an Odd Number of Electrons

Looking back at all of the structures we've shown so far, we see that valence electrons usually get paired up as either shared pairs (bonds) or lone pairs, but that's tough to do when the electron count is an odd number. For example, nitrogen dioxide has 17 valence electrons (5 from N, 6 from each O). Following the method from Part 2 gives us the following structure

$$:\overset{..}{\text{O}}\!\!-\!\!\dot{\text{N}}\!\!=\!\!\overset{..}{\text{O}}$$

That single electron on nitrogen is known as a radical or a **free radical**. At this point nitrogen only has seven electrons. Forming a second double bond or making the current double bond a triple will give it nine, which nitrogen can't have (for reasons we'll discuss momentarily), so it seems that nitrogen is stuck with seven.

However, there are a couple of ways that nitrogen can get an octet. One possibility is to react with a reducing agent to pick up an additional electron, forming nitrite (NO_2^-). If that's not possible, then another option is to have two molecules share their radicals to form a **dimer** (a molecule composed of two identical parts).

Many times, the dimer can be converted back to its free radical form by either heating or exposing them to certain frequencies of light (we'll discuss the energy required to break bonds at the end of the chapter).

Expanded Valences

There are many examples of molecules where the central atom has an **expanded valence**, meaning it has more than eight electrons. Take phosphorus pentachloride for instance. Forming single bonds with five chlorine atoms will give phosphorus a total of ten electrons.

$$\begin{array}{c} \text{Cl} \\ | \quad \text{Cl} \\ \text{Cl}-\text{P} \overset{\displaystyle}{\underset{|}{\diagdown}} \text{Cl} \\ \text{Cl} \end{array}$$

In general, atoms of atomic number 13 (Al) or higher have the ability to form expanded valences. This is why, in our earlier example, we couldn't draw NO_2 with two double bonds.

So why, you might be wondering, can phosphorus have more than eight, but not nitrogen? They're both in group 5A, after all. However, nitrogen's valence shell is $n = 2$, which only contains s and p subshells, meaning that shell can only hold a maximum of eight electrons. The valence shell of phosphorus, however, is $n = 3$, which also has a d subshell that can be used to hold additional electrons, if need be (how they might be used will be discussed in Chapter 12).

An expanded valence isn't just limited to shared pairs. For example, using the method discussed in Part 2 to draw the Lewis structure of sulfur tetrafluoride, you'll end up with two extra electrons after giving the outer atoms their eight.

$$\begin{array}{c} \ddot{\text{F}}{:} \\ | \\ {:}\ddot{\text{F}}-\text{S}-\ddot{\text{F}}{:} \\ | \\ {:}\ddot{\text{F}}{:} \end{array}$$

The next step says that any remaining electrons go on the central atom as lone pairs. Since sulfur is atomic number 16, it's allowed to have more than eight.

$$\begin{array}{c} \ddot{\text{F}}{:} \\ | \quad \ddot{\text{F}}{:} \\ {:}\text{S} \overset{\displaystyle}{\underset{|}{\diagdown}} \ddot{\text{F}}{:} \\ {:}\ddot{\text{F}}{:} \end{array}$$

Try It Yourself

P6. Draw Lewis structures for each of the following:
a) ClF_5, b) XeF_4, c) PCl_6^-

Test Your Skills

★The Rookie

1. Draw Lewis symbols for each of the following:
a) Si, b) K, c) Br, d) Mg

XP +4 each

2. Determine the number of valence electrons in each of the following: a) CCl_4, b) BrF_5, c) PO_4^{3-}, d) NH_4^+

XP +4 each

3. Draw a Lewis structure for each of the following molecules, showing all valence electrons as either lone pairs or shared pairs (bonds). a) $GeBr_4$, b) $BrCl_5$, c) NO_2^- d) OCl_2, e) O_2^{2-}

XP + 4 each

4. Which of the following molecules from question 3 is most likely to be a resonance structure?

XP +4

5. Using only the periodic table, arrange each of the following sets of atoms in order of increasing electronegativity:
a) Ca, N, P; b) Cl, In, Si

XP + 4 each

6. Each of the following Lewis structures is drawn incorrectly. Identify the error and redraw the structure.

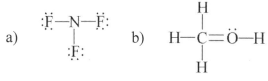

XP + 4 each

7. The structure of carbon dioxide can be drawn with either two double bonds or with one single bond and one triple bond. Use formal charges to determine the more correct structure.

XP +4

8. Three possible Lewis structures of sulfate are shown below.

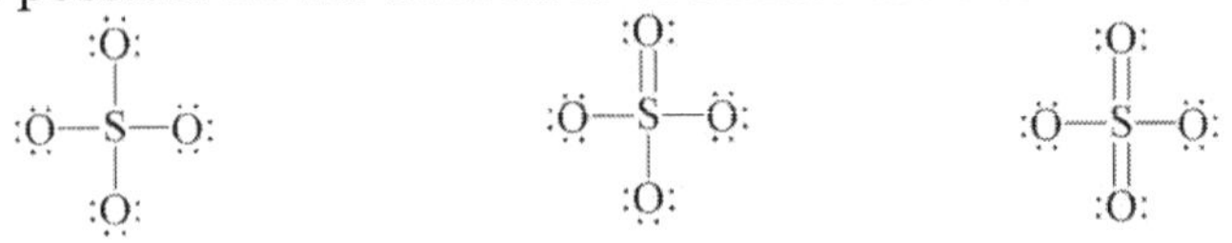

I   II   III

a) Calculate the formal charges of sulfur in each structure.
b) Calculate the formal charge of the double-bonded oxygens in each structure.
c) Calculate the formal charge of the single-bonded oxygens in each structure.
d) Which of the three structures is predicted to be the most correct?

XP + 4 each

9. Like boron trifluoride, beryllium chloride (BeCl$_2$) is also soluble in diethyl ether and will form coordinate covalent bonds with solvent molecules to give beryllium an octet. How many molecules of diethyl ether are need to give beryllium an octet? Draw a structure of this adduct.

XP +4

★XP: _____

If your XP is 75 or higher, maybe you have what it takes to be…

★★The Contender

10. Draw Lewis structures for each of the following compounds.
a) ClF_2^+, b) H_2O_2, c) XeF_2, d) HCN, e) CH_2O

XP +5 each

11. Draw a structure for perchlorate (ClO_4^-) where every atom has a zero formal charge except one (the atom carrying the negative charge)

XP +5

12. Aluminum chloride ($AlCl_3$) is a covalent compound that often exists as a dimer, Al_2Cl_6. Draw the Lewis structures of both $AlCl_3$ and Al_2Cl_6.

XP + 5 each

13. Calculate the formal charges of each of the following:
a) a carbon with two double bonds
b) a nitrogen with two double bonds
c) an oxygen with one lone pair and three single bonds
d) an iodine with three lone pairs and two single bonds

XP +5 each

14. Arrange the following molecules in order of increasing bond length: O_2, O_2^{2-}, O_3.

XP +5

15. Nitrogen monoxide (NO) has an odd number of valence electrons.
a) Use formal charges to determine which atom is more likely to carry the radical.
b) Draw the structure of a dimer formed from two NO molecules.

XP + 5 each

360

16. Draw the resonance structures of azide (N_3^-) and determine the major structure.

XP: +5 each correct structure.
+5 for major structure

★★XP: _____   Total XP: _____

If your total XP is 140 or higher, it's time to face...

★★★The World Champion

17. Pentazenium is polyatomic ion with the formula N_5^+ and the five nitrogen atoms arranged linearly (N-N-N-N-N). There are at least three different resonance structures. Draw them.

XP + 20 each

★★★XP: _____   Total XP: _____

If your total XP is 191 or higher: Level up!

Achievement Unlocked: Structurally Sound
Completed Chapter 10

It's time to learn more about chemical structures.

Chapter 11
Chemical Structures
(Part II)

Part 1: Organic Structures

Overall, organic compounds require a different approach than inorganic compounds because—besides methane (CH_4)—most organic compounds don't have the simple AX_n general formula. In such cases, coming up with a Lewis structure can be a trial and error process, but when you consider that roughly 95% of organic compounds are only made up of ten elements — C, H, N, O, P, S, and the four main halogens (F, Cl, Br, and I), it's not as bad as you may think at first.

The following trends should help you determine the structure of most organic compounds you'll encounter.

1. With the exception of hydrogen, all other atoms in an organic compound usually obey the octet rule.
2. Hydrogen and halogens are (almost) always outer atoms.
3. In neutral compounds, nitrogen and phosphorus will usually retain their lone pair. Likewise, sulfur and oxygen will usually keep their two lone pairs.
4. While phosphorus and sulfur have the ability to form an expanded valence, they rarely do when they're part of an organic compound.

Organic compounds are rarely shown as simple molecular formulas, since different compounds can have the same molecular formula, but different structures. Such compounds are known as **isomers**. For example, drinking alcohol (ethanol) has the formula C_2H_6O and the following structure:

$$
\begin{array}{ccc}
& H & H \\
& | & | \\
H-&C-&C-\ddot{\underset{\cdot\cdot}{O}}-H \\
& | & | \\
& H & H
\end{array}
$$

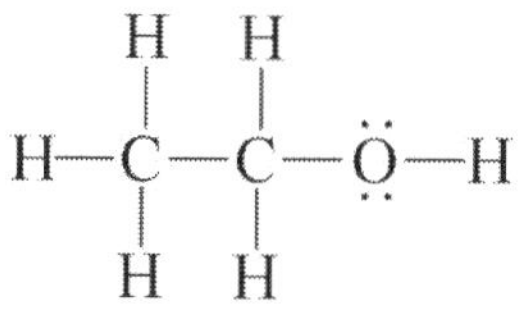

364

These nine atoms can also arrange themselves into the compound known as dimethyl ether.

$$H-\overset{\overset{\displaystyle H}{|}}{C}-\overset{..}{\underset{..}{O}}-\overset{\overset{\displaystyle H}{|}}{C}-H$$

As the number of atoms increase, so do the number of isomers. Back in Chapter 7, one of the Test Your Skills problems (the one about ANFO) involved a compound with the molecular formula $C_{17}H_{36}$. In reality, there are over *twenty-four thousand* possible isomers with that formula!

Chemists have devised a few tricks or shortcuts for drawing organic structures. One of the most common is to show molecules as **condensed structural formulas**. In general, hydrogens are written in front of the atom it's bonded to, while many or all of the single bonds (depending on the complexity of the molecule) are omitted for simplicity. The condensed structural formulas of ethanol and dimethyl ether would be

ethanol: CH_3CH_2OH
dimethyl ether: CH_3OCH_3

Multiple bonds are often shown, however,

$$CH_2=CH_2 \qquad CH\equiv CH$$

as well as bonds to groups that branch off of the main carbon chain.

$$\overset{\overset{\displaystyle OH}{|}}{CH_3CH_2CH_3} \qquad \overset{\overset{\displaystyle CH_3}{|}}{CH_3CH_2CH_3}$$

These side chains (as they're often called) can also be written in parentheses immediately after the carbon it's bonded to.

$$CH_3CH_2(OH)CH_3 \qquad CH_3CH_2(CH_3)CH_3$$

If the compound has a cyclic structure, like chlorocyclohexane,

chemists will simply draw the geometric shape that the compound resembles—a hexagon in this case—and won't bother drawing all of the hydrogens coming off each carbon.

You might also have noticed that lone pairs are often omitted for additional simplicity (outer atoms in particular), as seen with chlorine and oxygen in the above examples.

Try It Yourself

P1. Draw Lewis structures for each of the following compounds:
a) C_3H_8, b) C_3H_6

P2. Draw the structures from P1 as condensed structural formulas.

P3. In the previous chapter, the condensed structural formula of diethyl ether was given as $CH_3CH_2OCH_2CH_3$. Draw the complete Lewis structure of this compound.

Part 2: Bond Enthalpy

We talked quite a bit about the relationship between energy and reactions in Chapter 7 (and will talk even more about it in Chapter 19). Typically, breaking a chemical bond requires energy, which—if you think about it—really isn't that different from breaking anything else. I'm assuming at some point in your life, you've intentionally tried to break something. If not, and you have a pencil nearby, pick it up and snap it in half. Doing so requires you to exert energy, some of which gets transferred to what I'm hoping wasn't your only pencil.

Bond enthalpy is a measure of the energy required to break a bond between two atoms (in the gaseous state). For example, 436 kJ of energy are required to break the single bonds of a mole of hydrogen molecules.

$$H-H \rightarrow 2H \cdot \quad \Delta H = 436 \text{ kJ}$$

The average bond enthalpies of a few other common bonds are given below:

Bond	Bond Enthalpy (kJ/mol)	Bond	Bond Enthalpy (kJ/mol)
C—C	347	N≡N	941
C=C	620	N—O	176
C≡C	812	N=O	607
C—H	414	H—F	568
C—F	486	H—Br	366
C—Cl	327	H—Cl	432
C—Br	285	H—I	298
C—I	213	H—N	393
C—N	276	H—O	460
C—O	351	H—P	326
C=O	799 (CO_2)	H—S	368
	745 (others)	O—O	142
C≡O	1072	O=O	499
C—P	263	Br—Br	193
C—S	255	Cl—Cl	243
N—N	193	F—F	157
N=N	418	I—I	151

As we discussed in Chapter 7 (Hess' law), flipping an equation around causes the sign of its enthalpy change to "flip" as well. Therefore, the making of a bond should require the same amount of energy required to break it, but it would be an exothermic process.

$$2H\cdot \rightarrow H\!-\!H \quad \Delta H = \text{-}436 \text{ kJ}$$

Bond Enthalpies and ΔH_{rxn}

In Chapter 7, we saw how enthalpies of formation (ΔH_f) could be used to calculate the enthalpy change of a reaction. For example, to find the enthalpy change of

$$H_2(g) + F_2(g) \rightarrow 2HF(g)$$

we can take the enthalpies of formation for each substance (which we can find in our table of ΔH_f's in Chapter 7),

$H_2(g)$	0 kJ/mol
$F_2(g)$	0 kJ/mol
$HF(g)$	-271.6 kJ/mol

and calculate its ΔH_{rxn} as

$$\Delta H_{rxn} = 2(\text{-}271.6) - (0 + 0)$$
$$\Delta H_{rxn} = \text{-}543.2 \text{ kJ}$$

Another way to calculate ΔH_{rxn} is by examining the bonds that are broken and formed during the reaction. For the reaction above, we can imagine the two reactants breaking their respective single bonds

$$H\!-\!H + F\!-\!F \rightarrow 2H\cdot + 2F\cdot$$

and forming two hydrogen-fluorine bonds.

$$2H\cdot + 2F\cdot \rightarrow 2H{-}F$$

If breaking a bond is an endothermic process, and forming bonds are exothermic, the net change in bond enthalpy would be

Bonds broken:	H—H	436 kJ
	F—F	157 kJ
Bonds formed	H—F (x2)	2(-568 kJ)
Net change		-543 kJ

Using bond enthalpies can be especially useful for estimating the enthalpy change of organic reactions, since many involve the making or breaking of the same types of bonds (C-C, C-H, etc.), only in different structures.

Example: Calculate the enthalpy change of the following reaction:

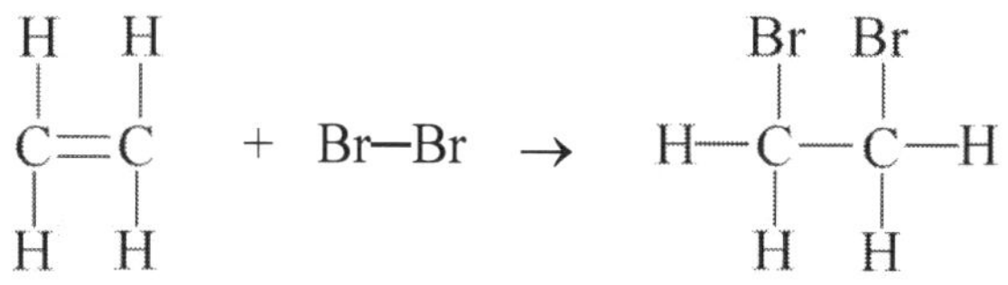

```
H  H                    Br  Br
|  |                    |   |
C==C   + Br—Br  →   H—C—C—H
|  |                    |   |
H  H                    H   H
```

Looking at the reaction, it seems that bromine is breaking its single bond and each bromine atom is forming a bond with one of the carbons.

Bonds broken:	Br—Br	193 kJ
Bonds formed	C—Br (x2)	2(-285 kJ)

The bond between the carbons is also changing from a double bond to a single. Since the bond enthalpy of a double bond isn't usually twice that of a single bond (and a triple bond isn't usually three times a single), the best approach is to imagine the two carbons breaking their double bond,

Bonds broken:	Br–Br	193 kJ
	C=C	620 kJ
Bonds formed:	C-Br (x2)	2(-285 kJ)

then coming back together as a single bond

Bonds broken:	Br–Br	193 kJ
	C=C	620 kJ
Bonds formed:	C–Br (x2)	2(-285 kJ)
	C–C	-347 kJ

The net change in energy would be

Bonds broken:	Br–Br	193 kJ
	C=C	620 kJ
Bonds formed:	C–Br (x2)	2(-285 kJ)
	C–C	-347 kJ
Net Change:		-104 kJ

Keep in mind that most of the bond enthalpies given in our table are average values measured from several different types of compounds, which can affect the accuracy of the above method, especially for organic reactions. And since bond enthalpies are measured in the gas phase, and most reactions occur in a solution, in many cases these calculated values are an estimate at best (albeit potentially useful ones).

Try It Yourself

P4. Using bond enthalpies, estimate the enthalpy change of the following reaction:

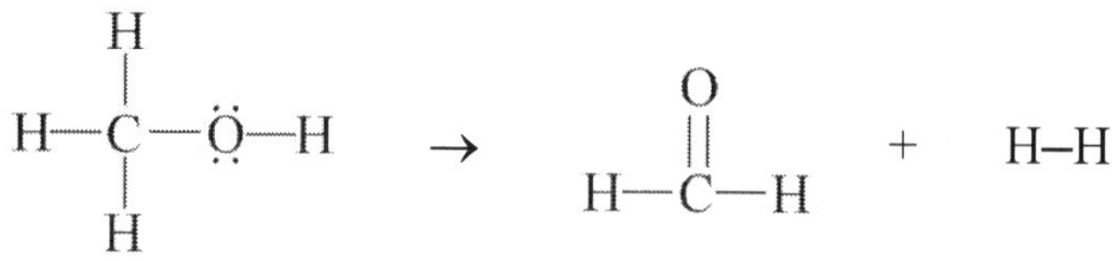

H—C(—H)(—H)—Ö—H → H—C(=O)—H + H–H

Part 3: The Shapes of Molecules

VSEPR Theory

Molecules, like most things in nature, are three-dimensional. Over the years, scientists have found ways to experimentally study the 3D shapes of molecules (using techniques such as X-ray crystallography) and discovered that molecules, on the whole, tend to conform to certain types of arrangements. The conventional theory that explains this behavior is **Valence-shell Electron-pair Repulsion Theory,** or *VSEPR* ("ves-per") *theory* for short, which states that molecules will conform to arrangements or shapes that minimize repulsive forces between the electron pairs (bonds *and* lone pairs) around an atom. To do this, any outer atoms around a central atom, as well as any lone pairs on that central atom, will spread themselves out as much as they possibly can.

In this section, we'll discuss many of the common arrangements and shapes that molecules typically conform to. The **arrangement** around a molecule describes how the electron pairs around an atom are arranging themselves around a given atom. The **shape** describes what the molecule actually looks like in three-dimensional space. To assist in our discussion, we'll use the general formula AX_mE_n. It's similar to the general formula we used in Chapter 10, where A is the central atom and X is the outer atoms, but here we'll add the symbol E to represent the number of lone pairs around A.

Two Outer Atoms, No Lone Pairs around a Central Atom (AX₂)

For arrangements of type AX_2, such as beryllium fluoride, there are only two atoms bonded to a central atom. It would seem to make sense that the two outer atoms will get the maximum amount of space possible if they're on opposite sides of the central atom, giving an ideal angle of 180°.

$$180°$$
:F̈—Be—F̈:

The name given to this arrangement is simply called **linear** (you'll find that most of the names we use for shapes and arrangements are pretty straightforward). It's commonplace to use the same name to describe both the arrangement and shape of a molecule when there are no lone pairs on the central atom, so the shape of the molecule is also said to be **linear**.

Three Things around a Central Atom

Three Atoms (AX₃)

When there are three atoms bonded to a central atom, they will spread out to ideal angles of 120°, as seen with boron triflouride.

The name given to both the arrangement and shape of such molecules is **trigonal planar**, *trigonal* because of the triangular look of the molecule and *planar* because the molecule is flat, with all atoms in the same two-dimensional plane.

Two Atoms, One Lone Pair (AX₂E)

When there are lone pairs on a central atom, they will occupy space just as an outer atom would. In sulfur dioxide, for example, the atoms cannot conform to a linear arrangement due to the presence of a lone pair on sulfur. The three things around sulfur must therefore conform to a **trigonal planar** arrangement.

Even though SO_2 and BF_3 have the same arrangement, it doesn't make sense to describe their shapes by the same name. After all, the shape describes what the molecule looks like, and without that third atom SO_2 doesn't *look* the same as BF_3. It looks like a linear molecule that's been **bent**, so that's the name given to this shape.

Four Things around a Central Atom

Four Atoms (AX₄)

Looking at a molecule like methane (CH_4) in two dimensions, it may first appear as if the hydrogen atoms can only spread out to maximum angle of 90°

Remember, though, we're not limited to two dimensions here. In three-dimensional space, the four outer atoms can spread out to an ideal angle of 109.5°

$$\begin{array}{c} H \\ | \quad 109.5° \\ C \\ H \quad | \quad H \\ H \end{array}$$

Those "dashes and wedges," as they're often called, are sometimes used to give some depth to an otherwise flat Lewis structure. Normal-looking lines indicate bonds in the plane of the paper. Dashed lines represent bonds that are behind this plane while wedge-shaped lines represent bonds sticking out of the plane. This arrangement of four things around a central atom is called **tetrahedral**, since it resembles a geometric shape called a tetrahedron.

As before, since there are no lone pairs on the central atom, the shape is also called **tetrahedral**.

Three Atoms, One Lone Pair (AX₃E)

When a lone pair occupies one of these four positions, as is the case with ammonia, the arrangement will still be tetrahedral. Again, arrangement is based on *everything* around that central atom, not just the atoms.

$$\begin{array}{c} \cdot\cdot \\ N \\ H \quad | \quad H \\ H \end{array}$$

The shape, however, is given the name **trigonal pyramidal**: *trigonal* because of the three outer atoms and *pyramidal* because the shape bears a resemblance to a three-base pyramid.

Two Atoms, Two Lone Pairs (AX₂E₂)

In a structure such as water's, where there are two lone pairs and two atoms around a central atom, the arrangement is once again tetrahedral.

$$H \overset{\ddot{O}}{\diagup \diagdown} H$$

As for its shape, notice that the molecule's shape basically looks the same as sulfur dioxide's, so it makes sense to give water's shape the same name: **bent**

The Effect of Lone Pairs on Bond Angles

As mentioned in the previous chapter, most of the covalent compounds studied in this course have the general formula AX_n, meaning all of the outer atoms are identical. Molecules like this typically exhibit the ideal angles discussed in this chapter. However, as you start replacing the outer atoms with lone pairs, the bond angles will begin to decrease. This can be seen by comparing the bond angles of methane, ammonia and water.

At first, this may not make sense, because a pair of electrons is obviously smaller than an entire atom, even hydrogen. Actually, this decrease in bond angle is due to the fact that electrons in a bond are interacting with two nuclei, which exhibit lower repulsive forces than those interacting with only one. The larger repulsive forces of the lone pairs will push the atoms away, and closer to each other.

Five Things around a Central Atom

Five Atoms (AX₅)

Five things will situate themselves around a central atom in an arrangement known as **trigonal bipyramidal**, as seen in the **trigonal bipyramidal** shape of phosphorus pentachloride.

In the other arrangements discussed in this chapter, all positions around the central atom are identical, but there are two distinct positions in a trigonal bipyramidal arrangement. The three "middle" positions that are 120° from each other are known as **equatorial positions**, while the two above and below this plane are called **axial positions**. You're probably familiar enough with a globe to see how they got their name.

Four Atoms, One Lone Pair (AX₄E)

As seen in our tetrahedral examples, lone pairs have larger repulsive forces than shared pairs, which effectively means that a lone pair will require more space than an outer atom. Of the two positions in a trigonal bipyramidal arrangement, the equatorial position gives a lone pair a bit more space, being perpendicular to only two other atoms whereas an axial position is perpendicular to three. We can see this in the structure of sulfur tetrafluoride.

Believe it or not, this shape is actually known as **seesaw**. Tilt the book on its side if you can't see why.

Three Atoms, Two Lone Pairs (AX₃E₂)

A second lone pair will also occupy an equatorial position, as it does in chlorine trifluoride, giving a shape we call **T-shaped** (again, tilt the book to its side).

$$:\ddot{F}:$$
$$|$$
$$:\ddot{Cl}—\ddot{F}:$$
$$|$$
$$:\ddot{F}:$$

Two Atoms, Three Lone Pairs (AX₂E₃)

Finally, a third lone pair will take the remaining equatorial position, resulting in a **linear** shape, as seen with an I₃⁻ ion.

Six Things around a Central Atom

Six Atoms (AX$_6$)

When there are six positions around central atom, the resulting arrangement is called **octahedral**, because the resulting shape resembles an eight-sided figure known as an octahedron.

Sulfur hexafluoride has an octahedral arrangement and shape

$$\ddot{F}$$

Five Atoms, One Lone Pair (AX$_5$E)

If a lone pair occupies one of the six positions in an octahedral arrangement, it gives a shape known as **square pyramidal**, as seen in the structure of bromine pentachloride.

Four Atoms, Two Lone Pairs (AX$_4$E$_2$)

Two lone pairs in an octahedral arrangement would place themselves on opposite sides of the central atom to give them the maximum amount of space. The resulting shape is called **square planar**, seen in a molecule of xenon tetrafluoride.

Summing Up

Electron Arrangement	Shape			
	No lone pairs	1 lone pair	2 lone pairs	3 lone pairs
Linear	Linear	-	-	-
Trigonal Planar	Trigonal Planar	Bent	-	-
Tetrahedral	Tetrahedral	Trigonal pyramidal	Bent	-
Trigonal bipyramidal	Trigonal bipyramidal	See-saw	T-shaped	Linear
Octahedral	Octahedral	Square pyramidal	Square Planar	-

Try It Yourself

P5. Lewis structures of each of the following were either given or drawn by you in the previous chapter. Now determine their arrangements and shapes: a) PCl_3, b) $SiCl_4$, c) NO_3^-, d) O_3

Part 4: Polarity

Even though covalent bonds are thought of as a sharing of electrons, many times it's not an equal sharing. In Chapter 10 we discussed electronegativity and how different atoms have different "desires" for electrons. In a case like elemental fluorine

$$F\!-\!F$$

the two atoms sharing electrons are of the same element. Since their electronegativities are identical, the electrons in that single bond are shared equally between them. Covalent bonds whose electrons are shared equally between atoms is said to be **nonpolar**. Since this is only a one-bond molecule, the entire molecule is nonpolar as well.

In a molecule like hydrogen fluoride, however,

$$H\!-\!F$$

fluorine has a higher electronegativity than hydrogen (see table in Chapter 10). As a result, fluorine will pull the electrons in that bond closer to it, giving fluorine a **partially negative** charge. Since the electrons are being pulled away from hydrogen, it in turn will become **partially positive**. The symbol for a partial charge is a lower case, Greek letter delta (δ). We don't usually bother noting the magnitude of a partial charge, like we do for ions (-2, +3, etc.), we simply note whether a given atom is partially positive ($\delta+$) or partially negative ($\delta-$).

$$\overset{\delta+ \quad \delta-}{H\!-\!F}$$

Hydrogen fluoride is an example of a **polar** molecule, meaning it has positive and negative ends. This separation of charge results in a magnetic force known as a **dipole moment**. In structures, dipole moments are often shown using a special arrow.

$$\overset{\delta+\quad\delta-}{H-F}$$

This arrow essentially shows you the direction the electrons are being pulled in. In an HF molecule, the electrons (and the resulting dipole moment) are being pulled from the hydrogen end to fluorine. Also, notice that the "plus sign" on the arrow is near the positive end of the polar bond.

Water

Looking at a (slightly) larger molecule,

water has two H−O bonds, with oxygen being the more electronegative atom.

$$\overset{\delta+\quad\delta-}{H-O}$$

Since water is a bent molecule, both dipole moments pull the electrons from the hydrogen end of the molecule to the oxygen end.

Because the electrons are being pulled towards one end of the molecule, there is an overall dipole moment, making water a polar molecule.

Ammonia

Ammonia is also polar for similar reasons.

In each N–H bond the electrons are being pulled towards the more electronegative atom (nitrogen).

$$\overset{\delta+}{H}\!-\!\overset{\delta-}{N}$$

Similar to water, there is an overall dipole moment as the electrons are being pulled from the hydrogen end of the molecule to the nitrogen end.

Dichloromethane

Finally, dichloromethane (CH_2Cl_2) is another example of a polar molecule.

In this case, there are two types of bonds in this molecule. In the C–H bonds, carbon is slightly more electronegative, so the electrons are pulled toward it.

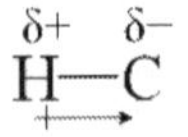

$$\overset{\delta+}{H}—\overset{\delta-}{C}$$

But in the C–Cl bonds the electrons are being pulled *away* from carbon because chlorine is more electronegative.

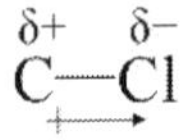

$$\overset{\delta+}{C}{-\!-\!-}\overset{\delta-}{Cl}$$

Overall, the electrons are being pulled across the molecule from the hydrogen end to the chlorine end.

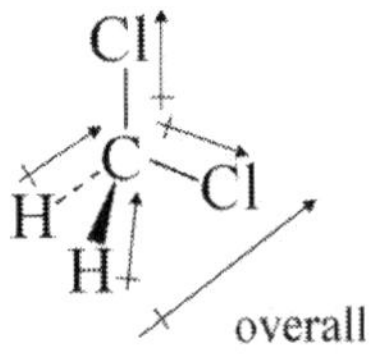

overall

Carbon Dioxide

However, just because a molecule contains polar bonds doesn't mean the molecule is polar. Take carbon dioxide, for instance.

$$O{=}C{=}O$$

In each C–O bond, the electrons are being pulled towards oxygen.

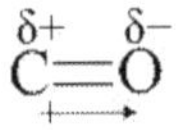

$$\overset{\delta+}{C}{=}\overset{\delta-}{O}$$

But since this is a *linear* molecule, the resulting dipole moments don't pull the electrons towards one end of the molecule.

$$O{=}C{=}O$$

Because the electrons aren't being pulled towards from one end of the molecule to the other, there's no overall dipole moment, meaning the molecule is actually *nonpolar* overall.

Boron Trifluoride

The same thing happens with boron trifluoride.

$$\underset{F \quad \ \ F}{\overset{F}{|}} B$$

Unlike ammonia, BF_3 is trigonal planar, meaning it's a flat, planar molecule. As it was with carbon dioxide, when the electrons are being pulled towards the more electronegative fluorine atoms, they're pulled outwards from the center, making it nonpolar overall.

Notice how important knowing the actual shape of the molecule is to determining its polarity. If you mistakenly draw water as a linear molecule, you might incorrectly predict it to be nonpolar.

Trends in Polarity

Comparing water and ammonia to CO_2 and BF_3, can you see the main structural difference between the two polar molecules and the two nonpolar ones?

Polar   H—O—H   H—N—H (with H below, lone pair on N)

Nonpolar   O=C=O   F—B (with F, F)

Water and ammonia both have lone pairs on the central atom, causing the outer atoms to bend out of the plane. As a result, overall the electrons are being pulled towards one end of the molecule, creating a dipole moment. Conversely, carbon dioxide and boron trifluoride are flat molecules, so the electrons are pulled symmetrically from the inside out.

Meanwhile, the other molecule we looked at, dichloromethane, didn't have a lone pair, but it was polar because it had different outer atoms with different electronegativities. This can also happen in planar molecules, as well. If you replace one of the fluorine atoms in BF_3 with a less electronegative element, the molecule will be slightly polar with the electrons leaning a little towards the fluorine side of the "triangle."

F — B — F (with I), overall

From these and similar examples, we get a general trend that allows you to predict polarity without having to worry so much about the actual shape of the molecule (you still, however, need to be able to draw a correct Lewis structure). Molecules with either a linear, trigonal planar, and tetrahedral arrangement are predicted to be nonpolar if

1) There are no lone pairs on the central atom
and 2) All outer atoms are the same

If one or both of these aren't true, then we predict the molecule to be polar.

This trend isn't as accurate for trigonal bipyramidal or octahedral arrangements, so you'll have to look at dipole moments, like we did earlier. Xenon tetrafluoride, for example, has lone pairs on the central atom, but the molecule has a flat, square planar shape. Therefore, the electrons would be pulled from the inside out as it did in BF_3.

Try It Yourself

P6. For of the following bonds, determine which end is partially negative and which is partially positive.
a) C-Cl, b) O-S, c) B-Br

P7. Predict the polarity of each of the following: a) ICl, b) PCl_3 c) SiI_4, d) BrF_5

388

Test Your Skills

★Bar Band

1. Draw Lewis structures for each of the following compounds.
a) $CH_3CH_2NH_2$, b) $CH_3CH_2CH(SH)CH_3$. c) $(CH_3)_2CHCH_2CH_3$

XP + 4 each

2. For the reaction below

a) Rewrite the two organic compounds as condensed formulas.
b) Estimate the enthalpy change of the reaction.

XP +4 each

3. Predict the electron arrangements for each of the following:
a) $SiBr_4$, b) $BrCl_5$, c) OCl_2, d) HCN

XP +4 each

4. Predict the shapes of each molecule from problem 3.

XP +4 each

5. For each of the following bonds, predict the partially charge of each end: a) N-F, b) O-P, c) B-Br, d) Ge-C

XP +4 each

6. Predict the polarity of each of the following:
a) CCl_4, b) HCN, c) OCl_2, d) SF_6

XP +4 each

★XP: _____

If your XP is 63 or higher, it's time to move up to…

★★Opening Act

7. Draw Lewis structures for each of the following compounds:
a) $CH_3CCl_2CH_2CH_3$, b) $CH_3CH_2COCH_3$, c) $CH_3CH_2CH=CH_2$
XP +5 each

8. Estimate the enthalpy change of the following reaction (the bond enthalpy of a C=N bond is 615 kJ/mol):

XP +5

9. It's important to be able to recognize whether two compounds are isomers or just the same compound drawn a little differently. Four structures with the molecular formula C_5H_{12} are given below. Which are actually the same compound?

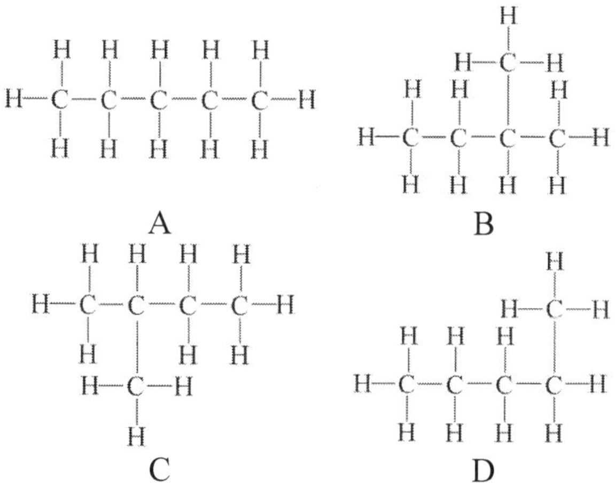

XP +5

390

10. Predict the electron arrangements of each of the following:
a) XeF_2, b) CH_2O, c) N_2O, d) ClF_2^+
$$XP +5 \text{ each}$$

11. Predict the shapes of each molecule from problem 9
$$XP +5 \text{ each}$$

12. Predict the polarity of each of the following:
a) XeF_2, b) CH_2O, c) N_2O, d) CH_3CH_3
$$XP +5 \text{ each}$$

13. When you use bond enthalpies to estimate a reaction's enthalpy change, why isn't it always necessary to factor in the bond energy of every single bond in every reactant and product?
$$XP +5$$

14. Estimate the enthalpy change of the following reactions:
a) $CO + Cl_2 \rightarrow COCl_2$
b) $2CH_3CH_2OH \rightarrow CH_3CH_2OCH_2CH_3 + H_2O$
$$XP + 10 \text{ each}$$

★★XP:_____   Total XP:_____

If your total XP is 145 or higher, maybe you can be a…

★★★Headliner

15. How many isomers can be drawn from each of the following molecular formulas?
a) C_6H_{14}, b) $C_3H_8O_2$
$$XP +10 \text{ each}$$

16. Lasers can sometimes be used to break chemical bonds, giving a chemist the ability to control or instigate certain types of reactions. Suppose a red laser with a wavelength of 655 nm could be used to break the bond between two chlorine atoms.

$$Cl_2 \rightarrow 2Cl\cdot$$

How many moles of photons would be needed to supply enough energy to break the bonds in a 2.0 L sample of chlorine gas at 23 °C and 1.8 atm?

XP +20

17. A compound was found to be 54.53% C, 9.15% H, and 36.32% O with a molar mass of 88.1 g/mol. Further analysis of the compound confirmed that all carbons were bonded to two hydrogens ($-CH_2-$) and one oxygen. Determine the structure of this compound.

XP +20

★★★XP: _____   Total XP: _____

If your total XP is 205 or higher: Level up!

Achievement Unlocked: Structurally Sounder
Completed Chapter 11

You're now ready to learn about bonding theories.

Chapter 12
Chemical Bonding

Part 1: Covalent Bonding Revisited

In Chapter 10 we discussed how covalent bonding is believed to form by an overlap of orbitals. In a few cases, one can envision these bonds occurring by simply overlapping the atomic orbitals introduced in Chapter 8. For example, with diatomic hydrogen (H_2) you can picture each hydrogen atom ($1s^1$) sharing its one electron by overlapping its 1s orbital.

Similarly, according to the orbital diagram of a chlorine atom there is an unpaired electron in a 3p orbital,

Cl   ⥮   ⥮   ⥮⥮⥮   ⥮   ⥮⥮↑

    1s   2s   2p   3s   3p

so one can imagine two chlorine atoms overlapping their 3p orbitals to form Cl_2.

And in the case of hydrogen chloride (HCl), we can picture chlorine overlapping this same 3p orbital with hydrogen's 1s orbital.

This "end-to-end" overlapping of orbitals that are seen in the above examples is known as a **sigma (σ) bond.** As we make our way through this chapter, you'll see that most single bonds form as sigma bonds.

While atomic orbitals can be used to explain bonding in diatomic molecules, it doesn't work as well for larger ones. Take methane, for instance. In Chapter 11, we discussed how the four C-H bonds are in a tetrahedral arrangement, 109.5° apart.

$$
\begin{array}{c}
H \\
| \\
H \cdots \overset{C}{\underset{H}{\bigg|}} H \\
\end{array}
$$

109.5°

The formation of these four bonds can't be explained using only s and p orbitals. In Chapter 9 we predicted that carbon's electron configuration is $1s^2 2s^2 2p^2$. Furthermore, from its orbital diagram we see that two of carbon's valence electrons are already paired up in a 2s orbital, while the other two are unpaired in two separate 2p orbitals.

C   ⬆⬇   ⬆⬇   ⬆ ⬆

     1s   2s   2p

And remember, 2p orbitals are perpendicular to each other (Chapter 8).

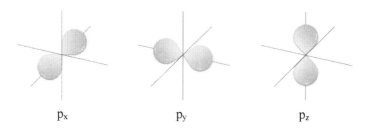

p_x $\qquad$ p_y $\qquad$ p_z

So how does a carbon atom take this electron configuration and form a molecule with this type of arrangement? Clearly, there's something else going on that we've yet to consider. In fact, there are two common theories to explain the bonding in compounds such as this, both of which we'll discuss in this chapter.

Part 2: Valence Bond Theory

In **valence bond theory**, atomic orbitals are combined or "mixed" to form new types of orbitals known as **hybrid orbitals**. Think of it as being similar to how one mixes different colors of paint to get a new color: white and red makes pink, blue and yellow makes green, and so on.

There are two important things to remember about hybrid orbitals. First, even when you're combining atomic orbitals of different energies, such as s and p orbitals, the resulting hybrid orbitals will be degenerate (equal energy), similar to how the three orbitals in a p subshell are degenerate. Also, the number of hybrid orbitals that form will equal the number of atomic orbitals that were hybridized. When you combine x number of atomic orbitals, you'll form x number of hybrid orbitals.

Two types of atoms are typically said to form hybrid orbitals: central atoms (those bonded to 2 or more other atoms) and outer atoms involved in multiple bonding. An outer atom that's only forming one single bond isn't predicted to hybridize. Whichever orbital is housing the unpaired electron to be shared will be the one doing the overlapping, like we saw with the diatomic examples in Part 1.

sp³ hybrid orbitals

Looking back at CH_4, carbon is sharing four valence electrons with four hydrogen atoms.

$$H$$
$$|$$
$$H\diagup \overset{C}{|} \diagdown H$$
$$H$$
$$109.5°$$

According to valence bond theory, carbon takes the four atomic orbitals in its valence shell (one 2s and three 2p's) and combines them to form four new orbitals known as **sp^3 hybrid orbitals**. The superscript *3* tells us that three p orbitals were hybridized (as usual, *1*'s are not written, so we don't call them s^1p^3 orbitals). Also notice that, unlike atomic orbitals, we don't usually bother noting the valence shell in the hybrid's name (in other words, we don't normally call them "$2sp^3$" orbitals).

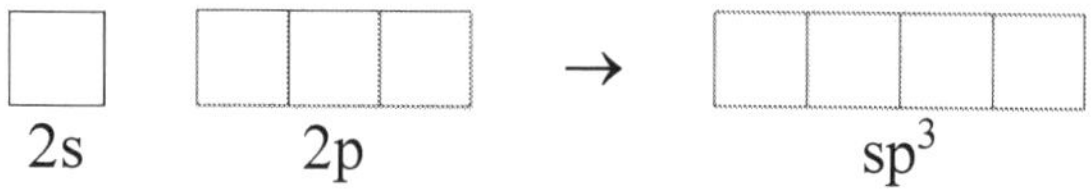
2s
2p
→
sp3

The orbital diagram of our four hybrid orbitals are shown as four connected boxes to emphasize that they're degenerate, just as we did with the *p*, *d*, and *f* orbitals in Chapter 9. Each of these hybrid orbitals holds an electron.

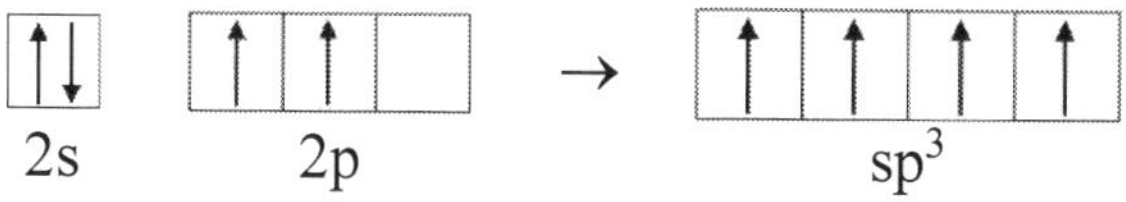
2s
2p
→
sp3

These four sp^3 orbitals will spread out in a tetrahedral arrangement.

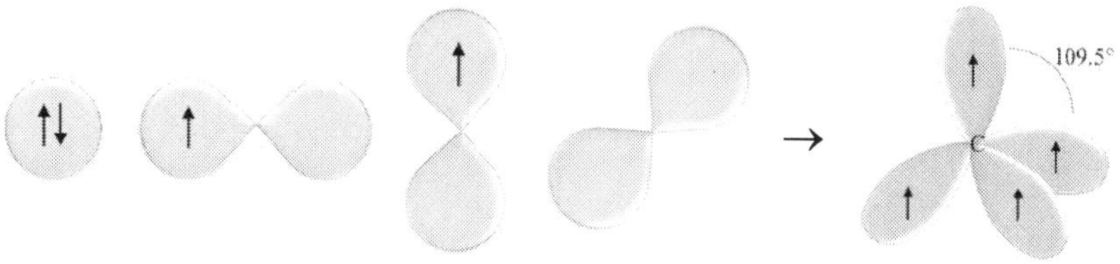
→
109.5°
C

So when carbon and hydrogen share electrons to form a bond,

C
H
→
C—H

hydrogen is overlapping its 1s orbital with one of carbon's sp^3 hybrid orbitals, forming a sigma bond.

Ammonia also has a tetrahedral arrangement, because—like methane—it has to accommodate four things around it (three atoms and a lone pair, in this case).

Therefore, it will also form four hybrid orbitals, just as carbon did in the previous example. Nitrogen's five valence electrons are rearranged into these new sp^3 orbitals. Three of the hybrid orbitals will contain an electron that can be shared with a hydrogen atom (via a sigma bond), while the fourth sp^3 orbital houses nitrogen's lone pair.

"Hang on," you may be saying, "nitrogen already had a lone pair and three unpaired electrons. Why bother hybridizing?" Don't forget, those three 2p orbitals are only 90° apart, while the hybrid orbitals are in a tetrahedral arrangement.

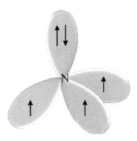

Therefore, the nitrogen-hydrogen bonds in ammonia are also sigma bonds between an sp^3 orbital of the central atom and hydrogen's 1s orbital.

sp^2 hybrid orbitals

As we discussed in Chapter 11, molecules with a trigonal planar arrangement, such as boron trifluoride, require three equal orbitals that are (ideally) 120° apart.

:F:
| ‚ 120°
B
:F   F:

Boron only needs three hybrid orbitals to accommodate the three atoms around it, so it only needs to hybridize three atomic orbitals in its valence shell. In any shell, the s subshell has the lowest energy (see Chapter 8), so this s orbital is normally used for any type of hybridization, meaning boron only needs to hybridize two of the three p orbitals in its valence shell. These new orbitals are called **sp^2 hybrid orbitals**.

Boron's three valence electrons are rearranged so that each sp^2 orbital holds an electron. The unhybridized 2p orbital remains empty (for now; we'll look at examples where that isn't the case a little later).

For those that prefer visualizing hybridization with those cute little balloon diagrams:

Fluorine isn't predicted to hybridize, as it's only forming a single bond with the central atom. Its unpaired electron is in a 2p orbital,

so this is the one that forms the single bond with boron.

$$\cdot B\bigcirc \ddot{F}: \quad \rightarrow \quad \cdot B-\ddot{F}:$$

According to valence bond theory, this bond is a sigma bond like the ones we saw earlier in HCl and Cl_2, only here the p orbital is forming an end-to-end overlap with a hybrid orbital.

sp hybrid orbitals

Beryllium fluoride has a linear arrangement, with the Be-F bonds being 180° apart.

$$180°$$
$$:\!\ddot{F}\!-\!Be\!-\!\ddot{F}\!:$$

Since beryllium only needs two degenerate, hybrid orbitals, it will only mix two orbitals in its valence shell: one *s* and one *p*. The resulting orbitals are therefore called **sp hybrid orbitals**.

Each of these hybrids will hold one of beryllium's two valence electrons so it can be shared with the unpaired 3p electron of fluorine.

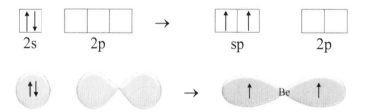

When beryllium forms a single bond with fluorine,

$$·Be\!\subset\!\ddot{F}\!: \quad \rightarrow \quad ·Be\!-\!\ddot{F}\!:$$

it forms a sigma bond between fluorine's 2p orbital (the same one as before) and one of beryllium's sp orbitals.

Atoms with an Expanded Valence

Recall from Chapter 10 that the reason elements of atomic number 13 and up can form an expanded valence is that they have a d subshell in its valence shell. According to valence bond theory, these d orbitals can also hybridize with the s and p orbitals, when needed.

In a molecule such as phosphorus pentachloride,

$$
\begin{array}{c}
:\ddot{C}l: \\
| \quad :\ddot{C}l: \\
:\ddot{C}l-P\!\!\!\diagup \quad)120° \\
| \quad :\ddot{C}l: \\
90° \quad :\ddot{C}l:
\end{array}
$$

the central atom needs five hybrid orbitals in a trigonal bipyramidal arrangement (see Chapter 11), so it must hybridize five atomic orbitals from its valence shell. Similar to our previous examples, phosphorus will use the s orbital and three p orbitals in its valence shell, but that only adds up to four. The fifth atomic orbital will come from the d subshell, and the resulting hybrids are called **sp³d hybrid orbitals**. Each hybrid orbital will hold one of phosphorus' five valence electrons that can be shared with the unpaired 3p electron of a chlorine atom via a sigma bond.

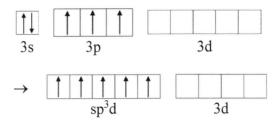

For a molecule with an octahedral arrangement, such as xenon tetrafluoride,

xenon will hybridize six atomic orbitals in its valence shell: the *s* orbital, the three *p* orbitals, and two *d* orbitals, forming six **sp³d²** **hybrid orbitals**. Two of these hybrid orbitals will hold xenon's two lone pairs, while the other four will hold one of xenon's remaining four electrons, which will be used to form sigma bonds with a 2p orbital of fluorine.

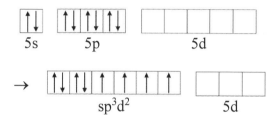

Summing Up

As you can see, the type of hybrids an atom forms will depend on the electron arrangement that's around it.

Arrangement	Hybridization
Linear	sp
Trigonal Planar	sp²
Tetrahedral	sp³
Trigonal bipyramidal	sp³d
Octahedral	sp³d²

An outer atom won't hybridize if it's only forming a single bond. When the outer atom is hydrogen, it will simply form a sigma bond using its 1s orbital, and when it's a halogen, it will use the p orbital containing the unpaired electron.

Try It Yourself

P1. What type of hybrid orbitals is the central atom forming in each of the following?

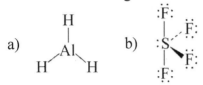

a)   b)

P2. What type of orbitals are being used for bonding by the outer atoms in the P1?

P3. For each structure in question P1, draw the orbital diagrams of the central atom's valence shell a) before hybridization, b) after hybridization.

Part 3: Valence Bond Theory & Multiple Bonding

Double Bonding

The Lewis structure of ethylene is given below

$$\underset{H}{\overset{H}{\diagdown}}C=C\underset{H}{\overset{H}{\diagup}}$$

Each carbon atom has three atoms around it and no lone pairs, giving it a trigonal planar arrangement. Therefore, it will form sp^2 hybrids, like boron did in BF_3.

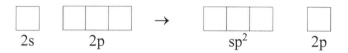

Looking at the Lewis structure of ethylene, it isn't possible for all four of carbon's valence electrons to occupy the three hybrids because that would mean that two of them would have to be paired up. That only happens when an atom has a lone pair (see ammonium and xenon tetrafluoride in Part 2), which neither carbon has. This means that the fourth electron must be in the unhybridized p orbital.

In each carbon, two of the sp^2 hybrids will form sigma bonds with two hydrogen atoms (similar to what we saw in methane).

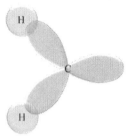

The third hybrid orbital will form a sigma bond with the other carbon's remaining hybrid.

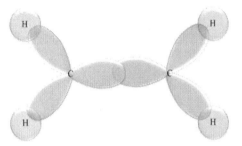

At this point, we've accounted for three of carbon's four electrons and only two of the four electrons that form the double bond. Remember, though, that each carbon has an electron in its unhybridized p orbital. The two carbons can line up these two p orbitals so they can overlap in a side-to-side fashion, which is called a **pi (π) bond** (for clarity's sake, I'll replace the sigma bonds with lines).

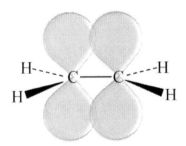

So according to valence bond theory, this double bond really is two bonds: a sigma bond between sp² orbitals and a pi bond between 2p orbitals.

Now let's look at the structure of formaldehyde

Once again, the carbon will form sp² hybrids to accommodate its trigonal planar arrangement. Since oxygen is involved in a multiple bond, it's also predicted to hybridize. Like carbon, oxygen also has to accommodate three things (2 lone pairs and a carbon atom), so it will also form sp² hybrids.

Two of the three hybrids will each hold one of oxygen's lone pairs, which accounts for four of its six electrons,

therefore the third hybrid and unhybridized 2p orbital must each hold one of the remaining two electrons.

As before, two of carbons sp² orbitals will form sigma bonds with the two hydrogen atoms. The third will form a sigma bond with the hybrid orbital of oxygen that contains the unpaired electron, forming half of the double bond.

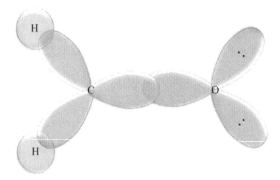

The other half of the double bond will again come from the two atoms sharing the electrons in their *p* orbitals via a pi bond.

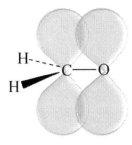

Notice that, like ethylene, the double bond is a sigma bond between hybrids and a pi bond between unhybridized *p* orbitals. This is the most common type of double bonding one encounters, though other types can occur (transitional metal compounds, for example, can form pi bonds between unhybridized *d* orbitals).

Triple Bonding

The structure of acetylene (C_2H_2) is

$$H—C≡C—H$$

Like BeCl$_2$, this molecule has a linear arrangement, so each carbon will form sp orbitals. Since there are no lone pairs on the carbons, two of its four electrons must be in the two hybrid orbitals while the other two are in the unhybridized p orbitals.

One of the hybrid orbitals will sigma bond with the 1s orbital of hydrogen while the other forms a sigma bond with the other carbon.

This accounts for two of the six electrons in the triple bond, but remember that each carbon has *two* unpaired electrons in a pair of *p* orbitals. Similar to what we saw with a double bond, two sets of *p* orbitals will align themselves in a way that allows the formation of two pi bonds (as before, I'm changing the sigma bonds to lines for the sake of clarity).

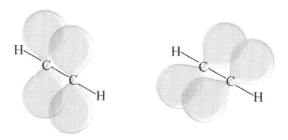

So according to valence bond theory, a triple bond really is *three* bonds: one sigma bond between hybrid orbitals and *two* pi bonds between two sets of p orbitals. Similar to double bonding, other types of triple bonds can form, but this combination of a sigma bond between hybrid orbitals and a pair of pi bonds between two sets of *p* orbitals is the one most commonly encountered.

Resonance Structures

Benzene (C_6H_6) is a common organic chemical whose structure is a resonance structure, shown below (using the organic shorthand discussed in Chapter 11). The two resonance forms only differ by the placement of three double bonds.

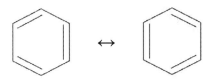

In both structures, all six carbons are trigonal planar and, therefore, sp^2 hybridized. Just as it was in ethylene and formaldehyde, each hybrid will contain one of carbon's four valence electrons, with the fourth going into the unhybridized p orbital.

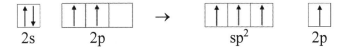

Each carbon will form a sigma bond with the 1s orbital of a hydrogen atom and two sigma bonds with the adjacent carbon atoms.

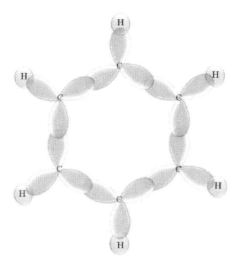

Each carbon also has a *p* orbital with an unpaired electron, all of which are perpendicular to the plane of the ring.

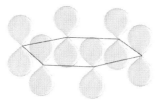

In ethylene and formaldehyde, the two adjacent *p* orbitals overlapped to form a pi bond. Something similar happens with benzene, except here all six *p* orbitals overlap one another.

This is why chemists will often draw benzene with a circle in the hexagon instead of three double bonds.

A pi bond that forms across three or more orbitals is called a **delocalized pi bond**. As you can see in the above figure, the double bond isn't really "resonating" between carbon atoms. Rather, all six carbons are forming one big double bond.

Looking at another example, we discussed nitrate's resonance structure in the Chapter 10.

$$:\ddot{O}: \qquad :\ddot{O}: \qquad :\ddot{O}:$$

Like the carbons of benzene, nitrogen becomes sp^2 hybridized to accommodate a trigonal planar arrangement, and since each oxygen is shown with a double bond in at least one of the above structures, they would also be sp^2 hybridized, similar to the oxygen in our formaldehyde example earlier. Each of nitrogen's hybrid orbitals is forming a sigma bond with the sp^2 of oxygen that holds the unpaired electron.

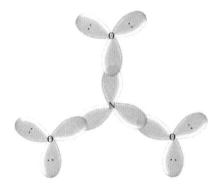

Like benzene, the "resonating" double bond is actually a delocalized pi bond that allows all four atoms to share an electron in their 2p orbital.

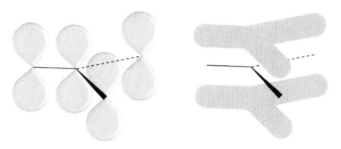

In both structures, notice that a resonating double bond is *still* a sigma bond between hybrids and a pi bond between *p* orbitals, only here the pi bond is delocalized.

Try It Yourself

P4. In Chapter 10, the structure of ozone was given as.

$$\ddot{O}{=}\ddot{O}{-}\ddot{O}: \quad \leftrightarrow \quad :\ddot{O}{-}\ddot{O}{=}\ddot{O}$$

How would valence bond theory describe the bonding in this compound?

Part 4: Molecular Orbital Theory

In general, the idea behind valence bond theory is that adjacent atoms share valence electrons by overlapping orbitals. Another popular bonding theory, **molecular orbital (MO) theory**, takes a slightly different approach. In MO theory, *all* electrons are shared over the *entire* molecule. The theory can be thought of as an extension of the atomic theory discussed in Chapter 8, where the Schrödinger wave equation was used to determine the most probable position of an electron in an atom, giving us the different types of atomic orbitals (s, p, etc.) we've been discussing for the past couple of chapters. Similar calculations can be done to find the most probable position of an electron in a *molecule*, giving us **molecular orbitals**.

Of the two bonding theories, MO theory is actually the more accurate. This is most often illustrated with elemental oxygen (O_2). In the Lewis structure of oxygen, all electrons seem to be paired up (:O=O:), making it appear to be a diamagnetic substance. However, oxygen is actually *paramagnetic*. Studies have shown that even though the bond in an O_2 molecule has a bond order of 2, confirming the presence of a double bond, there are actually *two* unpaired electrons in the molecule. If you're able to get your hands on some liquid oxygen, you can see this for yourself by pouring it between the poles of a magnet (if not, there's always YouTube). This can't be explained by valence bond theory, but it can—as we'll see—be explained by MO theory.

That doesn't make valence bond theory completely useless (I wouldn't have wasted two-thirds of a chapter talking about it if that was the case). It's still commonly used among chemists to explain chemical behavior. One reason might be that while MO theory is more accurate, it's also a bit more complex. For this reason, we'll only be looking at diatomic molecules— both real and theoretical—that are homonuclear (both atoms are the same element) from the first two periods. That's generally enough to give a first-year chemistry student an appreciation of how the theory works.

Formation of Molecular Orbitals

Recall from Chapter 8 that the quantum model of the atom was based on the idea that electrons exhibited wave behavior. Waves can combine in two ways: constructively or destructively. The constructive addition of two waves will cause the amplitude to increase,

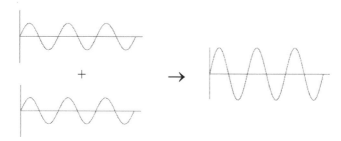

while two waves that combine destructively can cancel each other out

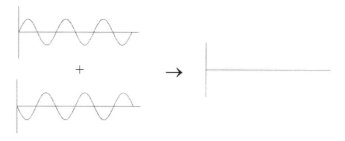

Just as it was with valence bond theory, MO theory is based on the idea that atomic orbitals are combined to form new types of orbitals (hybrid orbitals in valence bond theory, molecular orbitals in MO theory). And like valence bond theory, the number of atomic orbitals combined gives rise to an equal number of molecular orbitals. Combining two 1s orbitals will result in the formation of two molecular orbitals: a **bonding** orbital, from the constructive interaction between the two orbitals, and an **antibonding** orbital, from their destructive interaction (the dot in each picture represents the nucleus of each atom).

1s   1s   bonding orbital (σ_{1s})   antibonding orbital (σ^*_{1s})

The term *antibonding* can be somewhat misleading, since electrons can occupy these orbitals just as they can in any other orbital.

These new orbitals are said to be **sigma (σ)** molecular orbitals, as they form two orbitals combining in an end-to-end fashion, similar to the sigma bonds we discussed in the previous theory. An asterisk is used to differentiate between an antibonding sigma orbital (σ^*) and a bonding orbital (σ). Also, the type of orbitals that were combined is shown in subscript (σ_{1s} and σ^*_{1s} in this case).

Molecular Orbital Diagrams

In valence bond theory, we were able to illustrate the bonding between atoms through the use of balloon-type figures, but this isn't as easy with MO theory. Instead we're going to use a variation of the orbital diagrams ("box notation") that were introduced in Chapter 9. Redrawing the above balloon figures with boxes would look something like this:

That's not how we typically draw MO diagrams, however. In general, the energy of a bonding orbital is usually less than that of the original atomic orbitals, while antibonding orbitals are higher. To emphasize the differences in energy, molecular orbital diagrams are typically drawn vertically (instead of horizontally as we did with atomic orbital diagrams in Chapter 9).

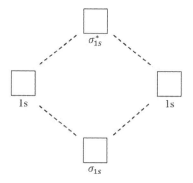

The dashed lines are used to emphasize that the two 1s orbitals have been combined to form two new molecular orbitals.

The MO Diagram of H$_2$

Molecular orbitals follow the same rules as the atomic orbitals discussed in Chapter 9, meaning no orbital can hold more than two electrons (Pauli exclusion principle) and orbitals are filled beginning with the lowest (Aufbau principle). In the case of elemental hydrogen (H$_2$), each hydrogen atom began with an electron configuration of $1s^1$.

When the two atoms come together to make a H_2 molecule, the 1s orbitals are combined and form two sigma-type molecular orbitals: one bonding and the other antibonding

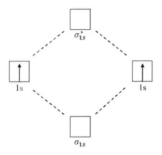

Following the Aufbau principle, the electrons in this molecule will fill these new molecular orbitals starting with the lowest (σ_{1s}).

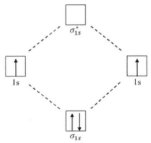

It's important to remember that two electrons in the σ_{1s} orbital are the same two electrons shown in the 1s orbitals on either side of it. Also notice that we still show the antibonding orbital even though there aren't any electrons in it, which isn't that different from how we draw atomic orbital diagrams (for instance, we always draw all three boxes of a p subshell, even when one or two orbitals are empty).

The electron configuration for a hydrogen atom is $1s^1$. From the above MO diagram, we see the electron configuration

for an H_2 molecule is $(\sigma_{1s})^2$. Since the two electrons are paired up, it's predicted to be a diamagnetic molecule.

Bond Order and MO Diagrams

You can determine the bond order of a molecule from its MO diagram by subtracting the number of antibonding electrons from the number of bonding electrons, then dividing by 2.

$$\text{Bond Order} = \frac{\text{bonding e}^- - \text{antibonding e}^-}{2}$$

For a H_2 molecule, the bond order is

$$\text{Bond Order} \frac{2-0}{2} = 1$$

Therefore, MO theory predicts a single bond in a H_2 molecule, which agrees with the predicted Lewis structure (H-H).

He₂ and He₂⁺

Let's look at a hypothetical example: diatomic helium (He_2). Each helium atom has a configuration of $1s^2$

As before, the two 1s orbitals will combine to form one bonding and one antibonding molecular orbital. He_2 has a total of four electrons, which are added to these molecular orbitals starting (again) with the lowest, σ_{1s}.

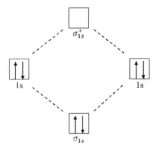

There are two more, which will go into the σ_{1s}^* orbital, giving us our final MO diagram.

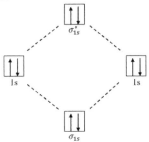

The predicted electron configuration of He_2 molecule is $(\sigma_{1s})^2(\sigma_{1s}^*)^2$. This means the predicted bond order would be

$$\text{Bond Order}\frac{2-2}{2} = 0$$

A bond order of zero means that no bond can exist, so it's theoretically impossible to make a He_2 molecule.

But what about a diatomic helium *ion*, such as He_2^+? Removing one electron from the molecular orbital diagram (and from either one of the atomic orbitals, to keep the overall diagram "balanced") gives us

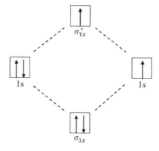

The electron configuration of an He_2^+ ion is predicted to be $(\sigma_{1s})^2(\sigma_{1s}{}^*)^1$, making the bond order

$$\text{Bond Order} \frac{2-1}{2} = \frac{1}{2}$$

As long as the bond order isn't zero, it can theoretically form, so it is possible to make a He_2^+ ion, though the bond would be weaker than a single bond. Also, since there's an unpaired electron present the molecule is predicted to be paramagnetic.

The MO Diagram of Li₂

A lithium atom has an electron configuration of $1s^2 2s^1$.

The 2s orbitals will combine to form σ and σ^* orbitals just as they do from the combination of two 1s orbitals. Since the 2s subshell has a higher energy than 1s, the σ_{2s} and $\sigma_{2s}{}^*$ orbitals will be higher than σ_{1s} and $\sigma_{1s}{}^*$.

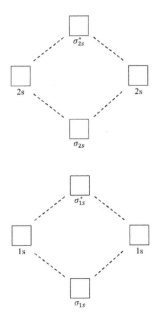

When two lithium atoms combined to form Li₂, you get the following MO diagram:

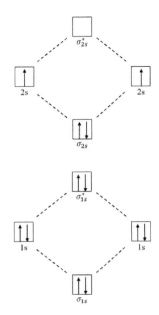

The electron configuration of a Li_2 molecule is $(\sigma_{1s})^2(\sigma_{1s}{}^*)^2(\sigma_{2s})^2$. Since all electrons are paired, the molecule is predicted to be diamagnetic, and the bond should be a single bond.

$$\text{Bond Order} \frac{4-2}{2} = 1$$

Therefore, diatomic lithium is theoretically possible (and has actually been observed in the gas phase).

Combining 2p orbitals

Back in Chapter 9, we learned that a p subshell has three degenerate (same energy) orbitals that are perpendicular to one another.

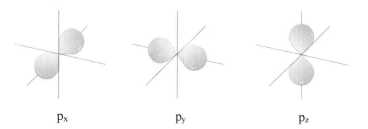

p_x $\qquad\qquad$ p_y $\qquad\qquad$ p_z

If one imagines two atoms coming together and combining their six p orbitals, one pair would interact in an end-to-end fashion while the other two would interact side-to-side.

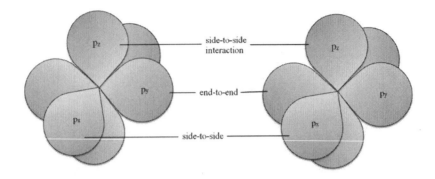

As it was with *s* orbitals, the two combining end-to-end would form two sigma molecular orbitals.

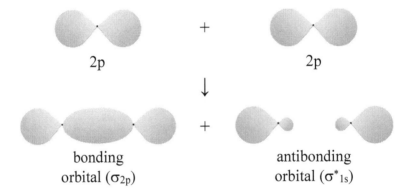

bonding
orbital (σ_{2p})

antibonding
orbital (σ^*_{1s})

The two sets of side-to-side interactions will result in the formation of two sets of **pi (π) molecular orbitals.**

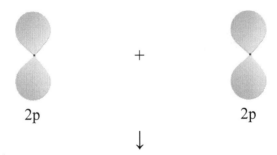

2p   2p

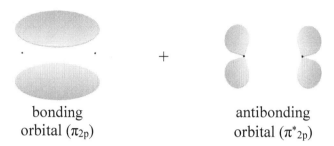

bonding
orbital (π_{2p})

antibonding
orbital (π^*_{2p})

The two pi bonding orbitals are degenerate, as are the two antibonding orbitals. As we did with atomic orbitals, degenerate molecular orbitals are shown as connected boxes.

$$2p \quad + \quad 2p \quad \rightarrow$$

$$\sigma_{2p} \quad + \quad \pi_{2p} \quad + \quad \sigma^*_{2p} \quad + \quad \pi^*_{2p}$$

As before, the antibonding orbitals are higher in energy than the original atomic orbitals while the bonding orbitals are lower. In most cases, the sigma orbitals are higher in energy than the pi orbitals, with both sets of pi orbitals being degenerate. Putting all this together gives the following MO diagram:

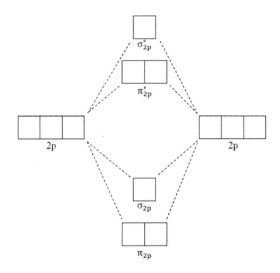

Two notable exceptions to the above diagram are O_2 and F_2, where the σ_{2p} orbitals are actually lower than the π_{2p} orbital.

The MO Diagram of O_2

The electron configuration of an oxygen atom is $1s^2 2s^2 2p^4$.

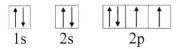

When two oxygen atoms come together to form an O_2 molecule, they'll form the molecular orbitals discussed above. We have a total of 16 electrons in this molecule, which are added to the molecular orbitals beginning with σ_{1s}, giving us an electron configuration of $(\sigma_{1s})^2(\sigma_{1s}*)^2(\sigma_{2s})^2(\sigma_{2s}*)^2(\pi_{2p})^4(\sigma_{2p})^2(\pi_{2p}*)^2$. The MO diagram would be

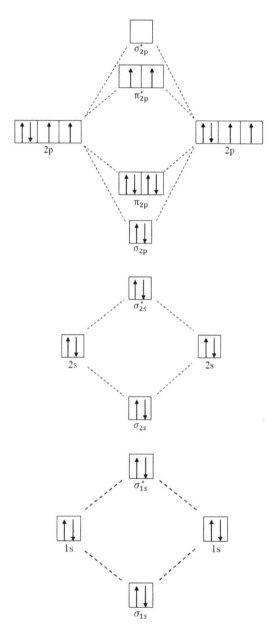

Just like the *p* orbitals of an atomic electronic configuration, the two electrons in π_{2p} will follow Hund's rule and occupy different orbitals. This means that MO theory correctly predicts O_2 to be paramagnetic. It also correctly identifies a bond order of 2.

$$\text{Bond Order} \frac{10-6}{2} = 2$$

Try It Yourself

P5. Draw a molecular orbital diagram for a C_2 molecule.

P6. Does MO theory predict C_2 to be diamagnetic or paramagnetic?

P7. What is the predicted bond order of a C_2 molecule?

Test Your Skills

★Cyborg Ninja

1. According to valence bond theory, what types of orbital overlap is occurring in the following bonds?
a) A–A, b) A=A, c) A≡A

XP + 4 each

2. According to valence bond theory, what types of hybrid orbitals is each of the following central atoms forming?

a) $\overset{\diagdown}{\underset{|}{A}}\diagup$ b) $-\overset{..}{A}-$ c) $\overset{\diagdown}{\diagup}\overset{..}{A}-$ d) $\overset{\diagdown}{\diagup}\overset{..}{A}=$

XP +4 each

3. According to valence bond theory, what types of orbitals is each of the following using for bonding?

a) $-\overset{..}{\underset{..}{F}}:$ b) $-H$ c) $=\overset{..}{S}$

XP +4 each

4. For each of the following, use valence bond theory to describe the bonding between the two atoms shown, noting which orbitals are overlapping and the type of overlap occurring (sigma or pi).

a) $-\overset{|}{\underset{|}{C}}-\overset{..}{\underset{..}{B}r}:$ b) $-\overset{|}{\underset{|}{P}}-H$ c) $-\overset{|}{\underset{|}{C}}=\overset{..}{N}$

XP +4 each

5. Without flipping back to Part 4, draw the predicted orbital diagram that results from the combination of a) two 1s orbitals, b) two 2p orbitals

XP +4 each

432

★XP: _____

If your XP is 45 or higher, get ready for…

★★Giant Mech

6. The structure of water is given below.

$$H-\overset{\cdot\cdot}{\underset{}{O}}-H$$

a) What type of hybrid orbitals is oxygen forming, according to valence bond theory?
b) Use orbital diagrams to illustrate how oxygen hybridizes the orbitals in its valence shell, and how its valence electrons are redistributed.
c) What type of orbitals are housing oxygen's lone pairs?
d) What type of orbital is each hydrogen using for bonding?
e) What type of bond (sigma or pi) is oxygen forming with each hydrogen?

XP + 4 each

7. The structure of sulfur hexafluoride is given below.

a) What type of hybrid orbitals is sulfur forming, according to valence bond theory?
b) Use orbital diagrams to illustrate how sulfur hybridizes the orbitals in its valence shell, and how its valence electrons are redistributed.

c) What type of orbital is each fluorine using for bonding?
d) What type of orbitals are housing fluorine's lone pairs?
e) What type of bond is sulfur forming with each fluorine?

XP + 4 each

8. The structure of chlorine trifluoride is given below.

a) What type of hybrid orbitals is chlorine forming, according to valence bond theory?
b) Use orbital diagrams to illustrate how chlorine hybridizes the orbitals in its valence shell, and how its valence electrons are redistributed.
c) What type of orbitals are housing chlorine's lone pairs?
d) What type of orbital is each fluorine using for bonding?
e) What type of orbitals are housing fluorine's lone pairs?
f) What type of bond is chlorine forming with each fluorine?

XP + 4 each

9. The structure of hydrogen cyanide is given below.

$$H—C≡N:$$

a) What type of hybrid orbitals is carbon forming, according to valence bond theory?
b) Use orbital diagrams to illustrate how carbon hybridizes the orbitals in its valence shell, and how its valence electrons are redistributed.
c) What type of orbital is nitrogen using for bonding?
d) What type of orbital is housing nitrogen's lone pair?
e) What type of orbital is hydrogen using for bonding?

434

f) What type of bonds is carbon forming with the two outer atoms?

XP + 4 each

10. Draw a molecular orbital diagram for each of the following:
a) H_2, b) H_2^-, c) B_2, d) N_2^{2+}, e) F_2, f) Ne_2

XP +5 each

11. For each molecule in question 10, write its electron configuration in standard notation.

XP +5 each

12. For each molecule in question 10, predict whether the molecule will be diamagnetic or paramagnetic?

XP +5 each

13. Calculate the bond order for each molecule in question 10.

XP +5 each

14. The structure of formate ion (HCO_2^-) is given below.

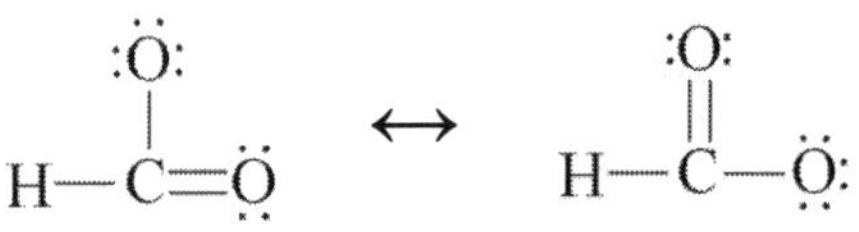

a) What type of hybrid orbitals is carbon forming, according to valence bond theory?
b) Use orbital diagrams to illustrate how carbon hybridizes the orbitals in its valence shell, and how its valence electrons are redistributed.
c) What type of orbitals are the oxygens using for bonding?
e) What type of orbital is hydrogen using for bonding?
f) What type of bonds are being formed in this structure.

XP + 5 each

★★XP:_____   Total XP:_____

If your total XP is 219 or higher, it's time to face the…

★★★Final Boss

15. The structure of phenylalanine is given below (lone pairs not shown):

Use valence bond theory to explain the bonding in this molecule.

$$XP + 50$$
(with partial credit as you see fit)

★★★XP:_____   Total XP:_____

If your total XP is 257 or higher: Level up!

Achievement Unlocked: Share and Share Alike
Completed Chapter 12

You're now ready to learn about the properties of liquids and solids

Epilogue

Answers to Try It Yourself Problems

CHAPTER 1

P1. a) homogeneous, b) heterogeneous, c) compound, d) heterogenous, e) compound, f) homogeneous, g) element, h) compound, i) element, j) compound, k) homogeneous, l) heterogeneous

P2. a) 3, b) 2, c) 2, d) 4, e) 7

P3. a) 122.3, b) 1640, c) 200, d) 89, e) 9.0

P4. a) $\frac{1 \text{ pt}}{473.2 \text{ mL}}$ or $\frac{473.2 \text{ mL}}{1 \text{ pt}}$, b) $\frac{1 \text{ gal}}{3.785 \text{ L}}$ or $\frac{3.785 \text{ L}}{1 \text{ gal}}$, c) $\frac{1 \text{ ng}}{10^{-9}}$ or $\frac{10^{-9}}{1 \text{ ng}}$, d) $\frac{1 \text{ cal}}{4.814 \text{ J}}$ or $\frac{4.184 \text{ J}}{1 \text{ cal}}$

P5. a) $48.5 \text{ in} \times \frac{2.54 \text{ cm}}{1 \text{ in}} = 123$ cm, b) $83.4 \text{ J} \times \frac{1 \text{ cal}}{4.184 \text{ J}} = 19.9$ cal, c) $105 \text{ nL} \times \frac{10^{-9} \text{ L}}{1 \text{ nL}} \times \frac{1 \text{ mL}}{10^{-3} \text{ L}} = 1.05 \times 10^{-4}$ mL, d) $80.30 \text{ m} \times \frac{1 \text{ km}}{10^3 \text{ m}} \times \frac{1 \text{ mi}}{1.609 \text{ km}} = 0.04991$ mi

P6. a) 151.5 L, b) 205 lb, c) 1.53×10^7 μm, d) 930 mi

CHAPTER 2

P1. a) 50, b) 122, c) +2, d) $^{122}_{50}\text{Sn}$, e) tin-122

P2. a) 123, b) 53, c) 70, d) 53, e) $^{123}_{53}\text{I}$

P3. a) uranium-238, b) 92, c) 238, d) 146, e) 86

P4. 28.09

P5. Boron-11

P6. a) P, b) Li, c) Br, d) I, Xe, e) Na, Mg, Al, f) C

CHAPTER 3

P1. NaCl, NaOH, $NaHCO_3$, CaO, $CaCO_3$, $Mg(OH)_2$

P2. a) 28.01, b) 87.97, c) 142.05, d) 179.87, e) 226.39

P3. a) +2, b) +3, c) +1, d) +4, e) +6

P4. Ionic: a, c, & d, covalent: b & e

P5.

Formula	First name	Last Name
CaS	**calcium**	sulfide
SO_2	sulfur	**dioxide**
Na_2O	**sodium**	oxide
P_2O_5	diphosphorus	**pentoxide**
$NiSO_4$	nickel (II)	**sulfate**
$NiCl_4$	**nickel (IV)**	chloride
NCl_3	**nitrogen**	trichloride
MgF_2	**magnesium**	**fluoride**
SF_6	**sulfur**	**hexafluoride**
Cu_3PO_4	**copper (I)**	**phosphate**

P6. sodium chloride, sodium hydroxide, sodium bicarbonate (or sodium hydrogen carbonate), calcium oxide, calcium carbonate, magnesium hydroxide

CHAPTER 4

P1. 99.00 doz, 1.973×10^{-21} mol

P2. 4.33×10^{23} doz, 8.64 mol

P3. 0.0787 mol, 4.74×10^{22} atoms

P4. a) 227 g K, b) 63.56 g SO_2

P5. a) 368 g Al, b) 9,130 g Br_2

P6. 0.13 mol Cl

P7. a) 43.12% Mg, 56.88% S; b) 11.44% P, 88.56% Br; c) 83.62% C, 16.38%H; d) 54.42% C, 9.513 % H, 36.32% O; e) 54.53% C, 9.153% H, 36.32% O

P8. CH_2

P9. $C_5H_{15}O_{10}$

P10. a) C_2H_3S, b) $C_{12}H_{18}S_6$

P11. a) $2Al + 3ZnO \rightarrow Al_2O_3 + 3Zn$, b) $N_2O_5 \rightarrow 2NO_2 + \frac{1}{2}O_2$ or $2N_2O_5 \rightarrow 4NO_2 + O_2$, c) $Na + H_2O \rightarrow NaOH + \frac{1}{2}H_2$ or $2Na + 2H_2O \rightarrow 2NaOH + H_2$, d) $Cr + 3Cl_2 \rightarrow CrCl_6$, e) $4H_3PO_3 \rightarrow 3H_3PO_4 + PH_3$, f) $H_2S + \frac{3}{2}O_2 \rightarrow H_2O + SO_2$ or $2H_2S + 3O_2 \rightarrow 2H_2O + 2SO_2$, g) $KClO_4 \rightarrow KClO_3 + \frac{1}{2}O_2$ or $2KClO_4 \rightarrow 2KClO_3 + O_2$

P12. a) 8 pieces of bacon, b) 16 patties, c) 24 slices of cheese

P13. a) 67.5 mol H_2, b) 1.5 mol N_2, c) 1.27×10^3 g NH_3, d) 15.8 kg N_2

P14.a) 10.9 g P_4, b) 34.69 g P_4O_{10}, c) 79.4%

P15. a) F_2 is limiting, 5 mol UF_6 produced, b) U is limiting, 22.2 g UF_6, c) 147.9 g UF_6

P16. a) $Ca_2C + 2O_2 \rightarrow 2CaO + CO_2$, b) $C_8H_{10}O_3 + 9O_2 \rightarrow 8CO_2 + 5H_2O$, c) $2KH + O_2 \rightarrow K_2O + H_2O$

P17. C_6H_{12}

P18. $C_3H_7O_2$

CHAPTER 5

P1. a) $CaI_2(s) \rightarrow Ca^{2+}(aq) + 2I^-(aq)$, b) $CuSO_4(s) \rightarrow Cu^{2+}(aq) + SO_4^{2-}(aq)$, c) $FeBr_3(s) \rightarrow Fe^{3+}(aq) + 3Br^-(aq)$, d) $NH_4NO_3(s) \rightarrow NH_4^+(aq) + NO_3^-(aq)$, e) $Mg(ClO_4)_2(s) \rightarrow Mg^{2+}(aq) + 2ClO_4^-(aq)$, f) $K_3PO_4(s) \rightarrow 3K^+(aq) + PO_4^{3-}(aq)$

P2. Soluble: a, b, d, & g; insoluble: c, e, & f

P3. a) $4LiBr(aq) + Pb(NO_3)_4(aq) \rightarrow 4LiNO_3(aq) + PbBr_4(s)$, b) $FeSO_4(aq) + 2NaOH(aq) \rightarrow Fe(OH)_2(s) + Na_2SO_4(aq)$, c) $CaCl_2(aq) + 2CuClO_4(aq) \rightarrow Ca(ClO_4)_2(aq) + 2CuCl(s)$, d) $K_3PO_4(aq) + CrBr_3(aq) \rightarrow 3KBr(aq) + CrPO_4(s)$

P4. a) $4Br^-(aq) + Pb^{4+}(aq) \rightarrow PbBr_4(s)$, b) $Fe^{2+}(aq) + 2OH^-(aq) \rightarrow Fe(OH)_2(s)$, c) $Cu^+(aq) + Cl^-(aq) \rightarrow CuCl(s)$, d) $Cr^{3+}(aq) + PO_4^{3-}(aq) \rightarrow CrPO_4(s)$

P5. a) hydroiodic acid, b) phosphoric acid, c) acetic acid, d) hydrofluoric acid, e) nitrous acid, f) chromic acid

P6. a) H_2CO_3, b) HBr, c) $HClO_2$

P7. a) $LiOH(aq) + HBr(aq) \rightarrow LiBr(aq) + H_2O(l)$, b) $H_3PO_4(aq) + 3NaOH(aq) \rightarrow Na_3PO_4(aq) + 3H_2O(l)$, c) $HF(aq) + NH_4OH(aq) \rightarrow NH_4F(aq) + H_2O(l)$, d) $Fe(OH)_2(s) + H_2SO_4(aq) \rightarrow FeSO_4(aq) + 2H_2O(l)$

P8. a, b, and c: $H^+(aq) + OH^-(aq) \rightarrow H_2O(l)$, d) $Fe(OH)_2(s) + 2H^+(aq) \rightarrow Fe^{2+}(aq) + 2H_2O(l)$

P9. a) $KHSO_3(aq) + HBr(aq) \rightarrow KBr(aq) + H_2O(l) + SO_2(g)$, b) $FeCO_3(s) + H_2SO_4(aq) \rightarrow FeSO_4(aq) + H_2O(l) + CO_2(g)$, c) $Al(s) + 3HClO_4(aq) \rightarrow Al(ClO_4)_3(aq) + {}^3/_2H_2(g)$ or $2Al(s) + 6HClO_4(aq) \rightarrow 2Al(ClO_4)_3(aq) + 3H_2(g)$, d) $3Cu_2S(s) + 2H_3PO_4(aq) \rightarrow 2Cu_3(PO_4)(s) + 3H_2S(g)$

P10. a) $HSO_3^-(aq) + H^+(aq) \rightarrow H_2O(l) + SO_2(g)$, b) $FeCO_3(s) + 2H^+(aq) \rightarrow Fe^{2+}(aq) + H_2O(l) + CO_2(g)$, c) $Al(s) + 3H^+(aq) \rightarrow Al^{3+}(aq) + {}^3/_2H_2(g)$ or $2Al(s) + 6H^+(aq) \rightarrow 2Al^{3+}(aq) + 3H_2(g)$, d) $3Cu_2S(s) + 2H_3PO_4(aq) \rightarrow 2Cu_3(PO_4)_2(s) + 3H_2S(g)$

P11. a) $H^+(aq) + CaSO_3(s) \rightarrow Ca^{2+}(aq) + H_2O(l) + SO_2(g)$, b) $S^{2-}(aq) + 2H^+(aq) \rightarrow H_2S(g)$, c) $Zn(s) + 2H^+(aq) \rightarrow Zn^{2+}(aq) + H_2(g)$, d) $Cu(s) + 4H^+(aq) + 2NO_3^-(aq) \rightarrow Cu^{2+}(aq) + 2NO_2(g) + 2H_2O(l)$

P12. a) Al = +3, F = -1; b) N = +4, O = -2; c) N = +3, O = -2; d) I = +5, O = -2; e) Na = +1, P = +5, O = -2; f) C = 0, H = +1, O = -2

P13. a) Fe is reduced, Zn is oxidized; b) C is oxidized, O is reduced; c) Fe is oxidized, Cr is reduced

P14. a) $FeCl_2$ is the oxidizing agent, Zn is the reducing agent; b) CH_4 is the reducing agent, O_2 is the oxidizing agent; c) Fe^{2+} is the reducing agent, $Cr_2O_7^{2-}$ is the oxidizing agent

P15. a) 1.0 M, b) 0.170 M, c) 0.125 M, d) 0.113 M

P16. a) 540 g, b) 490 g, c) 38.1 g

P17. a) 3.96 g Al, b) 43.5 mL, c) 2.67 M

P18. a) 2.5 M, b) 561 mL (final volume = 816 mL)

CHAPTER 6

P1. a) 988 mmHg, b) 815 torr, c) 1.354 atm

P2. a) 0.793 mol, b) 10.9 atm, c) 5.5 L

P3. a) 7.56 atm, b) 479 K, c) 2.056 L

P4. Charles' law: if $P_1 = P_2 = P$ and $n_1 = n_2 = n$, then $\dfrac{\cancel{P}V_1}{\cancel{n}T_1} = \dfrac{\cancel{P}V_2}{\cancel{n}T_2} \rightarrow \dfrac{V_1}{T_1} = \dfrac{V_2}{T_2}$

Avogadro' law: if $P_1 = P_2 = P$ and $T_1 = T_2 = T$, then $\dfrac{\cancel{P}V_1}{n_1\cancel{T}} = \dfrac{\cancel{P}V_2}{n_2\cancel{T}} \rightarrow \dfrac{V_1}{n_1} = \dfrac{V_2}{n_2}$

P5. 96.2 g/mol

P6. 1.05 g/L

P7. a) 0.157 mol, 15.2 atm, b) 10.4 L

P8. a) 2.04 atm, b) 341 mL

P9. a) P_{O2} = 2.70 atm, P_{CO2} = 4.86 atm, P_T = 7.56 atm; b) P_{H2} = 5.0 atm, P_{Kr} = 0.67 atm, P_{NO2} = 1.9 atm, P_T = 7.6 atm; c) P_{Ne} = 3.00 atm, P_{N2} = 3.14 atm, P_T = 6.14 atm

P10. a) Ne, b) 1.477 times, c) 1.46 x 10^{-3} m/s

P11. a) 604 m/s, b) 4.00 x 10^2 m/s, c) 4.80 x 10^2 m/s, d) 339 m/s

P12. Rate decreases as molar mass increases, which is what we'd predict.

CHAPTER 7

P1. a) 1,550 J, b) 490,000 J, c) -120,000 J

P2. a) 83 °C, b) 166 °C, c) 35 °C

P3. a) 21,000 J, b) 1.5 J/g·°C

P4. a) -164 kJ, b) 90,200 g

P5. a) -11.2 kJ, b) 42 L

P6. 257 kJ

P7. a) 184.6 kJ, b) -553.8 kJ, c) -92.3 kJ, d) 46.15 kJ

P8. 100 kJ

P9. -129 kJ

P10. a)177.8 kJ, b) -1233.7 kJ, c) -847.6 kJ

CHAPTER 8

P1. a) 3.70 x 10^{18} Hz, b) 6.79 x 10^{14} Hz, c) 3.99 x 10^{10} Hz

P2. a) 4.0042 x 10^5 m, b) 742 m, c) 0.02223 m, d) 3.25 x 10^{-7} m

P3. a) 4.9673 x 10^{-31} J, b) 2.681 x 10^{-28} J, c) 8.944 x 10^{-24} J, d) 6.12 x 10^{-19}

P4. a) 2.99 x 10^{-7} J, b) 1.61 x 10^{-4} J, c) 5.38 J, d) 3.68 x 10^5 J

P5. a) 9.496 x 10^{-8} m, b) 4.862 x 10^{-7} m, c) 1.094 x 10^{-6} m

P6. a) 2.093 x 10^{-18} J, b)   4.088 x 10^{-19} J, c) 1.817 x 10^{-19} J

P7. a) 9.50 x 10^{-8} m, b) 4.85 x 10^{-7} m, c) 1.09 x 10^{-6}

P8. a) 0,1,2,3; b) 0,1,2,3,4,5,6,7; c) 0,1,2,3,4,5,6,7,8,9,10,11

P9. a) s,p,d,f; b) s,p,d,f,g,h,i,j; c) s,p,d,f,g,h,i,j,k,l,m,n

P10. a) -3,-2,-1,0,1,2,3; b) -6,-5,-4,-3,-2,-1,0,1,2,3,4,5,6; c) -8,-7,-6,-5,-4,-3,-2,-1,0,1,2,3,4,5,6,7,8

P11. a) n = 3, l = 1; b) n = 5, l = 3; c) n = 7, l = 4; d) n = 9, l = 7

P12. a) 7, b) 11, c) 21

CHAPTER 9

P1. a) 3p, b) 4s, c) 5p, d) 5d

P2. a) 3, b) 2, c) 5, d) 10

P3. a) $1s^22s^22p^63s^23p^3$, b) $1s^22s^22p^63s^23p^64s^2$, c) $1s^22s^22p^63s^23p^64s^23d^{10}4p^65s^24d^{10}5p^5$, d) $1s^22s^22p^63s^23p^64s^23d^{10}4p^65s^24d^{10}5p^66s^24f^{14}5d^{10}$

P4. a) 5, b) 2, c) 7, d) 2

P5. a) [Ne]$3s^23p^3$, b) [Ar]$4s^2$, c) [Kr]$5s^24d^{10}5p^5$, d) [Xe]$6s^24f^{14}5d^{10}$

P6. a)

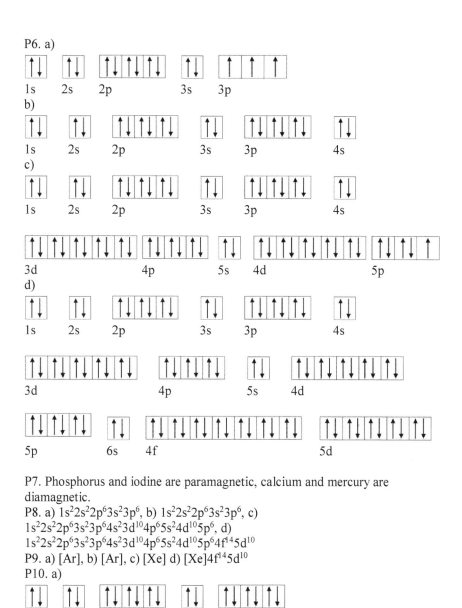

P7. Phosphorus and iodine are paramagnetic, calcium and mercury are diamagnetic.

P8. a) $1s^22s^22p^63s^23p^6$, b) $1s^22s^22p^63s^23p^6$, c) $1s^22s^22p^63s^23p^64s^23d^{10}4p^65s^24d^{10}5p^6$, d) $1s^22s^22p^63s^23p^64s^23d^{10}4p^65s^24d^{10}5p^64f^{14}5d^{10}$

P9. a) [Ar], b) [Ar], c) [Xe] d) [Xe]$4f^{14}5d^{10}$

P10. a)

444

c)

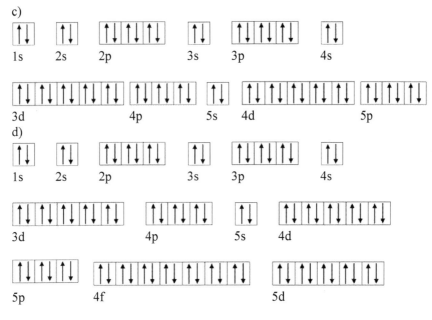

3d 4p 5s 4d 5p

d)

1s 2s 2p 3s 3p 4s

3d 4p 5s 4d

5p 4f 5d

P11. Mercury (II)
P12. N<Sb<Pb
P13. Na<C<Cl
P14. Na<C<Cl

CHAPTER 10

P1.

a) ·Ȧl·   b) Cs·   c) :S̈e·   d) :C̈l·

P2.

a) H−B̈r: b) Ö=c=Ö

c) :F̈−N̈−F̈:
              |
             :F̈:

P3.

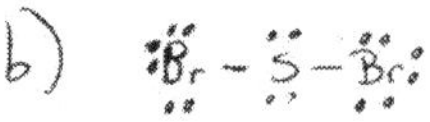

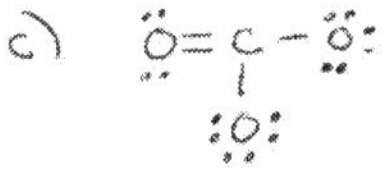

a) Lewis structure: Cl atoms bonded to central Si

b) Lewis structure: $Br - S - Br$

c) Lewis structure: $O = C - O$ with O below

P4. c

P5. a)

$:N \equiv N - \ddot{O}: \longleftrightarrow \ddot{N} = N = \ddot{O} \longleftrightarrow :\ddot{N} - N \equiv O:$

  A   B   C

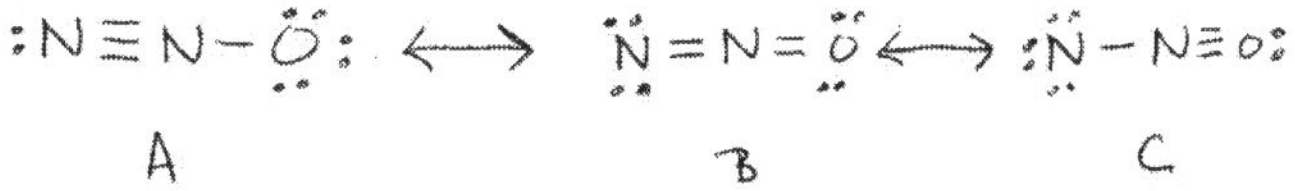

b) Left to right: A: 0, +1, -1; B: -1, +1, 0; C: -2, +1, +1

c) A

P6.

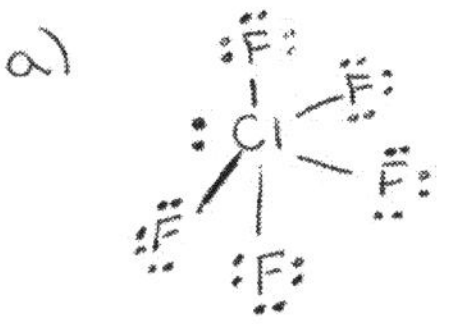

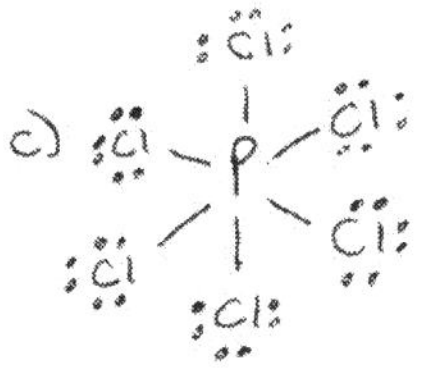

a) Lewis structure: ClF_5

b) Lewis structure: XeF_4

c) Lewis structure: PCl_5

CHAPTER 11

P1.

a) $H-C-C-C-H$ structure with H atoms

b) $H-C-C=C$ structure with H atoms

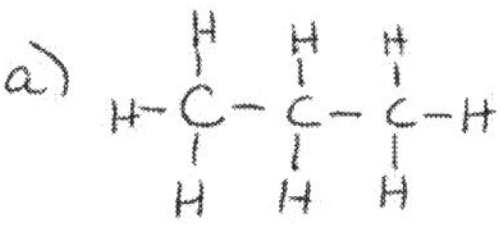

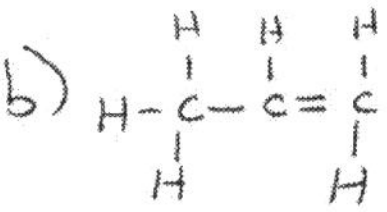

P2. a) $CH_3CH_2CH_3$ b) CH_3CHCH_2 or $CH_3CH=CH_2$

446

P3.

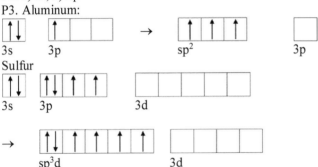

P4. 44 kJ

P5.

	Arrangement	Shape
a)	tetrahedral	trigonal pyramidal
b)	tetrahedral	tetrahedral
c)	trigonal planar	trigonal planar
d)	trigonal planar	bent

P6. a) carbon is positive, chlorine is negative; b) oxygen is negative, sulfur is positive; c) boron is positive, bromine is negative.

P7. c is nonpolar, the rest are polar

CHAPTER 12

P1. a) sp^2, b) sp^3d

P2. a) 1s, b) 2p

P3. Aluminum:

Sulfur

P4. Each oxygen is sp^2 hybridized, bonded by a sigma bond and a delocalized pi bond.

P5. a)

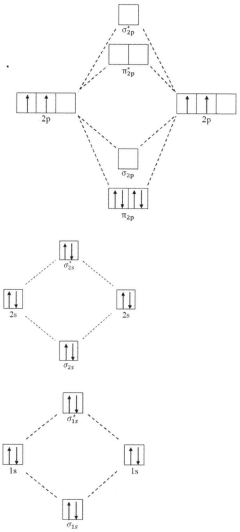

P6. diamagnetic
P7. 2

Answers to Test your Skills Problems

Because these problems are meant to be attempted one star-level at a time, the answers keys are divided up as such. That way, you don't accidentally get a peek at the next level's answers.

★ Problems

CHAPTER 1

1. a) Homogeneous, heterogeneous; b) hypothesis, theory; c) precision, accuracy
2. chemical: c, d, f, & g; physical: a, b, & e
3. a) 3, b) 1, c) 5, d) 3, e) 4, f) 4, g) 2
4. a) 9.1, b) 1230, c) 27, d) 0.014, e) 1,333,600, f) 6.0, g) 38.2, h) 20, i) 370, j) 44,000, k) 17,000
5. a) 13.6, b) 360.1, c) 86.9, d) 2,500, e) 14,000, f) 450
6. a) a) $\frac{1\ yd}{0.9144\ m}$ or $\frac{0.9144\ m}{1\ yd}$, b) $\frac{1\ mg}{0.001\ g}$ or $\frac{0.001\ g}{1\ mg}$, c) $\frac{1\ mi}{1.609\ km}$ or $\frac{1.609\ km}{1\ mi}$, d) $\frac{1\ \mu L}{10^{-6}\ L}$ or $\frac{10^{-6}\ LJ}{1\ \mu L}$
7. a) ft $\times \frac{in}{ft} \times \frac{cm}{in} = cm$, b) pL $\times \frac{L}{pL} \times \frac{\mu L}{L} = \mu L$, c) mg $\times \frac{g}{mg} \times \frac{kg}{g} = kg$,
8. a) pm, b) mg, c) m/s
9. a) 79 km, b) 550 cm, c) 719.2 L, d) 4,084 kg, e) 2,010 µg, f) 1.153 x 10^4 kg, g) 270 lb, h) 35.5 L, i) 8.093 x 10^{-4} Å, j) 331.5, k) 181.9 °C

CHAPTER 2

1. The law of conservation of matter
2. 11 grams, law of conservation of matter
3. a) 127 g, b) 308 g, law of definite proportions
4.

Atom	A	B	C	D
Protons	15	26	77	51
Neutrons	17	30	113	74
Electrons	16	23	73	53
Mass number	32	56	190	125
Charge	-1	+3	+4	-2

5. A) phosphorus-32, $^{32}_{15}P$; B) iron-56, $^{56}_{26}Fe$; C) iridium-190, $^{190}_{77}Ir$; D) antimony-125, $^{125}_{51}Sb$
6. a) 4 protons, 6 neutrons; b) 18 protons, 22 neutrons; c) 28 protons, 34 neutrons; d) 47 protons, 62 neutrons; e) 80 protons, 119 neutrons
7. (23.99 × 0.7899) + (24.99 × 0.1000) × (25.98 × 0.1101) = 24.31
8. a) E, H; b) C, E, I; c) F, H; d) E, H; e) B, E, H; f) D, E, H; g) E, I; h) G, H

CHAPTER 3

1. a) NO_3, b) S_2F_{10}, c) BrF_5, d) C_5H_{12}, e) $C_6H_{12}O_2$
2. a) 30.01, b) 38.00, c) 76.15, d) 187.57, e) 24.00, f) 52.08, g) 163.94
3. a-c are predicted to be covalent, d-g are predicted to be ionic
4. a) +2, b) -2, c) +1, d) -3, e) -1
5. a) +2, b) +2, c) +2, d) +1, e) +4
6.

	I^-	O^{2-}	N^{3-}
Li^+	LiI	Li_2O	Li_3N
Fe^{2+}	FeI_2	FeO	Fe_3N_2
Al^{3+}	AlI_3	Al_2O_3	AlN

7.

	I^-	O^{2-}	N^{3-}
Li^+	lithium iodide	lithium oxide	lithium nitride
Fe^{2+}	iron (II) iodide	iron (II) oxide	iron (II) nitride
Al^{3+}	aluminum iodide	aluminum oxide	aluminum nitride

8. a) carbon tetrachloride, b) disulfur decabromide, c) nitrogen dioxide, d) selenium hexaiodide, e) bromine pentachloride
9. a) nickel (II) chloride hexahydrate, b) magnesium bromide tetrahydrate, c) calcium sulfate dihydrate, d) barium hydroxide octahydrate

CHAPTER 4

1. a) 392 g C, b) 0.137 g Si, c) 1,710 g F_2, d) 45.7 g NaI, e) 750 g CF_2Cl_2
2. a) 0.235 mol Fe, b) 0.33 mol Mg, c) 0.00406 mol PCl_3, d) 0.02304 mol $CuCl_2$
3. a) 5.00 mol, b) 1.76 mol, c) 30.66 mol
4. a) 15.0 g, b) 32.1 g, c) 19.3 g
5. a) 868 g Ni, b) 110 g I_2, c) 16.99 g SF_6
6. a) 69.94% Fe, 30.06% O; b) 36.86% N, 63.14% O, c) 11.50% C, 54.57% F, 33.94% Cl, d) 66.75% Cu, 10.84% P, 22.41% O
7. a) $MnCl_5$, b) CH_3, c) N_2O_5
8. a) $C_{12}H_{28}$, b) $C_4H_{12}O_8$, c) $C_5H_{12}P$
9. a) $CS_2 + 3Cl_2 \rightarrow S_2Cl_2 + CCl_4$, b) $CS_2 + 3O_2 \rightarrow CO_2 + 2SO_2$, c) $P_4O_6 + 6H_2O \rightarrow 4H_3PO_3$, d) $Fe(OH)_3 + 3HNO_3 \rightarrow Fe(NO_3)_3 + 3H_2O$, e) $Ca + 2H_2O \rightarrow Ca(OH)_2 + H_2$
10. a) 43.5 mol C, b) 62.9 g CaC_2, c) 2.40 x 10^2 g C, d) 69.6%
11. a) $2Li + \frac{1}{2}O_2 \rightarrow Li_2O$ or $4Li + O_2 \rightarrow 2Li_2O$, b) $2AlH_3 + 3O_2 \rightarrow Al_2O_3 + 3H_2O$, c) $C_5H_{10} + {}^{15}/_2O_2 \rightarrow 5CO_2 + 5H_2O$ or $2C_5H_{10} + 15O_2 \rightarrow 10CO_2 + 10H_2O$, d) $C_{10}H_{14}O_3 + 12O_2 \rightarrow 10CO_2 + 7H_2O$
12. C_2H_5
13. $C_{10}H_{20}$

CHAPTER 5
1. Soluble = b, c, & d; insoluble = a & e
2. a) $CaCl_2(aq) + 2KOH(aq) \rightarrow Ca(OH)_2(s) + 2KCl(aq)$, b) $3Pb(ClO_4)_4(aq) + 4H_3PO_4(aq) \rightarrow Pb_3(PO_4)_4(s) + 12HClO_4(aq)$, c) $Na_2SO_4(aq) + BaBr_2(aq) \rightarrow 2NaBr(aq) + BaSO_4(s)$
3. a) $H_2SO_4(aq) + 2KOH(aq) \rightarrow 2H_2O(l) + K_2SO_4(aq)$, b) $3HI(aq) + Al(OH)_3(s) \rightarrow 3H_2O(l) + AlI_3(aq)$
4. a) $KHCO_3(aq) + HBr(aq) \rightarrow KBr(aq) + H_2O(l) + CO_2(g)$, b) $CuS(s) + 2HNO_3(aq) \rightarrow H_2S(g) + Cu(NO_3)_2(aq)$, c) $HCl(aq) + Mg(s) \rightarrow H_2(g) + MgCl_2(aq)$
5. a) Cu = +1, N = -3; b) Ca = +2, C = +4, O = -2; c) N = +3, O = -2; d) C = 0, H = +1, O = -2; e) H = +1, O = -1
6. a) Ce is reduced, F is oxidized; b) N is reduced, H is oxidized; c) Cl is reduced, Br is oxidized
7. a) 0.024 M, b) 0.0126 M, c) 0.0421 M
8. a) $NH_4^+(aq) + OH^-(aq) \rightarrow H_2O(l) + NH_3(g)$, b) 7.43 g $(NH_4)_2SO_4$, c) 380 mL NaOH
9. a) $CO_3^{2-}(aq) + 2Ag^+(aq) \rightarrow Ag_2CO_3(s)$, b) 83.8 g AgBr, c) 450 mL AgBr
10. a) 353 mL, b) 0.850 M

CHAPTER 6
1. 357 mmHg
2. 827 °C
3. 21.5 L
4. 2.01 atm
5. 313 mL
6. 7.01 atm
7. 165 g/mol
8. a) 2.00 g/L, b) 0.917 g/L, c) 6.63 g/L
9. a) 36.9 L, b) 114 g
10. 9.29 L
11. P_{O2} = 2.04 atm, P_{N2} = 0.373 atm, P_T = 2.41
12. a) Br_2, b) 1.50 times, c) 6.3×10^3 mm/min

CHAPTER 7
1. a) 1240 J, b) 361 J, c) 2520 J
2. a) 58.2 °C, b) 5.35 °C
3. 0.886 J/g·°C
4. a) 229.7 kJ, b) 1.66×10^5 g
5. a) -79.9 kJ, b) 9,240 g
6. a) 39 kJ, b) 192 kJ
7. -241.3 kJ
8. -187.8 kJ

9. Values should be the same as 7 and 8 (within reason).
10. a) 1130.2 kJ, b) -147.2 kJ, c) -322 kJ

CHAPTER 8

1. a) 59.8 m, b) 4.03×10^{-3} m, c) 1.03×10^{-6} m
2. a) 3.33×10^{-27} J, b) 4.93×10^{-23} J, c) 1.93×10^{-19} J
3. a) 3.43×10^{17} Hz, b) 4.54×10^{14} Hz, c) 3.74×10^{11} Hz
4. a) 7.16×10^{-26} J, b) 4.31×10^{-2} J, c) 0.216 J
5. a) 102.6 nm, b) 1,005 nm, c) 434.1 nm
6. a) 1.94×10^{-18} J, b) 1.977×10^{-19} J, c) 4.58×10^{-19} J
7. a) s, p, d, f; b) s, p, d, f, g, h, I; c) s, p, d, f, g, h, i, j, k
8. a) 9, b) 17, c) 19
9.

	Subshell	n	l	m_l
a)	4d	4	2	**-2, -1, 0, 1, 2**
b)	**3p**	3	1	**-1, 0, 1**
c)	**5f**	5	3	-3, -2, -1, 0, 1, 2, 3

CHAPTER 9

1. a) $1s^2 2s^2 2p^6 3s^2 3p^6$, b) $1s^2 2s^2 2p^6 3s^2 3p^6 4s^2 3d^{10} 4p^6 5s^2 4d^7$, c) $1s^2 2s^2 2p^6 3s^2 3p^6 4s^2 3d^{10} 4p^6 5s^2 4d^{10} 5p^6 6s^2 4f^{14} 5d^{10} 6p^6 7s^2 5f^{14} 6d^4$
2. a) $[Ar]4s^2 3d^{10} 4p^3$, b) $[Ar]4s^1$, c) $[Xe]6s^2 4f^{14} 5d^{10} 6p^3$
3. a)

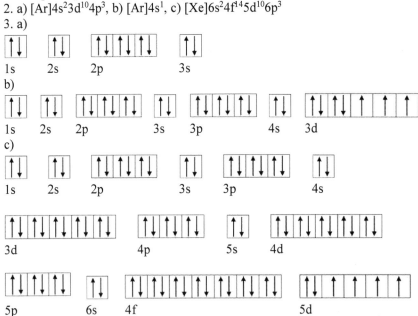

4. Magnesium

5. a) $1s^2 2s^2 2p^6 3s^2 3p^6$, b) $1s^2 2s^2 2p^6 3s^2 3p^6 3d^6$, c) $1s^2 2s^2 2p^6 3s^2 3p^6 4s^2 3d^{10} 4p^6 4d^{10}$

6. Al<Na<Ca<Ba

7. Pb>Ga>As>N

8. Bi<Be<P<F

9. O>Si>Li>K

CHAPTER 10

1.

2. a) 32, b) 42, c) 32, d) 8

3.

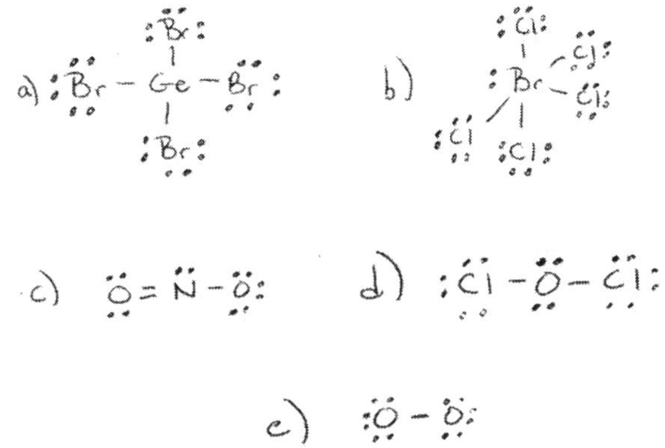

4. NO_2^-

5. a) Ca<P<N, b) In<Si<Cl

6. a) Missing valence electrons, nitrogen only has 6. b) Carbon has too many electrons. c) Too many valence electrons.

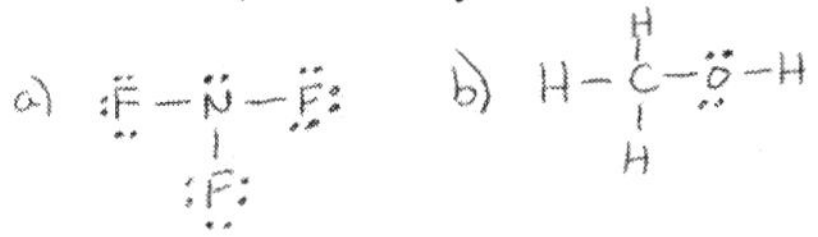

7. Two double bonds, as this gives all atoms a formal charge of zero.

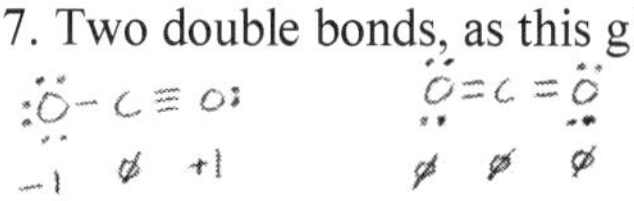

8. a) I = +2, II = +1, III = 0, b) 0 in each structure, c) -1 in each structure, d) III

9. Two

$$(R = CH_3CH_2\text{-})$$

CHAPTER 11
1.

2. a) CH_3CH_2OH, CH_3CH_2Br; b) -28 kJ
3. a) tetrahedral, b) octahedral, c) tetrahedral, d) linear
4. a) tetrahedral, b) square pyramidal, c) bent, d) linear
5. a) nitrogen is positive, fluorine is negative; b) oxygen is negative; phosphorus is positive, c) boron is positive, bromine is negative; d) germanium is positive, carbon is negative
6. a) nonpolar, b) polar, c) polar, d) nonpolar

CHAPTER 12
1. a) sigma, b) one sigma, one pi, c) one sigma, two pi's
2. a) sp^2, b) sp^3, c) sp^3d, d) sp^3
3. a) 2p, b) 1s, c) one sigma, one pi
4. a) sp^3 of carbon form a sigma bond with a 3p of bromine, b) sp^3 of phosphorus sigma bonding with a 1s of hydrogen, c) both atoms are sp^2 hybridized, form a sigma and a pi bond
5. See Part 4

★★ Problems

CHAPTER 1
10. a) helium, b) carbon dioxide, c) oil, d) anchor
11. Intensive properties: density, solubility, freezing point, boiling point, corrosiveness, air sensitivity, water sensitivity. Extensive properties: volume, color, mass. Chemical properties: corrosiveness, air sensitivity, water sensitivity. Physical properties: volume, color, mass, density, freezing point, boiling point, solubility.
12. Extensive properties: b and c; intensive: a, d, and e
13. a) 590, b) 66.0, c) 43, d) 2.0 x 10^2, e) 11, f) 360, g) 130, h) 3,000, i) 335.9, j) 33.6, k) 9400
14. a) 1.62 x 10^5 m^2, b) 1.512 x 10^6 kg/m^2, c) 0.52 g/mL

CHAPTER 2
9.

Isotope Symbol	$^{32}_{16}S$	$^{123}_{53}I$	$^{238}_{92}U$	$^{41}_{19}K$
Isotope Name	**sulfur-32**	iodine-123	**uranium-238**	**potassium-41**
Atomic number	**16**	**53**	92	19
Mass number	**32**	**123**	238	**41**
No. of neutrons	**16**	**70**	**146**	22

10. a) $^{32}_{14}Si$, b) $^{81}_{35}Br$, c) $^{44}_{20}Ca$, d) $^{75}_{33}As$
11. a) Hf, b) Ge, c) I, d) Sc
12. a) Ca, b) Cl, c) Rn, d) Nb, e) Cm
13. a) silicon, sulfur & iodine; b) hafnium, hydrogen & fluorine; c) lead; phosphorus & boron; d) cobalt; carbon & oxygen; e) indium; iodine & nitrogen
14. 64.94 amu, 30.83%
15. Cl$_2$ is a diatomic molecule, "2Cl" means two chlorine atoms.

CHAPTER 3
10. a) CH$_4$, b PCl$_5$, c) CH$_2$O
11. table salt is an ionic compound, and these don't exist as individual molecules.
12.

	NO$_3^-$	SO$_4^{2-}$	PO$_4^{3-}$
NH$_4^+$	**NH$_4$NO$_3$**	**(NH$_4$)$_2$SO$_4$**	**(NH$_4$)$_3$PO$_4$**
Cu^{2+}	**Cu(NO$_3$)$_2$**	**CuSO$_4$**	**Cu$_3$(PO$_4$)$_2$**
Ga^{3+}	**Ga(NO$_3$)$_3$**	**Ga$_2$(SO$_4$)$_3$**	**GaPO$_4$**
Mn^{4+}	**Mn(NO$_3$)$_4$**	**Mn(SO$_4$)$_2$**	**Mn$_3$(PO$_4$)$_4$**

113.

	NO$_3^-$	SO$_4^{2-}$	PO$_4^{3-}$
NH$_4^+$	ammonium nitrate	ammonium sulfate	ammonium phosphate
Cu^{2+}	copper (II) nitrate	copper (II) sulfate	copper (II) phosphate
Ga^{3+}	gallium nitrate	gallium sulfate	gallium phosphate
Mn^{4+}	manganese (IV) nitrate	manganese (IV) sulfate	manganese (IV) phosphate

14. a) S$_2$F$_{10}$, b) NH$_4$MnO$_4$, c) Cr(ClO$_4$)$_6$, d) Na$_2$CO$_3$·10H$_2$O, e) Se$_4$N$_4$, f) P$_3$I$_5$, g) Ni(CN)$_4$, h) NO$_3$

CHAPTER 4

14. a) 0.132 mol Na, b) 0.8014 mol H$_2$O, c) 1,140 g Fe(NO)$_3$, d) 6,716 g Cr(PO$_4$)$_3$

15. a) 179 g Ne, b) 1,037 g SrI$_2$·6H$_2$O, c) 2.80 x 10^{23} Cl atoms, d) 4.91 x 10^{23} ClO$_4^-$ ions

16. a) C$_2$H$_3$N, b) C$_2$H$_5$O

17. a) 68.4% Cr, 31.6% O; b) Cr$_2$O$_3$

18. a) CaCl$_2$ + Na$_2$CO$_3$ → CaCO$_3$ + 2NaCl, b) CuSO$_4$ + Fe → FeSO$_4$ + Cu, c) U + $^3/_2$O$_2$ → UO$_3$ or 2U + 3O$_2$ → 2UO$_3$, e) 2KClO$_3$ → 2KCl + 3O$_2$

19. a) 41.3 g Ag$_2$S, b) 26.1 g Ag, c) 2.02 g Al$_2$S$_3$

20. a) 1.00 x 10^9 g C. b) 565 g CO$_2$, c) Al$_2$O$_3$

21. CH$_4$ + $^3/_2$O$_2$ → CO + 2H$_2$O

22. C$_{12}$H$_{24}$O$_8$

CHAPTER 5

11. a) Fe(NO$_3$)$_2$, b) Na$_2$CO$_3$, c) Fe(NO$_3$)$_2$,

12. a) Fe^{2+}(aq) + S^{2-}(aq) → FeS(s), b) Mg^{2+}(aq) + CO$_3^{2-}$(aq) → MgCO$_3$(s), c) Fe^{2+}(aq) + 2OH$^-$(aq) → Fe(OH)$_2$(s)

13. a) 2HCl(aq) + Ca(s) → CaCl$_2$(aq) + H$_2$(g), b) 2HCl(aq) + Hg$_2$(NO$_3$)$_2$(aq) → Hg$_2$Cl$_2$(s) + 2HNO$_3$(aq), c) 6HCl(aq) + Ni$_2$(CO$_3$)$_3$(s) → 2NiCl$_3$(aq) + 3H$_2$O(l) + 3CO$_2$(g), d) 2HCl(aq) + K$_2$SO$_3$(aq) → 2KCl(aq) + H$_2$O(l) + SO$_2$(g), e) 2HCl(aq) + Ba(OH)$_2$(s) → BaCl$_2$(aq) + 2H$_2$O(l), f) 2HCl(aq) + (NH$_4$)$_2$S(aq) → 2NH$_4$Cl(aq) + H$_2$S(g)

14. a) 2H$^+$(aq) + Ca(s) → Ca^{2+}(aq) + H$_2$(g); b) 2Cl$^-$(aq) +Hg$_2^{2+}$(aq) → Hg$_2$Cl$_2$(s), c) 6H$^+$(aq) + Ni$_2$(CO$_3$)$_3$(s) → 2Ni^{3+}(aq) + 3H$_2$O(l) + 3CO$_2$(g), d) 2H$^+$(aq) + SO$_3^{2-}$(aq) → H$_2$O(l) + SO$_2$(g), e) H$^+$(aq) + OH$^-$(aq) → H$_2$O(l), f) 2H$^+$(aq) + S^{2-}(aq) → H$_2$S(g)

15. a) I$_2$ is oxidizing agent, S$_2$O$_3^{2-}$ is reducing agent, b) O$_2$ is oxidizing agent, Fe^{2+} is reducing agent, c) MnO$_4^-$ is oxidizing agent, Fe^{2+} is reducing agent

16. a) metal is reducing agent, acid is oxidizing agent, b) hydrocarbon is reducing agent, oxygen is oxidizing agent

17. a) 0.038 M, b) 0.038 M, c) 0.23 M

CHAPTER 6
13. 1.58 atm
14. 0.749 atm
15. 2.39 atm
16. 22.4 L
17. 52.4 g/mol
18. a) 1.86 atm, b) 12.0 g
19. 2.69 atm
20. a) 3.82 atm, b) 1.54 atm, c) 5.36 atm
21. At higher temperatures, volume increases. This causes its density to decrease. Since hot air's density is lower it will "float" on colder air.
22. At higher temperatures, there should be an increase in the number of collisions per area. If the volume is being held constant, this will cause the pressure to increase.

CHAPTER 7
11. 93.5 g H_2O, 109 °C
12. 24 °C
13. a) 1.75 kJ, b) 12 °C
14. 46.8 kJ
15. -241.4
16. a) $\frac{1}{2}H_2(g) + \frac{1}{2}Br_2(g) \rightarrow HBr(g)$, b) $Mg(s) + C(gr) + \frac{3}{2}O_2(g) \rightarrow MgCO_3(s)$, c) $6C(gr) + 5H_2(g) + 3O_2(g) \rightarrow C_6H_{12}O_6(s)$
17. No. Only the actual chemical reaction is absorbing or releasing heat. Having the spectator ions present shouldn't change anything.
18. -1432.7 kJ

CHAPTER 8
10. $E = \frac{hc}{\lambda}$
11. a) 2.96 x 10^{-19} J, b) 5.06 x 10^{-25} J, c) 2.03 x 10^{-18} J
12. 3.43 x 10^{12} Hz
13. $n = 4$
14. $n = 4$
15. a) 2.468 x 10^{15} Hz, b) 2.340 x 10^{14} Hz
16. a and d are allowed. b isn't because n cannot equal l, c isn't because m_l can't be greater than l
17. a and c are allowed. With b and d, the value of l is greater than the given n.

458

CHAPTER 9

10. a) Si, b) V, c) I
11. b) $[Ar]3d^2$, b) $[Kr]4d^5$, c) $[Xe]4f^{14}5d^2$
12. +3 and +5; +5
13. $1s^22s^22p^63s^23p^64s^23d^{10}4p^65s^14d^{10}$
14. Ca<K<Ar<Cl
15. a) 9 blocks, 4 with two electrons and 5 with one. b) 11 blocks, 7 with two electrons and 5 with one. c) 17 blocks, 8 with two electrons and 9 with one.

CHAPTER 10

10.

11.

12.

13. a) 0, b) +1, c) +1, d) -1
14. $O_2 < O_3 < O_2^{2-}$
15. The radical should be on nitrogen

a) :N̈=Ö   N̈=Ö
    ∅   ∅   -1   +1

b) (Lewis structure drawing)

16.

:N≡N-N̈: ⟷ N̈=N=N̈ ⟷ :N̈-N≡N:
∅ +1 -2   -1 +1 -1   -2 +1 ∅

The two outer structures are major.

CHAPTER 11
7.

a) (Lewis structure)   b) (Lewis structure)

c) (Lewis structure)

8. -4 kJ
9. B & C, A & D
10. a) trigonal bipyramidal, b) trigonal planar, c) linear, d) tetrahedral
11. a) linear, b) trigonal planar, c) linear, d) bent
12. a) nonpolar, b) polar, c) polar, d) nonpolar
13. The amount need to break is the same as the amount need to reform those bonds. The net change is zero.
14. a) -84 kJ, b) 0 kJ

CHAPTER 12
6. a) sp^3
b)

     →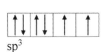

2s   2p sp^3

460

c) sp³, d) 1s, e) sigma
7. a) sp³d²,
b)

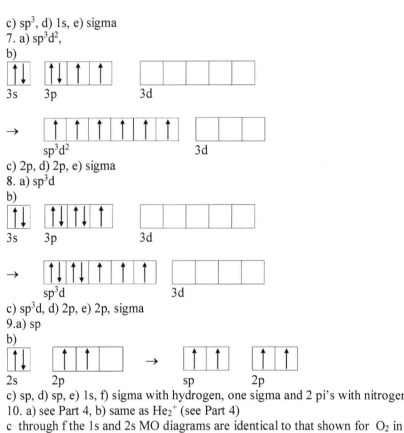

3s 3p 3d

→ sp³d² 3d

c) 2p, d) 2p, e) sigma
8. a) sp³d
b)

3s 3p 3d

→ sp³d 3d

c) sp³d, d) 2p, e) 2p, sigma
9.a) sp
b)

2s 2p → sp 2p

c) sp, d) sp, e) 1s, f) sigma with hydrogen, one sigma and 2 pi's with nitrogen
10. a) see Part 4, b) same as He₂⁺ (see Part 4)

c through f the 1s and 2s MO diagrams are identical to that shown for O₂ in
Part 4. To conserve space, only the 2p MO's will be shown
c)

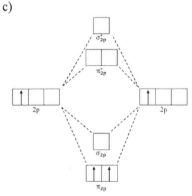

d)

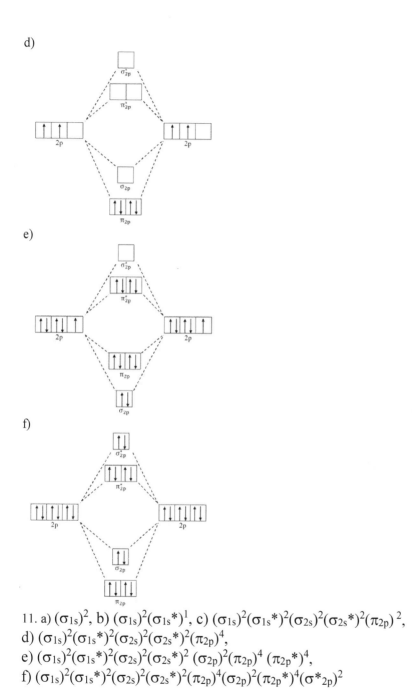

e)

f)

11. a) $(\sigma_{1s})^2$, b) $(\sigma_{1s})^2(\sigma_{1s}*)^1$, c) $(\sigma_{1s})^2(\sigma_{1s}*)^2(\sigma_{2s})^2(\sigma_{2s}*)^2(\pi_{2p})^2$,
d) $(\sigma_{1s})^2(\sigma_{1s}*)^2(\sigma_{2s})^2(\sigma_{2s}*)^2(\pi_{2p})^4$,
e) $(\sigma_{1s})^2(\sigma_{1s}*)^2(\sigma_{2s})^2(\sigma_{2s}*)^2(\sigma_{2p})^2(\pi_{2p})^4(\pi_{2p}*)^4$,
f) $(\sigma_{1s})^2(\sigma_{1s}*)^2(\sigma_{2s})^2(\sigma_{2s}*)^2(\pi_{2p})^4(\sigma_{2p})^2(\pi_{2p}*)^4(\sigma*_{2p})^2$

462

12. a) sp^2

b)

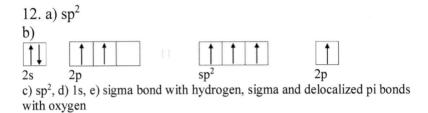

2s   2p   sp^2 2p

c) sp^2, d) 1s, e) sigma bond with hydrogen, sigma and delocalized pi bonds
with oxygen

★★★ Problems

CHAPTER 1
15. a) 3.6×10^5, b) 6.98×10^7, c) 9.87×10^7, d) 75.8, e) 5.4015×10^{14}
16. a) 5700 , b) 0.720 kf, c) 10.84 ce, d) 717 k, e) 5.8×10^4 g, f) 1200 jb/sz^2, g) 1.93×10^{15} c/ℓ^3

CHAPTER 2
16. Heat the compound (does it decompose in a substance with less mass?) or perhaps react the substance with other elements to test the law of definite proportions. Other answer are also possible.
17. a) 2.3×10^{-23} g, b) 2.3×10^{-17} µg, c) 2.3. $\times 10^{-11}$ g
18. a) 55.936 amu, b) iron-56 (and perhaps manganese-56)
19. Z never changes for a given element, but A can.
20. Boron-11, since the atomic weight is closer to this mass number.
21. ^{69}Ga = 59.8%, ^{71}Ga = 40.2%
22. a and c refer to O_2, b refers to O

CHAPTER 3
15. Nitride and oxide are both anions; like charges repel.
16. Yes. H_2O, CO_2, etc.
17. a) $Ca(HPO_4)_2$, b) $(NH_4)_2SO_3$, c) Hg_2Cl_2, d) K_2O_2
18. a) ammonium bicarbonate (ammonium hydrogen carbonate), b) mercury (I) nitrate, c) magnesium hydride, d) silver dihydrogen phosphate, e) titanium (II) dichromate
19. a) calcium chloride, b) titanium (IV) oxide, c) dinitrogen monoxide (or dinitrogen oxide), d) chromium (VI) oxide
20. 16 tubes
21. CaO

CHAPTER 4
23. Each side is 5.09 cm long
24. a) 3, b) bismuth (III) nitrate trihydrate
25. 88.2 g kg CO_2
26. a) $2NI_3(s) \rightarrow N_2(g) + 3I_2(g)$, b) $CaO(s) + 2C(s) \rightarrow CaC_2(s) + \frac{1}{2}O_2(g)$, c) Na(s), c) $PbS(s) + \frac{3}{2}O_2(g) \rightarrow PbO(s) + SO_2(g)$ or $2PbS(s) + 3O_2(g) \rightarrow 2PbO(s) + 2SO_2(g)$, d) $3Ba(NO_3)_2(aq) + 2Na_3PO_4(aq) \rightarrow Ba_3(PO_4)(s) + 6NaNO_3(aq)$
27. a) 30.8 kg CrO_3, b) 309 g CrO_3, c) 103 g Na_2CrO_4

CHAPTER 5

18. Ca^{2+} or Ba^{2+} would separate bromide from phosphate and sulfate. Any cation other than those under trends 1 and 3 could be used to separate sulfate and phosphate.

19. 1.55 M

20. $Zn_3(PO_4)_2$

21. Oxidation: gain of oxygen or loss of hydrogen. Reduction: loss of oxygen, gain of hydrogen

22. 0.059 M

23. a) 5.3×10^{-4} M, b) 17 L

24. a) $2NaCl(aq) + Pb(NO_3)_2(aq) \rightarrow 2NaNO_3(aq) + PbCl_2(s)$, b) 5.6 g $PbCl_2$, c) 0.80 M

25. KOH

26. a) 306 g/mol, b) $C_{14}H_{28}O_7$

CHAPTER 6

23. 0.116 g/mol

24. 1.42 atm

25. 40.0 g/mol

26. 5.97 atm

27. 1.28 mol

28. 2.03 g

29. 6.14×10^{-18} J

30. a) 1 L if HO, 2 L if H_2O, b) If all the O_2 reacts the O:H ratio is 1:1. If only half reacts, the ratio must be 2:1.

CHAPTER 7

19. 2.86×10^{24} J

20. $HA(aq) + MOH(aq) \rightarrow H_2O(l) + MA(aq)$ $\Delta H = 33$ kJ

21. a) -1.19 kJ, b) 210 L

22. a) -1.670×10^5 kJ, b) 6.74×10^5 kJ, c) 2.54×10^4 L

23. -4,014 kJ

CHAPTER 8

18. $n = 1$ has one, 2 has four, 3 has nine, 4 has sixteen, and 5 has twenty-five; number of orbitals in n equals n^2.

19. 20

20. $n = 3$

21. a) 6.7×10^{-12} J/photon, b) 4.0×10^{12} J/mol

CHAPTER 9

16. The 6th group in the d block (1st 8B group)

17. 7p8s5g6f7d8p9s7f8d9p

18. a) $1s^22s^22p^63s^23p^64s^23d^{10}4p^65s^24d^{10}5p^66s^24f^{14}5d^{10}6p^67s^25f^7$, b)
$1s^22s^22p^63s^23p^64s^23d^{10}4p^65s^24d^{10}5p^66s^24f^{10}$, c)
$1s^22s^22p^63s^23p^64s^23d^{10}4p^65s^24d^{10}5p^66s^24f^{14}5d^{10}6p^67s^25f^{12}$

19. a)

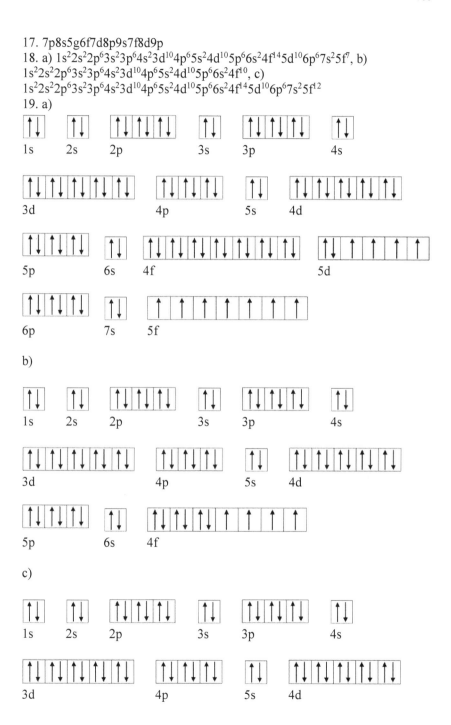

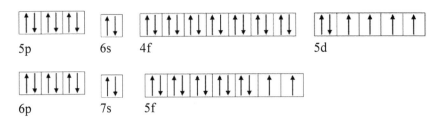

5p 6s 4f 5d

6p 7s 5f

20. a) Sulfur, b) Calcium

CHAPTER 10

17.

$$\ddot{N}=N=N=N=\ddot{N} \qquad :N\equiv N-\ddot{N}=N=\ddot{N}$$

$$:N\equiv N-\ddot{N}-N\equiv N:$$

CHAPTER 11

15. a) 4, b) 3
16. 0.197 mol
17.

$$\begin{array}{c}
\text{O} \\
\text{CH}_2 \quad \text{CH}_2 \\
\text{CH}_2 \quad \text{CH}_2 \\
\text{O}
\end{array}$$

CHAPTER 12

15.
- Benzene ring: all carbon's are sp^2, carbons are bonded by sigma bonds and a delocalized pi bond.
- Both carbons that are bonded to hydrogens are sp^3
- The carbon bonded to oxygens is sp^2
- Nitrogen is sp^3
- Double-bonded oxygen is sp^2, the other is sp^3
- ring-carbon bond: an sp^3 of carbon is sigma bonding with an sp^2 of one of the ring carbons
- All C-H bonds: an sp^3 of carbon sigma bonding with the 1s of hydrogen
- N-H bond: an sp^3 of nitrogen sigma bonding with the 1s of hydrogen
- C-N bond: an sp^3 of carbon sigma bonding with sp^3 of nitrogen

- CH_2-$CH(NH_2)$ carbons: each carbon is sigma bonding an sp^3
- $CH(NH_2)$-CO carbons: an sp^3 of the $CH(NH_2)$ carbon is sigma bonding with an sp^2 of the CO carbon
- C=O bond: both atoms are sigma bonding an sp^2 orbitals and pi bonding their 2p orbital
- C-O bond: an sp^2 of carbon is sigma bonding with an sp^3 of oxygen
- O-H bond: an sp^3 of oxygen is sigma bonding with the 1s of hydrogen

About the author

Mark Matthews grew up in Rockingham County, NC. A graduate of the University of North Carolina and the University of Louisville, he currently lives in Chapel Hill.

Made in the USA
Middletown, DE
19 March 2025

72967888R00280